Brewtown Tales

Brewtown Tales

More Stories from Milwaukee and Beyond

John Gurda

WISCONSIN HISTORICAL SOCIETY PRESS

Published by the Wisconsin Historical Society Press
Publishers since 1855

The Wisconsin Historical Society helps people connect to the past by collecting, preserving, and sharing stories. Founded in 1846, the Society is one of the nation's finest historical institutions.
Join the Wisconsin Historical Society: wisconsinhistory.org/membership

For permission to reuse material from *Brewtown Tales*
(ISBN 978-0-87020-999-4; e-book ISBN 978-1-9766-0000-5), please access www.copyright.com or contact the Copyright Clearance Center, Inc. (CCC), 222 Rosewood Drive, Danvers, MA 01923, 978-750-8400. CCC is a not-for-profit organization that provides licenses and registration for a variety of users.

Front cover image: Milwaukee River View Near Grand Avenue Bridge, WHI IMAGE ID 150534
Back cover images: Keg Man, MOLSON COORS MILWAUKEE ARCHIVES; John Gurda, PHOTO BY MAX THOMSEN

Printed in the United States of America
Cover design by Market Engineers LLC
Typesetting by Integrated Composition Systems

26 25 24 23   2 3 4 5

Library of Congress Cataloging-in-Publication Data

Names: Gurda, John, author.
Title: Brewtown tales : more stories from Milwaukee and beyond / John Gurda.
Other titles: Milwaukee journal sentinel.
Description: [Madison, WI] : Wisconsin Historical Society Press, [2022] | Includes index.
Identifiers: LCCN 2022013669 (print) | LCCN 2022013670 (ebook) | ISBN 9780870209994 (paperback) | ISBN 9781976600005 (ebook)
Subjects: LCSH: Milwaukee (Wis.)—History—Anecdotes. | Milwaukee (Wis.)—Social life and customs—Anecdotes.
Classification: LCC F589.M657 G855 2022 (print) | LCC F589.M657 (ebook) | DDC 977.5/95—dc23/eng/20220328
LC record available at https://lccn.loc.gov/2022013669
LC ebook record available at https://lccn.loc.gov/2022013670

♾ The paper used in this publication meets the minimum requirements of the American National Standard for Information Sciences—Permanence of Paper for Printed Library Materials, ANSI Z39.48–1992.

To my grandchildren—
Kai, Sula, Marin, Lilja, Kjell, and Silas—
so they'll have some idea of what Dziadzia
was up to all those years

Contents

In the Neighborhood

Landmarks and Landscapes

A CITY BUILT ON WATER

The Common Good

The Nature of Things

WISCONSIN WINTERS

THE PERSONAL PAST—LATE

Introduction

My father loved potluck dinners. On practically every Sunday in autumn, he and my mother would pile us four kids into the family station wagon and drive out to eat at one church or another in rural southeastern Wisconsin. Every potluck had its specialty—Swiss steak in Hartford, turkey in Eagle, ribs and kraut in Clyman—but the entrées never stood alone. From the Jell-O salads at the start of the line through the hot dishes in the middle and on to the pumpkin bars at the end, the food was always hearty, abundant, and certifiably homemade.

This book was prepared in the spirit of those fondly remembered potlucks. The main dish is Milwaukee history, served in a multitude of ways that I hope would have impressed the aproned ladies back in the kitchen. You will find in these pages the biography of a bridge, a requiem for a union, odes to both autumn and spring, a poem about aging, tales of two shipwrecks, a frank take on segregation, a visit to a junkyard, and memories of the summer of '68, among many other things. There are also side dishes that convey the distinctive flavors of Wisconsin and a few more exotic places, from Vilas County to Vietnam. My hope is that *Brewtown Tales* will satisfy your hunger, introduce you to some new and unexpected tastes, and whet your appetite for more homemade history.

Most of these offerings began as columns that appeared in the Milwaukee *Journal Sentinel* on the first Sunday of each month, a series that has been continuous since 1994. The Wisconsin Historical Society Press published a first collection called *Cream City Chronicles* in 2007. By 2021, the catalog of "new" essays had grown to more than 180. Liz Wyckoff of the WHS Press and I trimmed the possibilities down to 130 and kept winnowing them to a final number of 80. Although most of these essays are edited and updated newspaper columns, they also include one from an airline magazine (see if you can spot it), another that had its first incarnation as a speech, and a couple of previously unpublished pieces.

For all the similarities between the two books, *Brewtown Tales* is not a sequel to *Cream City Chronicles* but a continuation—a more generous helping from the same buffet. Certain lifelong passions and predilections are evident in both books—ethnic heritage, the natural world, the common good, and my abiding fascination with the interplay of past and present—but this collection highlights my evolving interest in race, polarization, and other contemporary issues as well. There's also a far greater emphasis on memoir here, a natural development for a writer much closer to sunset than dawn.

For more than a quarter century, my *Journal Sentinel* column has given me the opportunity to vent my political spleen, share moments of rare beauty, place current events in their historical context, call attention to some compelling fact, or simply tell what I consider a good story. I'm grateful for the platform, but the stories published in any newspaper will, by definition, end up either recycled into toilet tissue or cast into the icy vastness of cyberspace. The Wisconsin Historical Society Press has rescued my essays from oblivion for a second time and preserved them between the two warm covers of a book for posterity. *Brewtown Tales* is a permanent potluck. I hope you find these offerings nourishing and return to the line often for second helpings.

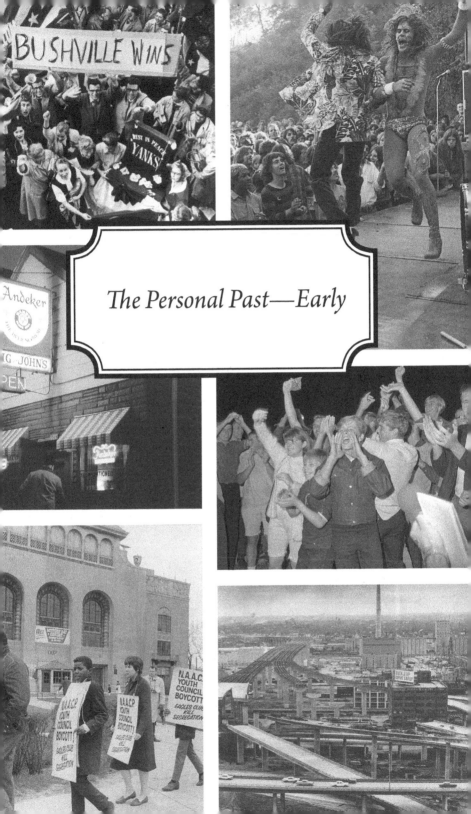

The Personal Past—Early

Sitting on Top of the World

1957 Braves Victory Was a Historic High Point

I am not, generally speaking, a nostalgic person. I don't look back wistfully to a vanished golden age of any sort, and the touchstones of a 1950s childhood, whether hula hoops or coonskin caps, don't have much resonance for me. History, in my view, is important not because it can lead us back to some dimly remembered past, but because it explains how we got to the present.

I'm not nostalgic, that is, with the exception of baseball. Many older Wisconsinites, myself included, have indelibly clear and incredibly warm memories of the autumn of 1957, when the Milwaukee Braves clinched the National League title and faced the New York Yankees in the World Series. For a generation of aging baby boomers, that titanic struggle is a defining memory of childhood.

I don't recall seeing County Stadium under construction, and the news that the Boston Braves were moving to Milwaukee in 1953 made absolutely no impression on me. I was, after all, only five years old at the time, still more interested in sandboxes than even sandlot baseball. What I do recall is literally growing up with the Braves. All through grade school and well into high school, I thought baseball was the only game worth playing and the Braves the only team worth following.

This iconic handmade sign celebrated upstart Milwaukee's triumph over the fabled New York Yankees in the 1957 World Series. MILWAUKEE JOURNAL SENTINEL

It is difficult to exaggerate the Braves' impact on their adopted city. After a half century in the minors, Milwaukee moved up to the big leagues overnight, and the players were greeted with a fervor that bordered on adoration. The team set a National League attendance record in its very first season, inspiring such rabid enthusiasm that one sportswriter called County Stadium "an insane asylum with bases."

I was one of the inmates on occasion. With four small kids and a tight budget, my parents weren't inclined to spend money on baseball, but our Aunt Johnnie was. At least once each summer, my mother's older sister would take the Chicago & North Western train down from La Crosse to Milwaukee, always timing her visit to coincide with a Braves home stand.

While my parents relaxed on South Thirty-Fourth Street, this intrepid former nurse would take all four of us, and sometimes an extra cousin or two, out to the ball game. Peanuts and

Cracker Jack, soda and pretzels—everything was possible with Aunt Johnnie. Snacks were so rare in our house that my brother Mike once took home an empty peanut bag as a souvenir.

Night games were especially memorable. If our seats were in the lower deck, we'd wind through the dimly lit concourses of County Stadium and emerge to a view of the field so bright it was practically blinding: the grass impossibly green, the white foul lines so vivid that they almost vibrated. *This,* I thought, *is what heaven must look like.*

Another aunt, this one my father's sister, brought us even closer to an actual Milwaukee Brave. In the mid-1950s, Aunt Rosemarie and Uncle Al lived in a modest four-family apartment building at 6703 West Blue Mound Road, directly above

The Braves inspired such fan frenzy that Milwaukee County Stadium was described as "an insane asylum with bases." MILWAUKEE JOURNAL SENTINEL

Del Crandall and his family. Professional ballplayers mingled with mere mortals in those days, and the Braves' star catcher shared meals, conversation, and tickets with Rosie and Al. I never got to meet Del Crandall, but I remember pausing at his door in wonder, just one step removed from royalty.

For the rest of the season, a little gold-and-white transistor radio was my primary link with the Braves. Night after night, in the room I shared with my two brothers, I'd fall asleep to the sound of Earl Gillespie and Blaine Walsh broadcasting the play-by-play. In the morning, more often than not, we'd wake up and play baseball ourselves. I spent my childhood years on the old South Side and then in Hales Corners, at a time when that suburb was rapidly being transformed from cow pastures into subdivisions. There were plenty of vacant lots within a few blocks of our house on Brookside Drive, and the flattest of them served as homemade baseball diamonds—until the builders came.

We also played on a more formal diamond created by the Hales Corners Little League. As a pitcher with a strong arm but precious little control, I struck fear into opposing batters for all the wrong reasons. I did, however, get to wear the number of my hero, pitcher Lew (a.k.a. Lou) Burdette. That "33" sewed onto my uniform was a badge of particular honor.

When the boys in the neighborhood weren't playing or listening to baseball,

Lew Burdette was the hero of my Little League years. MILWAUKEE COUNTY HISTORICAL SOCIETY

we were usually buying, trading, or flipping baseball cards. Every kid had at least one shoebox under his bed or in his closet filled with Topps cards. Braves players, of course, were the ones you hoped to find when you bought a pack of bubble gum at Drews or Woolworth's. I once owned an Andy Pafko card that I ended up selling for one dollar, a princely sum in the late 1950s. (Pafko has not aged well; the card would bring no more than ten bucks today.)

The non-Braves cards were usually fair game for flipping. One boy would send his card spinning to the ground, where it came up either heads or tails. If the second player matched it, heads for heads or tails for tails, he took his opponent's card; if he flipped the opposite, he lost his own.

Flipping and trading were suspended for the duration of the 1957 World Series. Milwaukee had always followed its Braves with consuming interest, but the community was absolutely mesmerized in October of 1957. At my grade school—St. Mary's in Hales Corners—classes were actually canceled during day games, when we all trooped down to the lunch room to watch our team on the biggest black-and-white TV the nuns could find.

It took seven games, but the Braves finally prevailed. Lew Burdette—my hero and my role model—was the MVP, pitching three complete games against the Yankees, including two shutouts, and racking up an impossible 0.67 earned run average. Pandemonium reigned on the streets of downtown Milwaukee, and even in the cul-de-sacs of Hales Corners.

Memories of that collective delirium still linger in Wisconsin, decades after the Braves decamped for Atlanta in 1966. The flames were rekindled in 1982, when the Brewers went to the World Series, and they rise again whenever the team is on a hot streak. But there's no time like the first time.

Marching with Father Groppi

Before Open Housing, It Was the Eagles Club

S ome might have called it a loss of innocence, others, perhaps, an overdue reckoning. In the 1960s, when most white residents still considered their city an oasis of racial tranquility, the civil rights movement came to Milwaukee, blowing that delusion to smithereens. Ironically, the movement's most visible leader at the time was Father James Groppi, a white Catholic priest who served as advisor to the local NAACP Youth Council. A native son of Bay View's Italian community, he was an unlikely figure who quickly earned a national reputation.

I marched with Father Groppi near the start of his eventful career as an activist. In 1966, the priest and his Youth Council decided to protest the whites-only membership policy of the Eagles Club, one of Milwaukee's largest fraternal groups. Hundreds of prominent citizens, including what might have been a quorum of Milwaukee County judges, were active Eagles, and Groppi wanted them to resign. How, he asked, could a magistrate sit in judgment of Black Milwaukeeans when he belonged to an organization that had already judged them inferior?

Judge Robert Cannon was the Youth Council's first target. Cannon was known for his relatively liberal views on race, and organizers hoped that he would be quick to see the logic of their position. To help the judge make up his mind, they picketed his house in a particularly leafy section of Wauwatosa for eleven

Father James Groppi (second from right) began his storied career as a civil rights activist by protesting the whites-only membership policy of the Milwaukee Eagles Club. MILWAUKEE JOURNAL SENTINEL

straight nights. The marches, which began on Friday, August 19, were quiet at first, but interest grew rapidly, fanned by nonstop media attention. Within a week, the number of spectators approached four thousand, many of them openly, even rabidly, hostile.

I had turned nineteen earlier that summer. I don't recall what drew me to the scene—budding sympathy or just idle curiosity—but I found myself on the West Side, near the line of march, one warm August evening at the peak of the demonstrations. As the picketers approached, I thought, *Well, you can watch, or you can march.* Seconds later, I was one of the relatively few white people in a group of perhaps two hundred headed to Wauwatosa.

The mood was light at first, even festive, but the atmosphere changed dramatically after we crossed the Wauwatosa line at Hawley Road. By the time our group reached Cannon's home at Seventy-Eighth and Wisconsin, we were in the eye of a storm, separated from a mob of jeering, taunting spectators by a cordon of police officers and National Guard troops.

What I recall is not so much fear as a powerful sense of righteousness. Many in the crowd were smiling, even smirking, as if they found some odd pleasure in venting their hatred. *If that's what the opposition looks like*, I thought, *I'm obviously on the right side of the line.*

After we had marched back and forth for perhaps an hour, Father Groppi said a few words and we headed back to town. It is at this point that my memories become indelible. One of the organizers, thinking, no doubt, of the symbolism, put me and a Black teenager at the head of the line, carrying an American flag between us.

We marched directly behind a wedge of National Guardsmen in full battle dress, with their rifles at the ready and bayonets fixed. The scene was surreal, almost dreamlike, and verging on nightmarish. As we headed east on Wisconsin Avenue, a crowd of young white men shadowed us from the sidewalk like running dogs. Some of their taunts were directed at me personally. "[N-word] lover" was the most common, but I also heard "Do you want your sister to marry one?" Never before had I felt so angry, so scared, and so exhilarated all at the same time.

Both the goons and the Guardsmen were gone by the time we crossed the Wisconsin Avenue viaduct. Our ragtag group of demonstrators made it all the way back to the Freedom House on North Fifth Street, where the mood, after the evening's adrenaline had worn off, was decidedly quiet. Father Groppi himself seemed just plain tired, but I recall being impressed by his obvious physical courage as well as his moral stamina. A Youth Council member gave me a ride to my car, and I was soon back in the suburban safety of Hales Corners, where it seemed—that night, at least—as if nothing had happened since the beginning of time.

White counter-protesters heckled and jeered the marchers, including me, as we picketed Judge Robert Cannon's home in suburban Wauwatosa. Note the Confederate flag. MILWAUKEE JOURNAL SENTINEL

A few days later, I was a thousand miles away, starting my sophomore year at Boston College. Early in the semester, I ran into another Milwaukee kid in the cafeteria, a football player known for both his size and his temper. When I remarked that I hadn't seen him all summer, he fixed me with a look of unblinking contempt and said, "I saw you." My hometown buddy, it turned out, had been one of the running dogs on the sidewalks of Wauwatosa. Our friendship, such as it was, came instantly to an end.

By the time the next summer rolled around, Milwaukee's civil rights leaders had shifted their focus from the Eagles Club to open housing. Although I followed the events of 1967 with interest, I didn't march. It was the "summer of love" for many young whites, and I was engrossed, for a time, in the softer side of the 1960s.

A couple of years later, I was ready for some harder realities. Determined to be "part of the solution" after graduation in 1969,

I took a job at Journey House, a youth center a few blocks south of the Sixteenth Street viaduct. We spent nearly every day with kids who had been part of the raucous, brick-throwing mobs that greeted Father Groppi, Vel Phillips, and members of the Youth Council when they marched down Sixteenth Street in 1967.

None of the young people we worked with were demons. They and their parents were largely low-income whites with roots in rural Wisconsin. Marginalized themselves, they found it easy to demonize those a rung or two below them on the social ladder. America's problems, it seemed, were more than a matter of Black and white.

Many years later, the handful of Journey House kids I'm still in touch with are retired adults who wouldn't dream of throwing bricks at anyone. The Sixteenth Street they knew is now Cesar Chavez Drive, a stronghold of Latino commerce, and there are hundreds of Black residents living nearby. In a neighborhood that once greeted Black protesters with blind rage, racial integration is now an accomplished fact.

The more revolutionary change involves public attitudes. Although my own involvement was incidental, almost accidental, marching with Father Groppi helped to change my mind. The protests of the 1960s exposed many of us, including middle-class white kids from the suburbs, to the realities of discrimination and the raw face of racial hatred.

We still have a long way to go, as recent events have clearly demonstrated, but we now live in a world where whites-only membership clauses and whites-only housing policies are not only illegal but unthinkable. That, I believe, is a change we can all agree was worth marching for.

The Long Hot Summer of 1967

When Flower Power Met Black Power

It was a three-ring circus of a summer. In 1967, a juggernaut of forces—youthful white idealism, growing Black militancy, and blind inner-city rage—combined to roil the waters of the Republic as they had rarely been roiled before. Everywhere the old order seemed under attack, and gauzy visions of a new one competed with cries for violent revolution. Looking back, it's hard to believe that the "summer of love," the high tide of the local civil rights movement, and the worst urban unrest of the twentieth century occurred in the same three-month span.

I was almost twenty and at the end of my sophomore year at Boston College when the summer began. Faithful to the spirit of the times—at least as that spirit revealed itself to middle-class white kids—I took the long way home, hitchhiking down the East Coast to New York, Washington, and Miami, then thumbing back through St. Petersburg and Biloxi to New Orleans before heading home. I had no set itinerary on my month-long journey, and nothing resembling a daily routine. College friends put me up most of the time, but I also slept in my share of fleabag motels and spent one night in the back seat of an old Buick on a used-car lot in Pascagoula.

I had some memorable experiences in 1967, including a couple of days spent with a ragtag band of hippies around Jackson Square in New Orleans, but one of my sharpest memories is

The schizoid summer of 1967 witnessed both the full flowering of the largely white counterculture, typified by a "love-in" in Lake Park, . . .

. . . and a violent conflagration in the largely Black inner city. TOP: MILWAUKEE COUNTY HISTORICAL SOCIETY; BOTTOM: MILWAUKEE JOURNAL SENTINEL

musical. I was perusing the records in a Georgetown head shop when *Sgt. Pepper's Lonely Hearts Club Band* came on the stereo. The album was just a few days old, and I sat transfixed as "Fixing a Hole" wafted out through the open doors onto Wisconsin Avenue. Listening to *Sgt. Pepper's* was a revelation, and I don't use that word lightly. After years of the pop pap that dominated the nation's Top Forty, here was music that made everything before it seem obsolete.

Sgt. Pepper's wasn't just a really good album. The Beatles seemed to have created a self-sufficient world, one that echoed with themes and glowed with colors we'd never seen before. There were answers in their songs, or so I thought at the time— answers to questions our parents had never taught us to ask. *Sgt. Pepper's* earned a permanent place in the era's soundtrack, and every verse of every song is still imprinted in the memories of millions of aging baby boomers.

I came home in early July to a construction job on one of the freeways that were transforming the landscape of Milwaukee County. I was still humming Beatles tunes, but it soon became apparent that other soundtracks were playing in my hometown. The NAACP Youth Council was picketing the homes of aldermen who opposed an open housing ordinance. "We Shall Overcome" and "Ain't Gonna Let Nobody Turn Me Around" were heard on the line of march every night—a far cry from "A Day in the Life" and "Lucy in the Sky with Diamonds."

I had marched with the Youth Council and their advisor, Father James Groppi, during the Eagles Club protests the year before, but I didn't join the 1967 demonstrations. The counter-culture was fast developing two equal and somewhat complementary dimensions: an inward side focused on questions of personal meaning and an outward side galvanized in opposition to the Vietnam War, racial prejudice, and a generic bogeyman called The Establishment. I was already taking the inward path.

All the navel-gazing came to a temporary halt on the evening of July 30. I was driving home from a date with a girl who
lived on upscale Lake Drive, of all places. Traveling across the
North Side to a freeway entrance that led home to Hales Corners, I passed within a mile of Third Street and North Avenue,
where, I learned the next morning, a riot had been underway.
Although it had largely escaped my notice, America's inner
cities were tinder boxes in the summer of 1967. Newark had
gone up in flames on July 12, and Detroit followed on July 23—
the worst of 164 separate disturbances that shattered the nation's
peace that year. Milwaukee could hardly have escaped a spon-
taneous combustion of its own. The final toll: 3 dead, nearly 100
injured, 1,740 arrested, and more than 700,000 traumatized.

The trauma was magnified by the city's official response.
When I tried to go to work on Monday, July 31, I was turned
away before I reached the jobsite. Mayor Henry Maier and his
suburban counterparts had put the entire metro area on lockdown; roads were closed, businesses were shuttered, and the
North Side was essentially occupied territory. Like nearly every
other local resident, I was left to sit at home and wonder what
might come next.

What came next was fear and more fear. With all normal
activities suspended indefinitely, imaginations ran riot, and
staid suburbanites prepared for an onslaught from the inner
core that never came. Without in the least downplaying the
gravity of the riot, the city's response was, in hindsight, a case of
overkill whose psychological impact lingers to this day.

One month later, against the advice of the usual authorities,
Father Groppi and the Youth Council resumed their open-
housing marches, this time targeting individual neighborhoods.
The group drew an especially hostile response on the South
Side, my home turf. The demonstrations continued for two hun-
dred consecutive nights, through the long winter months and

well into March. I was back in Boston when they started, trying to muddle my way through the rest of my college career. Even before Woodstock, I was feeling the fatigue that would later overtake many in my generation.

Two generations have passed since Flower Power and Black Power—the odd couple of American social movements—shared the national spotlight. Does the summer of 1967 have any relevance to the America of the present? Not much, as it turns out. The 1960s, in my opinion, remain a decade that's still largely undigested and perhaps even unforgiven. The revolution never came—neither the peaceful new world of the counterculture nor the righteous new order of the civil rights movement.

Progress was made—open housing became the law of the land, and attitudes have changed perceptibly—but too much remains the same. Although the hippies-vs.-hardhats dichotomy of 1967 seems antique today, American society is arguably even more polarized now than it was then. Millions of countercultural types bowed to destiny after graduation, taking establishment jobs from which they have retired in droves—too often with their 401(k)s in better shape than the world around them. And inner-city conditions are even more dire than they were in 1967, a fact brought home with every police shooting and every bleak statistical report.

What gives me hope on the last score is a rising awareness of the problems, especially on the local level. Issues of racial justice and income inequality are receiving more attention in the 2020s than they have at any time since the 1970s. Instead of "What's wrong with them?," more people are asking, "What is my responsibility?" All that rhetorical smoke will, I hope, finally lead to fire, and this time to flames that temper and transform rather than destroy.

Coming Unglued with America

A Personal Look Back at the Summer of 1968

If you had to identify a watershed period in modern American history, the summer of 1968 would be a leading candidate. The season began with the assassination of Robert F. Kennedy on June 5, which came just two months after Martin Luther King Jr. had met the same fate. It ended with the televised mayhem outside the Democratic National Convention, where young Vietnam War protesters faced the uniformed violence of the Chicago police. America spent the entire season off balance, whirling in a maelstrom of violence, protest, experimentation, and reaction.

And what was I doing during that long, hot, significant summer? I was working as a professional stripper. That might require a little explanation. The late 1960s were the peak of the freeway-building era in Milwaukee. It was easy for any able-bodied man (no women yet) to walk onto a worksite and be hired on the spot. Shortly after coming home from my junior year at Boston College, I went to the top of the High Rise Bridge over the Menomonee Valley and had a job within five minutes.

The bridge was almost finished at that point. My crew's task was to remove, or strip, the plywood forms on which the concrete had been poured, hammer off any excess material, and touch up the various dings with silver paint. We worked second shift, from four to midnight, on a movable wooden platform clamped to the I beams that supported the deck—under the

18

Working on the High Rise Bridge over the Menomonee Valley was the high point of my summer in 1968. MILWAUKEE PUBLIC LIBRARY

bridge, in other words. Our pay was $4.50 an hour, which would be equivalent to about $37 in today's dollars. I paid my dues to Local 113 of the Laborers Union with gratitude.

Not that we didn't earn those princely wages; the work was physically demanding and frequently hazardous. I can recall holding a ladder on the very end of the pier cap that held up the bridge and looking straight down to the valley floor 120 feet below—no belt, no net, no brains. "Some day," I remember thinking, "I'm going to look back and realize that this was really scary." I have, and it was.

The job was also surprisingly odorous. On the hottest, stillest nights, the rotting-grease smell from the rendering plant just beneath the bridge would waft up to our platform and just hang there, practically marinating our clothes, our hair, and our skin. Friends were known to comment.

I spent my summer in blissful ignorance of the tragedy that would end it. For a kid brimming with testosterone, the job was ideal, and not just for its physical demands. When our shift ended at midnight, a group of strippers would usually descend on the bars in nearby Walker's Point and stay until last call. Some of the places we frequented were on the tougher side, but no one ever bothered a bunch of smelly, sweat-stained, hardhat-wearing roughnecks with hammers hanging from their belts.

I was also exposed to worlds I had barely known existed. My best friends on the job were John Hayes and Arthur Small, two of the Black workers on our integrated crew. John was the soul of friendliness, despite the diagonal knife scar that creased his face from right temple to left jawbone. On more than one weekend, John invited me to join him and Arthur for a night on the town. We'd start at Arthur's place, where his wife, Willie Mae, would fry up a meal of catfish, and then we'd hit a succession of North Side bars. I recall ending one long night, significantly impaired, at an after-hours place whose location I couldn't begin to find today. I remember only John vouching for me—the solitary white guy in the room—and floating around tables filled with boisterous gamblers and young women urging them on. "Slumming"? Voyeurism? True friendship? It was what it was.

I had my foot in another world as well. The counterculture was approaching high tide in the summer of 1968, and one of my best friends, Frank Miller, had a job delivering pizzas for Angelo's Restaurant in his 1963 Chevy Biscayne. We'd meet fairly regularly when I was through stripping forms and Frank had made his last delivery. We would visit friends or stop at bars—none on the North Side—but our final destination was often Water Tower Park, a magnet for our particular demographic. One night someone put laundry soap in the park's new fountain, generating a quivery mountain of foam. On another we stayed until dawn. As the sun rose over Lake Michigan and a freighter pulled into the harbor, someone put Canned Heat on a portable stereo. The moment was perfect. Whenever I hear "Going Up the Country," I'm transported straight back to that hillside above Bradford Beach.

The wonder is that, on nights when I wasn't staying with friends, I'd return from all those early-morning adventures to my home in the impossibly placid backwater of suburban Hales Corners. My parents proved themselves to be either very tolerant or very myopic—probably more the latter.

By the time summer ended, I had gained a few pounds—all muscle, which typically happened when I worked construction—and lost all enthusiasm for returning to college. Whatever else it did for me, the summer of '68 was a visceral break from my headwork as an English major. The only way I could make myself go back was to take a half-fare standby flight to Boston before the fall term and find an apartment in the North End, which, in those pre-gentrified days, was the city's Little Italy. Even then I was drawn to neighborhoods with rich histories, preferably ethnic.

A few days later, I hitchhiked home from Boston, a regular practice made possible only by the network of superhighways like the one I'd spent the summer finishing. My last ride deposited me on Twenty-Seventh and Morgan. When I called home from the nearest pay phone, my mother asked ominously, "Are you ready for a shock, John?" She then told me that my sister Susan had died in a one-car accident while I was traveling. Older than me by two years, Susie was coming home from her first teaching job in Rockford to see my brother Paul and me before we headed back to college. A malfunction of some kind, perhaps a blown tire, had caused her car to roll near East Troy. Her skull was fractured, and she never regained consciousness.

As I sat on the curb on that bright August day, stunned and shattered, waiting for my dad to pick me up, I knew in my bones that nothing, absolutely nothing, would ever be the same. All the days on the job and nights on the town that marked the summer of 1968 were instantly meaningless. Decades later, they seem like ancient history, but my sister, my big sister Sue—she might have left us yesterday.

My Life as a Barfly

Becoming a South Sider at Big John's Tap

Of the two thousand bars in Milwaukee, Big John's Tap was one of the smallest. "Seating Capacity 12,000," claimed the tavern's matchbook covers, adding in fine print, "12 at a Time." That was about the size of it when I first saw the place in 1972: twelve stools lined up against a plain Formica bar, a table in one corner, a jukebox in the other, and between them an electric bowling machine that was eventually replaced by an upright piano that John's brother, Tony, banged away on every Saturday night.

Modest as it was, Big John's Tap played a formative role in my life at a time when I was decidedly a work in progress. Nearly fifty years later, my appreciation has only grown. Some people go to mountain peaks or desert islands to find themselves; for me, it was a twelve-stool Milwaukee bar.

The "Big John" emblazoned on the neon sign above the front door was John Kwiatkowski, an appropriately plus-size South Sider who ran the tavern as a sort of recreational adjunct to his small roofing business. John and his wife, Esther, shared cramped quarters behind the bar, and their son, Billy, the night bartender and eventually my good friend, lived in a tiny bedroom directly above.

This mom-and-pop-and-son establishment missed being a classic corner tavern by about a hundred feet. Big John's was

A tiny tavern with an outsized impact on my life, Big John's Tap served
my South Side neighborhood as a communal living room. (*Inset*) Big
John Kwiatkowski was the de facto mayor of South Twelfth Street.
BOTH PHOTOS: JOHN GURDA

shoehorned into a thirty-foot lot at 2508 South Twelfth Street,
two doors off the intersection of Twelfth and Arthur in the very
heart of the old South Side Polish district. The street was lined
with Polish flats and small duplexes from the early years of the
twentieth century. Holy Name Polish National Catholic Church
was two blocks away, St. Josaphat's Basilica four blocks farther. In
1980, 51 percent of the residents of Big John's census tract claimed
Polish ancestry, one of the highest concentrations in the city.

John did not have the shot-and-a-beer market to himself in
such a crowded working-class neighborhood. There were, by
actual count in the 1975 city directory, sixty-seven taverns in the
surrounding square mile, each dispensing its own combination

of community and escape. Most were practically interchangeable with Big John's: small, family-owned thirst emporiums
with names like Stan & Verna's, Tom's Place, Ted and Marilyn's,
Hank's on Sixth, and Gordy & Kathy's.

I lived across the street from Big John's Tap for five years in
the mid-1970s, renting the upper rear unit of a brick four-family
owned by Roman Marzec, an ancient Polish immigrant who
had retired from the International Harvester factory decades
earlier. Roman wore thermal underwear in season and out, and
there was a permanent dent in his lower lip from an ever-present
cigar. For $125 a month, I had the use of four small rooms, with
a bathroom in the hall and a back porch just large enough for a
single lawn chair. I was twenty-five when I moved in, a long-
haired kid three years out of college, precariously employed
and, it turned out, on the verge of grad school. I was just starting
to immerse myself in Milwaukee's story; Big John's made that
story a living, breathing reality.

I don't remember the first time I pulled up a stool at the
tavern; it was probably just to watch a ball game and have a beer.
I do recall the moment when I knew I was a regular. I walked
in one fall evening to find that Esther Kwiatkowski had made
me a liver sausage sandwich, complete with onions and a pickle.
Esther had me pegged as a somewhat disorganized young man
of uncertain dietary habits, which was pretty accurate. Later I
learned that she would see me walking across the street from my
apartment and say, "John's coming. I better make a sandwich."

My walk may have been the shortest, but nearly all of my
fellow regulars lived within a few blocks of the bar, and their
ethnic profile was hard to mistake. My bedroom window looked
out over the postage-stamp backyards of the Ciszewskis, Zielinskis, Przybylskis, and Rzatkiewiczes, all of them Big John's
patrons. The major exceptions to the walking-distance rule were
the Perfex guys, coming off second shift at a radiator factory on

nearby Oklahoma Avenue. After bending metal at their turret lathes and punch presses for eight hours, they were ready to spend a few more bending elbows. My closest friends on the Perfex crew were Tommy and Larry Chaulklin, brothers built like middleweight wrestlers with rough-and-tumble dispositions to match. Tommy and Larry's roots were Up North, and to the north they would return.

I was different from most of Big John's regulars in two respects: I'd spent more time in school, and I didn't work with my hands. Those differences were acknowledged and accepted with a bare minimum of fuss. Big John's Tap served all of us as a community living room, the place where we socialized, watched the Brewers and Packers, played games, and wasted time at our own chosen speeds.

What I discovered, after a month or two of Esther's liver sausage sandwiches, was that I had happened into an urban village. If Milwaukee was indeed a "big small town," that identity was due in part to the abundance of small towns in the city's neighborhoods. For the regulars, Big John's Tap was a self-contained and impressively complete social system. We knew each other by our stories, and they flowed like Pabst Blue Ribbon in the unforced intimacy of the bar. Big John recounted more than once the terrors of driving a tank against the Nazis in World War II. He was wounded in one attack, and, while he was recovering behind the lines, the GI who took his place was decapitated in another firefight. Nick Zielinski wistfully relived his teen years as a CCC worker in northern Wisconsin. Tommy and Larry Chaulklin loved to describe the cat-and-mouse games they played with their supervisors at Perfex. At any point on any evening, one regular or another might have been talking about his high school glory days, her unfortunate first marriage, or why the hell Bart Starr was such a great player and such a lousy coach.

What the villagers created and renewed each night was a community of interest, and John and Esther kept it strong with a full calendar of social events: an annual picnic in Greenfield Park, occasional pig roasts in the backyard, a yearly buffet at Pabst for the brewery's best customers, chartered buses to the horse track in Arlington Heights, and bar-sponsored softball teams. I played on every one of Big John's teams, always in the outfield, and I still have a team jacket somewhere in the attic— too frayed to wear, too precious to toss. My favorite coach was Ziggie Majchszak, who took his manager's role every bit as seriously as Craig Counsell with the Brewers. Irene, Ziggie's wife and our devoted fan, was known for the huge purse she lugged around. I once asked if she had a hammer in there; without a moment's hesitation, Irene fished around in the depths of that enormous satchel and pulled one out.

There were enough characters in Big John's crowd to fill a caricaturist's sketchbook. The regulars included Harry the Hat, Richie Fingers, Kissing Ray, Gino the Mailman, and Bubsie, a New Berlin farmer whose entire wardrobe consisted of flannel shirts and bib overalls. Billy Kwiatkowski himself was the soul of the evening shift. While I had been studying literature at Boston College, Billy was attending art school in Brooklyn, with a specialty in scene painting for the theater. There were precious few openings in that field when he came home, but the tavern became Billy's canvas. He once spent weeks covering the entire back bar with a scene from the Tatra Mountains of southern Poland, placing carefully crafted buildings—a castle, an inn, a church—in the foreground. The regulars were genuinely impressed, but after a year or two the mural became wallpaper. Meaning no disrespect to his son, Big John hung a trophy walleye between the two highest peaks. Billy eventually painted over the entire panorama with a more predictable Up North scene.

John's son, Billy Kwiatkowski (standing), covered the tavern's back bar with a Polish mountain scene. JOHN GURDA

I delighted in bringing friends down to Big John's, including the occasional tenured professor. Billy was always good for a round or two. When my future wife, Sonja, became a mainstay in my life, she naturally became a Big John's regular as well, and she and Billy and I developed an especially close friendship. He was always making bets he knew he couldn't win—quitting smoking, losing weight—as a flimsy pretext for taking us out to dinner, usually at the Lone Pine Inn on Sixteenth and Grant.

Those dinners were high points in my years as a regular, but there were so many others. I once arm-wrestled Tommy Chaulklin to a draw, although he was straining so hard that his nose bled. I slaughtered chickens with the whole Chaulklin clan at Bubsie's farm and capped the experience by helping to gut, scald, and truss the pig Bubsie was supplying for Big John's backyard roast the next day. One night I substituted for Billy in the duckpin bowling league at Koz's on Becher Street. He had to pay for the bowling, I won every beer frame, and I took home a free turkey in the Thanksgiving raffle. That trifecta was a South Sider's perfect evening.

One of my proudest moments at Big John's illustrated the power of the written word. I was already writing about Milwaukee in the late 1970s, and *National Geographic* tracked me down when the magazine was preparing a profile of the city. My first thought, naturally, was to take the *Geographic* reporter, Louise Levathes, down to Big John's Tap on a Saturday night. She was enthralled. Levathes gave the tavern a full two paragraphs in the August 1980 issue, borrowing my "community living room" line and highlighting Tony Kwiatkowski's informal piano concerts. For weeks after the article appeared, complete strangers, most of them passing through from other states, would drop by on Saturday nights to hear Tony play his learned-by-ear renditions of "Harbor Lights," "Blueberry Hill," and other standards. I basked in the reflected glory.

Was there a dark side to this urban idyll? Oh, yes. Big John's was the closest I'll ever come to living in a small town, with the same continuum of strengths and weaknesses. The tavern had all the stereotypical virtues of a rural community—a relaxed pace, mutual support, inherent modesty—but some of the faults as well, including insularity: a prohibitively foreshortened view of the world. In that little hothouse on Twelfth Street, most people's favorite subject was other people. Gossip was currency, feuds played out in the open, and a pair of infidelities on my block seriously disrupted the established social order for a time. I also witnessed more than one near-fight. Whenever violence seemed imminent, John would bellow, "Cut it out or I'll sit on you!," which usually settled the matter. These uniformly white villagers held some insular attitudes as well, including a reflexive racism. One regular patron drew an especially crude comparison between, in his terms, a Black man and a [N-word], the first deserving utmost respect and the second utter scorn. My stoolmate did not make a comparable distinction among his white co-workers at Perfex.

There were also physical hazards. Big John's was, remember, a tavern. Practically every regular smoked in the 1970s, and the few who didn't might as well have. And we all drank. The balm for our tensions, the solvent for our inhibitions, was alcohol. Most of us stayed safely on the near side of oblivion, but there were nights when the bar's collective mood became irrepressibly buoyant and Billy started pouring shots. He'd raise a glass from his left side and say, "First one today—with this hand." His shooter of choice was the *aber gut*—German for "but good"—which consisted of brandy poured to the line and then topped with peppermint schnapps. Two or three of those usually meant a 2:30 a.m. breakfast with Billy at Cunningham's on Thirteenth Street and a headache later that morning.

Hazards and hangovers aside, I wouldn't have traded my years as a regular for a Fulbright scholarship. Big John's Tap is where I became a true South Sider. Not that I didn't have a solid head start. My grandfather was born in Poland, my father spoke the language, and I was raised on South Thirty-Fourth Street and then in Hales Corners. I also had vivid childhood memories of Gurda patriarchs breaking out the sheepshead deck and firing up cigars after Christmas dinner. But I was in some ways a casualty of the 1960s, preoccupied with Big Questions and adrift in the firmament with the likes of T. S. Eliot and James Joyce. I had moved to Twelfth Street as a refugee from both academia and the Age of Aquarius. I was already a self-proclaimed "born-again ethnic," looking to my roots for a firmer connection with the world than anything the counterculture could offer. Big John's provided that and more; the tavern community did me the great favor of bringing me down to earth. I had begun to find my feet at Journey House, the South Side youth center where I worked for three years after college, but that tiny tavern on Twelfth Street is where I started walking.

Learning how to play sheepshead at one end of the bar and when to farm aces with a dice cup at the other were only superficial accomplishments. The real lesson was learning to live in an authentic community that was rooted in my own ancestral culture, one that rose from the very foundation of Milwaukee. It meant following my grandfather's occasionally tipsy footsteps into the late twentieth century. I had obviously been a South Sider all my life. Big John's Tap added the critical dimension of *belonging*; I could feel in my bones what I knew in my brain. My education, I realize, was radically incomplete—people of color were totally absent, for one thing—but an informed and open grounding in my own world has proven to be a powerful starting point for understanding and appreciating other worlds.

Memories of that world are indelible. When Sonja and I got engaged in 1977, Big John's was the first place we went to share the news. One of my tavern softball teammates supplied the films for my stag party a few weeks later, and Big John himself helped make our wedding reception a success, providing barrels of PBR at cost and booking our two-piece polka band. Of the three hundred or so people who celebrated with us at the old Sons of Norway hall on Greenfield Avenue, a dozen or two were fellow regulars. And there were those incandescent nights at the bar when the cards were falling right, one story led seamlessly to another, and the table was brimming with goodwill. There was no place in the world I would rather have been on those occasions, no people on earth whose company I would have preferred. What I felt on those evenings was freedom. What I felt was family.

Eventually, perhaps inevitably, the family broke up. Esther Kwiatkowski died of a heart attack in 1978 at the impossibly

Billy and me at the bar, circa 1973. SONJA NELSON

young age of fifty-three, and with her passing the bar's soul was materially diminished. I was a pallbearer at her funeral—small repayment for all those sandwiches. Perfex closed its plant and moved production to Mississippi, eliminating more than two hundred jobs. The casualties included Tommy and Larry Chaulklin, who moved north to Fremont, a town of seven hundred on the Wolf River. One by one the regulars left the neighborhood, Sonja and I among them. In 1978, we bought the last thirty-six-thousand-dollar house in Bay View and started to have kids. Big John finally sold the tavern in 1981 and retired. Billy decamped for West Allis as the manager of a bar attached to a Chinese restaurant, where he somehow resisted the temptation to paint a mural of the Great Wall. We stopped at his place and the old bar on Twelfth Street once in a while, but it was never the same. The weeks between visits became months, and the months became years.

It's been almost half a century since I lifted my first twenty-cent tapper at Big John's, nearly fifty years since I was a scruffy-looking kid walking across the street to catch a Brewers game.

I went for a stroll around the old neighborhood on a recent evening. Big John's has long since been converted to a small residence, but Twelfth Street otherwise looks largely the same. What has changed is the culture. The population of my old census tract was more Latino in 2019—63 percent—than it was Polish in 1980—51 percent. The Ciszewskis and Zielinskis on my former block were replaced by Garcias and Santiagos years ago. I stopped at one of the few surviving taverns for a beer—*cerveza* now, no longer *piwo*—and felt a glimmer of the old sense of community, but that world is closed to me, forever sealed off by a daunting language barrier.

I'll never be a regular again; I simply don't have the stamina, the desire, or the time. But I look back on my life as a barfly with nothing but fondness. The person who comes most often to mind is Billy Kwiatkowski. The last time I saw him was at the Wilson Park Senior Center, where I was giving a talk and he had just directed a play starring his fellow seniors. He told me that he was battling health problems and living alone in subsidized housing on the South Side. There was more than a whisper of disappointment about him, but Billy told stories during the question-and-answer session as if he were right back at the bar.

Then, in March of 2019, I received the sad news from his sister-in-law that Billy had died. His funeral was stark evidence of how completely our old world had disintegrated. There was no reunion of aging barmates, not even a service—just a handful of relatives and friends at the funeral home, sharing wistful memories of a singular figure in their lives. I found myself wanting a heartier send-off for a person who had played such a vital role at such a pivotal point in my life. And so this story's for you, Billy. With it I raise a glass to your memory, old friend. First one today—with this hand.

Getting Around

The Slow Road Home

Getting Off the Freeway, Going Back in Time

I go time traveling whenever I can. I don't use experimental machines or mind-altering drugs. Doc Brown and his marvelous DeLorean from *Back to the Future* are nowhere in sight. All I have to do is get off the freeway.

One of my favorite excursions to the past began in Eau Claire. I was there on a fall morning at the end of a work trip, hoping to bike the Chippewa River Trail for a few hours, but a persistent light rain put a damper on that idea. With the entire day before me and no reason to hurry back to Milwaukee, I followed my nose onto Highway 12, the main-traveled road through west-central Wisconsin before Interstate 94 virtually put it out of business.

I was only a few miles outside Eau Claire when I began to feel that I had returned to the 1950s or an even earlier time. This was the road my parents' generation had traveled when they drove from Milwaukee or Chicago to the Twin Cities. It had two lanes, a fifty-five-mile-per-hour speed limit, and enough curves and corners to embarrass a modern transportation engineer.

Highway 12 also went through the heart of nearly every town on its route—no bypasses, thank you. It was, in fact, the main street in Fall Creek, Augusta, Fairchild, Humbird, Merrillan, Black River Falls, and a succession of other towns strung along its corridor like beads on a necklace.

The quiet was breathtaking. Highway 12 is well maintained and wide enough for plenty of cars, but it felt like the scene of a party after everyone had left. Where they had gone, of course, was I-94, which was never more than a few miles away. With very little company (and blessedly few trucks), I had ample leisure to enjoy the countryside. I rolled through the gentle hills of Eau Claire and Jackson Counties, with their trees ablaze in early October, and onto the broad floor of Glacial Lake Wisconsin. There was always something to see: mountains of snow-white frac sand bound for the oilfields of North Dakota, acres of tank cars at rest on their sidings, more pumpkins than I could count heaped on roadside stands, cranberry bogs red with the season's harvest, towers of sandstone rising like castles above the plain, and the obligatory brick banks and church steeples of small-town Wisconsin.

I stopped for lunch at Tugger's Café in Augusta, a classic eatery where you can order the hamburger plate special for $7.95 and top it off with a piece of homemade pecan pie. At the table next to mine was an elderly Amish couple—she with a bonnet, he with white chin whiskers—who had tied up their horse and buggy outside—not a sight you'd find in a freeway rest area. Just outside town, to my surprise, was the mammoth canning factory of Bush's Best Baked Beans.

When I continued to see railroad tracks alongside the highway, I suspected, and later confirmed, that I was on the route of the fabled Twin Cities 400, a Chicago & North Western passenger train that could travel the four hundred miles from Chicago to Minneapolis in four hundred minutes. Launched in 1935 to regain some of the ground C&NW was losing to automobiles, the Twin Cities 400 could hit more than a hundred miles an hour on a straightaway. That speed, combined with superior service, kept it in operation until 1963, when the passenger train,

(*Above*) Taking the road less traveled can put you in close contact with a curious calf...

(*Right*) ... or a lone oak standing sentinel in a misty cornfield. BOTH PHOTOS: JOHN GURDA

like Highway 12 itself, succumbed to the pressures of the freeway era. A mainline became a sideline and then disappeared.

The longer I stayed on 12, the more I liked its pace. If I saw something that begged to be photographed, I pulled over. If a particularly brilliant maple or a picturesque graveyard seemed to call my name, I stopped. On the freeway, that would be not just unsafe but illegal. I passed under I-94 three or four times on my way south, and each time the contrast was jarring. Compared to state roads, expressways are like gerbil tubes. Each is a hermetically sealed world of its own, with stout fences, frequent patrols, and officially sanctioned stops. Freeway interchanges are, in a word, interchangeable, offering the same banal blend of fast food, fast gas, and standard lodgings. They are, by design, little more than pit stops on a racetrack.

Expressways are all business; state roads are about leisure. Expressways turn the passing landscape into wallpaper; trunk highways provide an immersive experience. Expressways are fine for getting where you're going; state highways are ideal for being where you are. Expressways allow you to be in one state and only one: a state of motion. On Highway 12 and its two-lane counterparts, you know you're in Wisconsin.

The route I took may be somewhat unusual for its state of preservation and its proximity to the superhighway that replaced it, but there's no shortage of comparably quiet roads in our backyards. In 1918, responding to the automobile's growing popularity, Wisconsin adopted a master plan for its state trunk highway system. Capped initially at five thousand miles, the system was designed to connect every county seat and every settlement with a population of at least five thousand. Not even 20 percent of the system's designated miles were paved at the time, but they were steadily upgraded to highway standards.

That system is still very much in place, even if superhighways move more people. Some of my favorite segments include Highway 10, a "long cut" from Hudson to Osseo in northwestern Wisconsin; Highway 14 through the heart of the Driftless Area; Highway 16 west of Oconomowoc; and Highway 57 east of Lake Winnebago. Other trunk highways survive only as byways running parallel to the freeways that replaced them. Highway 15 persists as County ES, which shadows I-43 between New Berlin and East Troy, and Highway 141 lives on as County R between Manitowoc and Green Bay.

St. Patrick's Catholic Church in Mauston was a visual treat at the end of my slow road home. JOHN GURDA

All these routes and many others represent the road less traveled. How much time did I "lose" by taking Highway 12? Excluding random stops and a few side trips, perhaps an hour— surely a small price to pay for such a privileged view of Wisconsin during its loveliest season.

But the sun was about to set when I was still hours from home. With the landscape receding into darkness, I opted for the freeway. As I pulled onto I-94 at Mauston (which has a gorgeous Catholic church, by the way), I was surprised to find myself saying "Good-bye" out loud. Good-bye to the slow lane, good-bye to the historic view, good-bye to serendipitous wandering. But only until next time.

Pedal Power

Bicycles Have Been Moving Milwaukee since 1876

For nearly a decade, I was known in some circles as The Guy on the Bike. From 2011 through 2019, when production ceased, I was the on-camera historian for *Around the Corner with John McGivern*, a popular Milwaukee PBS series that profiled a different Wisconsin community every week. At the beginning of each show, I would pedal up to John at some likely spot and tell him the backstory of the place we were visiting—in three and a half minutes or less. I could gauge *Around the Corner's* popularity by the number of people who stopped me on the street and asked, "Where's your bike?"

The truth, then and now, is that it's never far away. Ever since bad knees forced me to hang up my running shoes, biking has been my preferred form of exercise, and I ride in both summer and winter. I put more than a thousand miles on my aluminum steed in a typical year, tooling around town, exploring the Wisconsin countryside, and traveling farther afield with my wife and a group of like-minded friends. Over the years, we've pedaled the Katy Trail across Missouri, the Erie Canal Trail from Buffalo to Albany, the OTET (Ohio to Erie Trail) across Ohio, and—still my favorite—the Great Allegheny Passage/C&O Canal Trail from Pittsburgh to Washington, DC.

The routes closest to home are most familiar, of course. Every time I take my bike out of the garage, I know I'm continuing a

Terry Andrae, a Wisconsin racing champion, posed with his high-wheeler in the days before he switched to safety bicycles. His family's summer retreat in Sheboygan County was donated to become Terry Andrae State Park. MILWAUKEE COUNTY HISTORICAL SOCIETY

venerable tradition, riding in the tracks of countless Milwaukeeans who pedaled before me. The first bicycle, in fact, appeared in 1876, when the city was just thirty years old. The *Milwaukee Sentinel* reported that the contraption "was gazed at with undisguised amazement by the startled natives, who hurried to their windows and crowded upon the sidewalks to get a look at the strange thing that sped noiselessly by." We'd probably do the same. That first bicycle was a classic "boneshaker," with a front wheel nearly five feet in diameter and a minuscule rear wheel. Riders found the vehicles hard to get on and even harder to get off. "As soon as the speed of the bicycle is checked," reported the *Sentinel*, "it begins to wobble like a dying top, and if the inexperienced rider can manage to dismount without falling off, he is exceptionally lucky." Unless there was someone nearby to help him, continued the paper, "the unskillful bicyclist has to choose between riding on forever and stopping the machine and dismounting in that miscellaneous manner that is so fatal to limbs and clothing."

The hazards of the high-wheeler didn't stop people from riding them. The Milwaukee Bicycle Club was founded in 1880 and grew quickly to sixty-five members, making it the largest in the nation for a time. The group raced on occasion, but its real passion was touring the dusty roads of Waukesha County. The club thoughtfully published its route before each ride so that farmers with skittish horses knew which roads to avoid.

Although it became a fairly familiar sight, the inherent difficulty of the high-wheeler limited its appeal. The sport's real breakthrough came in the 1880s, when manufacturers introduced the "safety bicycle," with two wheels of equal size, air-filled rubber tires, a chain drive, and coaster brakes. It was, in other words, a simpler, heavier version of the bicycle that every baby boomer learned to ride as a child. Easy to use, faster than walking, and cheaper than the streetcar, safety bicycles became a coast-to-coast craze. By 1900, four million Americans were riding them—in a country of seventy-six million.

Milwaukee shared in the general excitement. Local ridership soared to fifteen thousand in 1895, up from an estimated two hundred fifty in the high-wheeler era. Every celebration, it seemed, had to showcase bicycles in some fashion. On the Fourth of July in 1896, the Cream City Wheelmen held their first-ever road race over a twelve-mile course that ran from Twenty-Eighth and Vliet Streets to Wauwatosa and back. The winner was Edward Rosenberg, a fifteen-year-old who had borrowed his brother's bike. Nearly eight thousand spectators turned out to watch the contest.

The Milwaukee Country Club, then located in Shorewood, took the opposite tack, holding a "slow bicycle race" on the same 1896 holiday. The object, reported the *Sentinel*, "was to be the last to cross the line, without dismounting or deviating from the general direction toward the finish." The victor was George Merriweather, who was the only rider still on his bike after one hundred yards.

As the sport's popularity grew, nearly everyone got on board. A Protestant minister praised the bicycle as "the

Members of the League of American Wheelmen (and women) gathered for a Milwaukee meet in 1900. MILWAUKEE COUNTY HISTORICAL SOCIETY

two-wheeled evangelist of health and happiness" and declared that it was "doing for man's health what steam has done for industry." But the preacher was also disturbed by the number of enthusiasts who did most of their riding on Sunday. "The wheel," he warned, "is seeking to run the Sabbath out of the week."

Doctors touted the health benefits of cycling. "The effete materials in the tissues are rapidly removed," wrote one, "and oxidation, which is essential to health, is more perfectly performed." His meaning may be lost on modern readers. The physician was clearer when he addressed the sport's psychological benefits: "No one can ride a bicycle and not have his thoughts taken out of himself, and at the same time have his attention pleasantly engaged." That's something I experience nearly every time I get on a bike.

The new vehicles weren't particularly cheap. One of Milwaukee's larger dealers was Julius Andrae, whose son, Terry, was a state racing champion—and the man for whom a popular state park is named. In 1893, the Andrae shop sold the Featherstone, an entry-level bike, for $35—about $875 in today's currency. That was a significant sum in a blue-collar town like Milwaukee, but thousands made the investment.

A high point of sorts was reached in 1895, when three thousand cyclists were the featured attraction in a civic parade that drew more than a hundred thousand spectators. There were elaborate costumes, colorful bunting, and even a woman rider wearing bloomers. "Never in the history of the Northwest was there a more pleasing parade," gushed the *Sentinel*, "and Milwaukee may live and thrive another fifty years before the cycling interests of Wisconsin are marshalled again in such a dazzling array."

That proved to be an understatement. I doubt that Milwaukee has ever had another parade featuring three thousand cyclists. Just as the safety bicycle pushed the bone-shaker into oblivion, a new vehicle—one with four wheels—ended the bicycle craze. The first mass-produced automobiles appeared at the turn of the century and quickly took the market by storm. Henry Ford's Model T sold for as little as $260—not much more than a high-end bicycle. Why settle for a bike when you could have twice as many wheels and an engine besides?

The bicycle never really went away, but it was relegated to secondary status: a toy for kids, not a vehicle for grown-ups. Only in recent decades has the cycle come round again. For reasons of health, economy, environmental stewardship, and just plain fun, millions of us are riding, and there are more bikes on the road every year. Thousands of them are in Wisconsin. Our state has become a national leader in rail-to-trail conversions, and Milwaukee is steadily enlarging its reputation as a bike-friendly city. The Guy on the Bike may ride only in reruns today, but this guy on a bike is still pedaling, and he has plenty of company on the road that starts just outside our doors.

From Steel Wheels to Skinny Tires

First Trains, then Bicycles on Milwaukee's Lakefront

Trains are not the first transportation mode you'd associate with Milwaukee's magnificent lakefront. Cars, yes, and bicycles, too—not to mention sailboats, yachts, and the occasional kayak. But to modern Milwaukeeans, smoke-belching, earth-shaking locomotives would seem distinctly out of place on one of the finest stretches of urban shoreline on the Great Lakes.

The surprising fact is that a railroad made the first down payment on the development of today's lakefront, and its presence there was the result of a titanic battle between two transportation giants. From the day it was organized in 1863, the dominant railroad in southern Wisconsin was the homegrown Milwaukee & St. Paul, more popularly known in later years as the Milwaukee Road. Its chief rival in the region was the Chicago & North Western, headquartered ninety miles south. The two lines were proxies in the larger rivalry between Milwaukee and Chicago. As both expanded into new territory, their trains sometimes ran practically next to each other.

The C&NW was handicapped by its lack of a direct line into downtown Milwaukee, a link that became more and more difficult to forge as the city grew. The railroad was knocking on the door in 1872, when it completed an "air line" from Fond du Lac to northern Milwaukee County, and it had plans to go even farther. Frederick von Cotzhausen, the company's general counsel,

In 1910, a smoke-belching locomotive chugged up the incline that is now the Oak Leaf bicycle trail. The flushing station on the left houses Colectivo Coffee today. MILWAUKEE PUBLIC MUSEUM

tried to bargain with the Milwaukee Road for shared use of its right-of-way into the center of town. "However," he recalled in 1919, "my negotiations signally failed." The Milwaukee Road, von Cotzhausen wrote, was "the almighty ruler in State and local politics," and Alexander Mitchell, the tycoon who ran the line, "did not feel that his company ought to grant us any facilities adverse to their interest."

Rebuffed by its rival, the C&NW looked high and low for another point of entry. Its chief engineer suggested running a line across the East Side and then down the bluff to the lakefront at North Point. From there, after extensive landfill operations, trains would follow the shoreline to the Third Ward, "where lands were then at a low price," wrote von Cotzhausen. "At first I was shocked at the idea," the lawyer recalled, "because the expense of grading and protecting the track against the encroachment of the waves seemed enormous. But as the prop-osition was revolved in our minds it gained strength. The right-of-way along the beach was certainly cheap."

It's hard to believe that what is now perhaps the most cher-ished public space in our region—the downtown lakefront—was once so little valued. In 1872, however, Lake Michigan's waves lapped against the foot of steep bluffs that made the beach practically inaccessible; every cubic inch of today's lakefront is landfill.

It took just over a year to finish the first installment of "made land" on the shoreline. Working from the north, C&NW crews laid tracks along the east bank of the Milwaukee River to Locust Street and then traversed the East Side to Lafayette Place, where they cut a canyon down to the beach. All the dirt they excavated was tamped into place on top of the sand to form a stable road-bed, which the railroad protected from the waves with a highly engineered system of pilings and cribwork. The tracks led to a depot at the foot of Wisconsin Avenue and then continued through the Third Ward to a swing bridge at Jefferson Street, where they crossed the Milwaukee River and joined the North Western's existing right-of-way to Chicago.

The new lakefront line was dedicated on September 6, 1873, when nearly six hundred visitors chugged into town from Fond du Lac and other communities on the "air line" route. "Large numbers of our citizens had gathered at points along the bluff," wrote the *Milwaukee Sentinel*, "and the welcoming hurrah soon resounded along the shore." The out-of-towners were treated to band music, city tours, and dinner at several down-town hotels, where speaker after speaker extolled the virtues of the new competition that existed between the Chicago & North Western and the Milwaukee Road.

The region's two major railroads were approaching a state of parity that took architectural form in 1889, when the C&NW

(*Top*) The Chicago & North Western railroad's tracks remained in service even as landfill created Juneau Park. (*Bottom*) The completion of Lincoln Memorial Drive in 1929 gave Milwaukee one of the finest expanses of urban shoreline on the Great Lakes. BOTH PHOTOS: MILWAUKEE JOURNAL SENTINEL

completed a depot on the lakefront equal in splendor to the Milwaukee Road's central station near Fourth and Clybourn Streets. Both landmarks, lamentably, are long gone, but the North Western's swing bridge, unused for years, still splits the river at Jefferson Street.

The lakefront right-of-way remained a work in progress. The original tracks across the East Side were laid at street level, creating a serious safety hazard as the district grew. According to James Yanke, a former C&NW conductor who authored a detailed history of the line, the East Side grade was lowered nearly twenty feet in 1905, creating a continuous stone-walled canyon from the lakeshore to Riverside Park.

For nearly a century, the shriek of locomotive whistles and the smoke billowing from their stacks were fixtures of life along the line. The tracks, however, became farther and farther removed from the shore as the city filled land to the east for Lincoln Memorial Drive. By the time the drive opened in 1929, automobiles had begun to challenge trains as America's dominant transportation mode.

The lakefront line was a casualty of the competition. After years of attrition, passenger service ended in 1964, and Milwaukee County promptly purchased the right-of-way closest to downtown. The corridor was paved and opened to bicycle and foot traffic in the 1980s, quickly becoming one of the most popular units of the Oak Leaf Trail.

The lakefront segment is still a crown jewel in the county trail system. Slicing through one of Milwaukee's most congested districts without a single stop sign or red light, the trail connects lake and river, high ground and low, but it also connects past and present. Traces of its rich history abound: in the silent witness of the occasional telegraph pole, in the blast holes scoring the stone retaining walls, and in a length of wrought-iron fence that once marked some wealthy family's backyard.

The old right-of-way tells an even larger story, and its central theme is change. Milwaukee's lakefront trail represents a transformation. Steel wheels have given way to skinny rubber tires; a roadbed created as an artery of commerce has become a corridor of recreation. Like a fickle lover, the world is always abandoning one technology and embracing another. Which fixtures of our own era will meet the same fate? Freeways? Smartphones? Social media? The generations will tell.

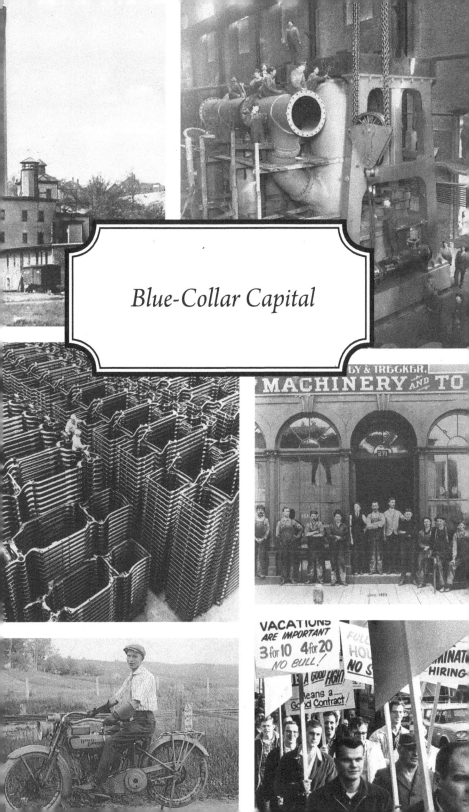

Blue-Collar Capital

Milwaukee the Innovator

Walker's Point Intersection Spawned Some Giants

The intersection of South First and Florida Streets looks anything but historic. A vaguely Irish bar crowds one corner, and a paint store and two underused parking lots fill the others. The surrounding Walker's Point landscape is an agglomeration of shops, small industries, and converted factory lofts, with an elevated rail line curling through the ensemble like a snake across a jungle floor.

First and Florida may never make the visitor bureau's list of must-see Milwaukee destinations, but the intersection was every bit as important to the city as Hollywood and Vine is to Los Angeles or Forty-Second and Broadway is to New York. It was there, in the late 1800s, that a world-class constellation of industries began to shine. Together, they helped to make Milwaukee a global capital of innovation and enterprise.

Edward P. Allis was the first star. In 1867, he opened his Reliance Works on the southeast corner of First and Florida, producing flour mill equipment, sawmill machinery, and, in time, the largest steam engines on earth. Within twenty years, the Reliance Works employed more than a thousand men and stretched from Florida Street to National Avenue—a distance of four blocks. The company took a new name in a 1901 merger: Allis-Chalmers. Even before its final move to—where else?—West Allis in 1923,

A steam pump under construction at E. P. Allis's Reliance Works dwarfed the men who were assembling it. WHI IMAGE ID 9490

the firm was one of the largest manufacturers of heavy equipment in the world.

In 1869, two years after Allis put down roots, Delos Filer and John Stowell moved into a machine shop on the northwest corner of First and Florida—diagonally across the street from the Reliance Works. After exploring a number of other lines, including steam engines, the partners made sawmill machines their specialty, and Filer & Stowell became one of the most trusted names in the American lumber industry.

The neighborhood's pace accelerated later in the century. In 1884, Henry Harnischfeger and Alonzo Pawling opened a small machine shop on the northeast corner of First and Florida. The partners were pioneers in the development of electric cranes, and the business grew so fast that they soon built a larger shop exactly one block north, on Oregon Street.

The pair also offered job-shop services, making machinery to order for other fledgling industrialists. One of them was Bruno Nordberg, a Finnish-born engineer who brought in drawings for a new type of steam-engine governor. Another was Christopher Levalley, whose bright idea featured endless chains of metal links that would eventually replace many of the leather belt drives in the nation's factories.

Harnischfeger and Pawling built superlative products for both men, making possible the birth of two more industrial giants: the Nordberg Company and the Chain Belt Company. Both leased space in the Harnischfeger shop at first but eventually rose to greatness on their own: Nordberg in mining equipment and marine diesels, Chain Belt in link drives and construction machinery. Harnischfeger, in the meantime, became the largest manufacturer of traveling overhead cranes on the planet.

One block north of the Harnischfeger plant, at what is now First and Pittsburgh Streets, two friends who had met at a Bay View machine shop started a business of their own in 1898. Edward Kearney and Theodore Trecker had an idea for a better milling machine. As Kearney & Trecker, they became major suppliers of machine tools to industries around the globe.

Down the block from First and Florida, at Bruce Street, another kind of enterprise was taking shape. In 1902, working out of his father's bicycle parts factory, Arthur Oliver Smith built America's first pressed-steel automobile frame. The A. O. Smith Company would become the largest car and truck frame manufacturer in the world.

Another inventor was hard at work nearby. In 1902, Lynde Bradley finished one of his first motor controllers in a space he had rented (for three dollars a week) at Second and Florida. With help from his kid brother, Harry, and backing from family friend Stanton Allen, Lynde eventually perfected the device, and Allen-Bradley became a global leader in industrial controls.

Starting in 1898, friends Edward Kearney and Theodore Trecker parlayed an idea for a better milling machine into a globally important machine tool business. MILWAUKEE JOURNAL SENTINEL

Two blocks north of the Allis works was a little forge shop run by the Obenberger family. Herman Ladish ran a nearby malting plant, and he had persistent trouble with a crankshaft in one of his machines. In 1905, he brought his problem to the Obenbergers, who forged a shaft that worked perfectly. Ladish was so impressed that he first bought into the firm and then bought it out. In 1913, renamed for its new owner, the Ladish Company moved to Cudahy and became the largest forge shop in America.

Let me recap the progression for you. In the eight square blocks around First and Florida Streets, between 1867 and 1905, the following industries took their first steps to success: Allis-Chalmers, Filer & Stowell, Harnischfeger, Nordberg, Chain Belt, Kearney & Trecker, A. O. Smith, Allen-Bradley, and Ladish. That's an all-star cast on such a minuscule stage. Every company rose to the top of its chosen field, and most were numbered at some point among the Fortune 500. All but Allen-Bradley, still doing business in the neighborhood as Rockwell Automation, grew to maturity elsewhere in town, but every one started within two blocks of First and Florida.

When you consider the variety of goods those companies produced, the tens of thousands of jobs they created, and the billions of dollars they pumped into the economy, you have to wonder how many comparable eight-block areas there are in the entire world. Silicon Valley? Milwaukee was in the same league a century earlier.

How did it happen? It helped that the wind was at Milwaukee's back. In the later 1800s, the Midwest was America's industrial frontier, attracting, like all frontiers, the young, the ambitious, and the talented. Walker's Point became an unplanned, unzoned industrial incubator. A small army of tinkerers set up shop there, drawn by the area's superb rail connections, the enormous local work force, and each other. What emerged around

First and Florida was a culture of mechanical enterprise. There was always someone with a new way to solve a problem and always someone who could bend the metal to make that solution a reality. In 1902, for instance, one of Allen-Bradley's first motor controllers was tested on a Harnischfeger crane in the Allis-Chalmers plant, and tales of similar synergy abound.

Can such creative lightning strike Milwaukee again? It is fashionable to lament the passing of the entrepreneur from the American scene, particularly in a region still in the throes of deindustrialization, but the species is hardly extinct in southeastern Wisconsin. Look no further than Harry Quadracci of Quad Graphics, Michael Cudahy of Marquette Medical, or John Mellowes of Charter Manufacturing. All rose to national leadership in their fields by developing better ideas, perfecting the right technologies, and then rolling the dice—exactly what the pioneers of Walker's Point did.

How can we replicate their success? Government can help, but I suspect that the market plays a much larger role—the market, and something far less tangible: the heady blend of ideas, skill, and ambition that once flowered on First and Florida. As Milwaukee struggles to reinvent itself in the twenty-first century, its leaders can look to that ordinary street corner for extraordinary inspiration.

End of the Line for A. O. Smith Plant

America Once Rode on Milwaukee-Made Frames

There are times, I must say, when I feel like an obituary writer for deceased Milwaukee industries. Over the years, I've paid final respects to Allis-Chalmers, Pabst, Pfister & Vogel, Harnischfeger (in its original form), Nordberg, the Milwaukee Road shops, and other vanished enterprises—all mainstays of local manufacturing.

I added a conspicuous fatality to the list in 2006, when the sprawling A. O. Smith plant on North Twenty-Seventh Street—owned for a decade by Tower Automotive—closed its doors for good. There is still an A. O. Smith Corporation, and it's still a giant, with billions of dollars in sales, but that company makes water heaters, and none of them in Milwaukee. The A. O. Smith most of us remember is the one that turned out more car and truck frames than anyone else on the planet.

The company's first success came with an entirely different mode of transportation. In 1874, an English immigrant named Charles J. Smith opened a small machine shop on Humboldt Avenue. He accepted all sorts of repair and fabrication orders at first, but Smith's dream was to find a manufacturing line he could call his own.

The entrepreneur actually found two. The first was baby carriages, and Smith turned out springs, axles, hubcaps, and other perambulator parts by the thousands. The second and more

In the 1950s, car frames were stacked by the thousands at the Twenty-Seventh Street complex. A. O. SMITH CORPORATION

important was bicycles. Americans developed an absolute mania for two-wheeled transportation in the 1890s, and Smith helped fuel their passion, producing a full range of bicycle frames, forks, handlebars, sprockets, pedals, and wheel rims. By 1895, Charles J. Smith was the largest manufacturer of bicycle parts in America, every one of them made in an up-to-date factory in the Walker's Point neighborhood.

The craftsman-turned-capitalist had four sons, all of whom showed definite business ability, but it was Arthur Oliver Smith who carried the enterprise to the next level. Working first in the family bicycle plant and then on his own, A. O. Smith moved to the cutting edge of transportation technology. In 1902, responding to a customer request, he made the first pressed-steel automobile frame in America. It obviously met a need. The A. O. Smith Company, organized in 1904, was soon deluged with orders from Pope-Toledo, Packard, Cadillac, and Locomobile. In 1906, Henry Ford himself visited Milwaukee and placed an order for ten thousand frames. The Walker's Point plant was so jammed that incoming steel had to be stockpiled on the sidewalk outside. In 1910, finally, A. O. Smith built a new factory on North Twenty-Seventh Street at Hopkins Avenue—well beyond the settled limits of Milwaukee. The company continued to turn out car and truck frames there at a breakneck pace, even after Arthur O. Smith's death in 1913. His son and successor, Lloyd Raymond Smith, kept raising the bar. In about 1915, he directed the company's engineers to find a way to make automobile frames automatically.

After an exhaustive round of trials and errors (and an investment of $8 million, more than $120 million today), the engineers were ready to unveil their creation in 1921. A. O. Smith's automatic frame plant was a mechanical marvel, combining 552 separate operations, from cutting and bending to riveting and painting, in a seamless flow that produced one frame every eight seconds—more than ten thousand a day. *Fortune* magazine called the Twenty-Seventh Street facility "the most advanced single exhibit of automatic function in the world."

Applied research became A. O. Smith's hallmark. In 1930, the company completed its seven-story research building, a modernist icon whose clean lines and accordion glass walls still seem contemporary many decades later. Some of the ideas developed and refined in the research building had nothing to do with cars or trucks. The most significant involved a technology for rolling sheets of steel into tubes and then closing them with welds that were practically seamless.

That basic technology underpinned product lines that were extraordinarily diverse and hugely successful. Joined at their ends, A. O. Smith tubes formed pipelines that moved oil and gas all over the world. Lined with glass and closed at their ends, the same cylinders became brewery storage tanks when Prohibition ended in 1933. Fitted with nose cones and tail fins, the smaller cylinders became bomb casings; A. O. Smith produced 80 percent of the nation's supply during World War II. The same techniques were applied to agriculture after the war, and the company's tall blue Harvestore silos still dominate the skyline in countless rural communities.

It was in the postwar decades that A. O. Smith hit its stride. As demand for all of its products soared to record levels, the complex on North Twenty-Seventh Street swelled to well over a hundred buildings on 140 acres of land. The Smith plant was practically a city in itself, supporting nearly nine thousand employees on all three shifts. Many were Black Milwaukeeans who were finally earning the high wages and generous benefits that constituted one version of the American Dream.

More recent decades have been less kind to both A. O. Smith and its workers. The 1982 recession shook the company to its foundation, but a shift in automotive technology caused even more problems. Struggling to keep pace with their Japanese competitors, American carmakers abandoned conventional steel frames in favor of less costly (and lower-quality) unibody construction. As demand for its core product plummeted, the company simply saw more opportunity in its non-automotive

On the plant's last day in 2006, Eddie Ballard struggled for composure after forty-one years on the job.
MILWAUKEE JOURNAL SENTINEL

markets. In 1997, Smith sold the frame business and related lines to Tower Automotive for $625 million.

The post-sale story was sadly familiar: layoffs, wage cuts, bankruptcy, and then, in 2006, the end of the line for the Twenty-Seventh Street plant. As building after building was either mothballed or demolished, the historic Smith complex looked undeniably forlorn. In 2009, after acquiring most of the site, the City of Milwaukee announced plans to turn it into a "modern business park" called Century City. It has attracted businesses that make everything from passenger trains to beer cans, but the development of Century City has proceeded at a snail's pace.

The A. O. Smith plant was once a world-class metal-bender that provided a smooth ride for millions of American drivers and smooth sailing for thousands of Milwaukee workers. An earlier generation undoubtedly thought it would last forever. We know better, but the knowledge brings no comfort. As the story of another industrial giant ends in an obituary, we're left to wonder, once again, what comes next.

Hog Heaven

Harley-Davidson Makes the Most of Its History

E very five years, ready or not, the Harley hordes rumble into town. Workaday concerns are put aside as riders converge on Milwaukee, the company's birthplace, by the tens of thousands, sparking impromptu parades on local freeways and turning bar-district sidewalks into showcases of tattoos and leather. The company keeps the fun going with factory tours, an open house at its Menomonee Valley museum, picnics, and big-name concerts, but the riders are more than capable of generating their own entertainment. Milwaukee's children fall asleep to the steady thunder of two-cylinder engines.

I remember the 2003 reunion in particular. Billed as the centennial celebration, it was appropriately grand. On Labor Day weekend that year, a city unaccustomed to national attention found itself in the limelight, happily besieged by two hundred fifty thousand Harley-Davidson riders and a small army of journalists covering every twist of the throttle. My brother Mike was part of the spectacle, riding down from Minnesota on his 1970 Electra Glide (turquoise with cream panels) as head of the Nobody's Motorcycle Club. ("Who's in your club?" "Nobody.")

It was a great party, but I remember wondering how many of the Harley horde had a clear idea of what they were celebrating. A centennial, yes, but a centennial of what? Precisely what happened back in 1903 is still something of a mystery, and

Harley-Davidson could actually pick any number of dates to celebrate its inception. William Harley drew his first plans for a motorcycle engine in 1901. The earliest commercial cycles—the ones sold to actual customers—rolled out in 1903 or 1904 (although "Model 1" dates to 1905). The company was officially incorporated in 1907. The year 1903 works as well as any, and so it has come to be celebrated as the official date when Harley-Davidson started its engines.

A number of other myths and mysteries surround the company's early years. The first carburetor may or may not have been a tomato can. The Harley and Davidson families are described as next-door neighbors in some accounts, even though they lived almost three miles apart. The firm's first "factory," a ten-by-fifteen-foot shed in the Davidsons' backyard, was either built by an indulgent father for his sons or usurped by those sons from a resistant parent.

Given Harley-Davidson's legendary status, it's not surprising that its origins are shrouded in legend. The heart of the story is

Harley-Davidson has always been synonymous with the freedom of the open road. The sign on the post reads "5 Miles to Milwaukee Limits." MILWAUKEE COUNTY HISTORICAL SOCIETY

compelling enough. In the early 1900s, William Harley and Arthur Davidson decided to build a motorized bicycle. The friends were mechanically inclined, and at least one had worked in a local bicycle factory. They were, at twenty-one and twenty, less than half the age of the company's average customer today.

The pair's early work showed promise, and they soon graduated to the fabled shed behind the Davidson family's house at Thirty-Eighth Street and Highland Avenue. (Bill Harley lived at Twelfth and Burleigh.) The enterprise also attracted two more Davidson brothers: Walter, who served as first president; and William, the eldest, who took charge of manufacturing. Bill Harley remained the company's chief engineer, and Art Davidson concentrated on building a dealer network.

They were a formidable team, and the company prospered from the start. When the expanded backyard shed proved too small, Harley and the three Davidsons moved to a new shop one block north, at Thirty-Eighth and Juneau. The company's headquarters, much enlarged, is still there—a testament to tenacity in the best Milwaukee tradition.

What set Harley-Davidson apart from its hundreds of competitors was the sheer practicality of its machine. Many early motorcycles built by other companies were little more than bicycles with engines strapped to their frames, and the bumps of the open road often jolted them to pieces. Harleys were built to last from the beginning. The debut of the V-twin engine in 1909 (with a major upgrade in 1911) gave Harley-Davidson the power to run with the leaders. Long hours, savvy marketing, and attention to quality did the rest. By 1920—not even two decades after the earliest sketches—Harley-Davidson was the largest motorcycle manufacturer in America.

The company's success was evident in more than its sales performance. Harley-Davidson became one of those rare businesses that develops a genuine mystique. Highly publicized

The company began in a ten-by-fifteen-foot shed at the Davidson family's
West Side home. MILWAUKEE COUNTY HISTORICAL SOCIETY

racing successes, stylish designs, and pop-culture endorse-
ments, from James Dean to Peter Fonda, lent the brand a mantle
of glamor, and the Hell's Angels and their satanic brethren
added a potent outlaw element. The amalgam of speed, style,
and raw power, with an added hint of danger, appealed to den-
tists and dropouts alike. Harley-Davidson bikes became the icons
of a new romanticism, attracting riders who relish the wind in
their hair—and don't mind the bugs in their teeth.

And so a legend is celebrated every five years in the place of its
birth. The well-attended orgies of chrome have an important local
dimension. Harley-Davidson fits squarely in the metal-bending
tradition that made Milwaukee the Machine Shop of the World
for much of the twentieth century. The community's stock in
trade was heavy equipment—machine tools, mining shovels,
tractors, gears, construction machinery, and other items rarely
purchased by the average consumer. That left beer—a German
contribution—to shape Milwaukee's well-advertised image in

the popular imagination. Harley-Davidson's success added another dimension to the city's image in the wider world.

The pairing of beer and motorcyles is expressed geographically on Milwaukee's West Side. The headquarters of Harley-Davidson and Miller Brewing are literally one block apart, separated only by Highland Boulevard, and the (unmarked) site of that famous ten-by-fifteen-foot shed where Bill Harley and Art Davidson built their first machines is just outside Miller's main offices. The two consumer products on which the community hangs its reputation are close indeed.

Not that either company has had it easy. Now part of Molson Coors Beverage Company, Miller has overcome any number of obstacles to become the last major brewery operating in Milwaukee. Harley had a near-death experience of its own in the 1970s, sinking so close to bankruptcy that a stiff tariff on Japanese bikes was necessary to keep it afloat. New management brought the company roaring back to dominance in the motorcycle world's heavyweight division. Fifty years later, the graying of Harley's core ridership and the sales resistance of younger prospects represent another threat, prompting the company to develop an extensive Learn to Ride program and its first-ever electric bike.

Corporate strategies will continue to evolve, but the similarities between Milwaukee and its homegrown machine remain more than skin deep. Both city and cycle are more substantial than streamlined, more steak than sizzle. Both are rooted in a warts-and-all tradition of hard work and elemental honesty. Harley-Davidson is an American classic based in a Genuine American city. The leather bras and black T-shirts may come out of the dresser only once every five years, but Harley-Davidson remains a tradition to celebrate. Whatever bumps emerge in the road ahead, the legendary status of "Milwaukee Iron" is secure.

Strong Spirits, Stronger Aroma

Red Star Yeast Was an Olfactory Landmark

The company was never a major employer. No tourists were invited to visit the plant, and it's doubtful that many would have accepted. Red Star Yeast kept a decidedly low profile, and yet it was one of Milwaukee's most conspicuous industries for decades. Perched on the north rim of the Menomonee Valley at Twenty-Seventh Street, the plant was practically on the shoulder of Interstate 94, seen by tens of thousands of motorists every day. What most people remember, however, is not the sight but the smell. As an olfactory landmark, Red Star had few equals in Milwaukee or anywhere else.

The aroma was in the love-it-or-hate-it category: pungent, organic, suggesting origins in wetness and warmth. It was probably a little too rich, a little too ripe, for most passersby on I-94, but the smell certainly made an impression. Although the plant was demolished in 2012, it remains etched in Milwaukee's collective memory—and in our nasal passages.

Red Star made a different sort of impression on the local economy as one of the relatively few food and beverage companies that wasn't a brewery. It was no surprise that beer makers would find a ready market in a community as German as Milwaukee, but there were always consumers with a taste for the harder stuff. In late 1882, a group of local entrepreneurs, all of them Germans, founded the Meadow Springs Distillery. Within

Red Star Yeast began as the Meadow Springs distillery on the north rim of the Menomonee Valley in 1882. WHI IMAGE ID 54551

months, they had purchased a small parcel of land on the northern edge of the Menomonee Valley and put up a two-story building, using stone quarried from the adjacent bluff. The location was comfortably remote but still close enough to attract workers. By the end of 1883, Meadow Springs had sent one hundred eighty thousand gallons of whiskey out into a thirsty world.

Renamed National Distilling in 1887, the company's product line expanded from straight whiskey to such bygone brands as Mistletoe Old Tom Gin, National Rye Malt Gin, and Livingston Bourbon. Useful byproducts were created as well, particularly yeast. During the fermentation process, this magical microorganism digests the sugars in grain, for instance, and converts them to alcohol and carbon dioxide. It continues to eat—and continues to multiply—until there's nothing left to consume, and a surplus of live yeast always remained in National Distilling's vats after the liquor was drawn off.

The company decided to sell it. Compressed into cakes and packaged under the Red Star label, Milwaukee-made yeast became a mainstay of bakers throughout Wisconsin and far beyond. The valley plant's annual output topped two hundred thousand pounds as early as 1885. "It is pure," declared an early Red Star ad, "and makes wholesome bread."

Spent grain was another abundant byproduct. Rich in proteins, fats, and fibers, it was an ideal animal food, and the distillery doubled as a feedlot. National's owners fattened their own herd of 239 cows and 69 bulls in the mid-1880s, but there was still used mash to spare. Some was sold or given to neighboring farmers, and the remainder was left to rot on the distillery grounds.

In that era of reckless disregard for the environment, the unpleasant result was a monumental pollution problem. One local resident wrote an angry letter to the *Milwaukee Sentinel* in 1891, condemning what he described as "the nuisance caused by depositing the surplus slops of the distillery on the ground south of the railroad track, which fermented and festered there until they had become almost a living mass of putridity." The pile was so poisonous, he complained, "that the gases arising from it destroyed all vegetable life surrounding it."

National Distilling's owners responded that their firm was "a simon pure home institution" whose operations were not polluting the valley "to any appreciable extent"—at least no more than the tanneries, slaughterhouses, and soap factories nearby. The distillers did install equipment to dry their spent grain, but waste liquids still flowed into the Menomonee River, which bubbled its malodorous way toward Lake Michigan, unfit for fish, waterfowl, or human beings.

Production, and pollution, continued to grow in the twentieth century, as National Distilling became a truly national supplier of both liquor and yeast. It was Prohibition that prompted a major shift in the company's direction. Barred by law from making its primary product, National turned to its primary byproduct. Yeast became, in a sense, the tail that wagged the dog, and in 1919—the year Prohibition began—National Distilling changed its name to Red Star Yeast and Products.

When the drought finally ended in 1933, the valley plant resumed gin production for a few years, but Red Star's leaders ultimately decided that there was a more secure future in yeast. Molasses replaced grain as the nutrient for the hungry microbes, and the company's national distribution network expanded rapidly.

Red Star's signature product had always been cut into cakes and wrapped in foil, but experiments with dry yeast in granular form yielded a less-perishable product. When America entered World War II in 1941, dry yeast became a staple in every army kitchen, and Red Star supplied five million pounds to the military before the fighting was over.

The company's focus broadened steadily in the decades following World War II. Concluding that they were in a mature industry with little long-term growth potential, the firm's leaders began to look elsewhere for opportunities to expand, usually by acquiring other companies. New business lines ranged from frozen eggs to ready-mix rolls. The campaign reached its first climax in 1962, when Red Star adopted the name of a recent acquisition: Universal Foods. The new name, said then-CEO Russell Wirth, "will better reflect the company's increasingly diversified product line in the food field."

There was no looking back after that corporate decision. Universal Foods absorbed companies that made Italian cheese, frozen french fries, soft drinks, pretzels, and dehydrated onions, among other products, but it eventually settled on flavors, colors, and fragrances—value-added specialty products that were used in cosmetics, printer inks, and pharmaceuticals as well as foods. In 2000, still based in Milwaukee, Universal Foods changed its name once again, to Sensient Technologies. "It clearly is a new company," said Kenneth Manning, the CEO at the time. "The businesses we're in today we were not in twenty years ago."

There was no room for an old standby in the new global enterprise. In 2000, Sensient sold its Red Star division to Le Saffre, a French yeast maker, for $125 million and exited the business that had long been its reason for being.

It was ironic, given Red Star's shrinking role in the parent company after World War II, that the division's profile in its hometown grew dramatically. That newfound prominence was largely the result of a transportation planning decision. The founders of the Meadow Springs Distillery couldn't have guessed in 1882 that a high-speed, high-volume superhighway would one day slice through their backyard. If Red Star had been tucked away in a quieter corner of the valley, its distinctive aroma might have blended into the general air currents wafting over central Milwaukee. In the mid-1960s, however, when I-94 was completed to downtown, a substantial portion of the region's population breathed the plant's discharges every day. The smell was inescapable, enveloping motorists on their journeys in and out of the city.

The discharges ended in late 2005, nearly forty years after I-94 opened. Citing "overall plant economics," Le Saffre closed Red Star's valley plant and moved production to a brand-new facility in Cedar Rapids, Iowa. The smell vanished, and so, seven years later, did the plant that produced it.

I doubt that many Milwaukeeans really miss the odor, but it's not hard to feel a touch of nostalgia for Red Star Yeast. The plant was a Milwaukee icon for well over a century, a fixture of daily life that added something distinctive to the landscape, and to the atmosphere. But even the most aromatic icons can't stand forever. The Red Star property has become what it was before 1882: raw land, awaiting a new story to tell.

Requiem for Local 1111

Shifting Paradigms on Greenfield Avenue

S ometimes entire epochs end with a whimper. That was the case on July 31, 2010, when Local 1111 of the United Electrical, Radio and Machine Workers ceased to exist. For nearly seventy-five years, the union had represented workers at Allen-Bradley and its successor, Rockwell Automation, both world leaders in the production of industrial controls. At the stroke of midnight on July 31, the handful of dues-paying members who remained—electricians, maintenance crews, cafeteria staff—were terminated, and their jobs were taken by contract workers earning dollars less per hour.

The outward appearance of the massive Rockwell plant changed not at all. The former factory contains two million square feet of floor space spread across four square blocks on Milwaukee's near South Side. Crowned by an illuminated clock tower that was the world's largest for decades, the complex is still one of Milwaukee's most prominent landmarks. Inside, however, a transformation had been underway for years. White-collar employees steadily replaced production workers; space once occupied by machinists and assemblers was redesigned for the cubicles of software engineers and account managers. Thousands of people still reported for work every day, but with one critical difference: no one made anything. With the demise of Local 1111, the Industrial Age was over, at least on South Second Street.

These assemblers were among the Allen-Bradley employees who organized Local 1111 of the United Electrical Workers in 1937. MILWAUKEE COUNTY HISTORICAL SOCIETY

The existence of a labor union at the original Allen-Bradley plant was highly ironic. When brothers Lynde and Harry Bradley were at the helm, the company was a famously benevolent employer. In the 1920s, the factory had marble washrooms, a wood-paneled reading room, and a rooftop sundeck where employees could dance, box, play badminton, or tee off into nets suspended above Greenfield Avenue. Other opportunities ranged from bowling leagues to a national-caliber basketball team and, after World War II, the celebrated Allen-Bradley Orchestra and Chorus, a "show band" that served as an ambassador for both the company and the community.

If Allen-Bradley was famously benevolent, the company was just as famously paternalistic. The lavish facilities and ambitious programs were designed to promote a sense of family, and no one had to ask who the fathers were: the Bradley brothers and their chief lieutenant, Fred Loock. The trio stood alone at the top of the corporate hierarchy, and they firmly believed that Father knew best.

In the 1930s, a pivotal decade for American labor, the employees of Allen-Bradley developed a taste for independence. The Wagner Act of 1935, which recognized the right of workers to organize and bargain collectively, touched off an epidemic of labor fever all across America, including the South Side of Milwaukee. In May 1937, over the heartfelt objections of management, a solid majority of employees voted to form Local 1111 of the United Electrical Workers.

The Bradleys accepted the new order graciously. "Collective bargaining with our employees through a Union," wrote Harry, "is a new experience for the company and our employees, and it is only fair that we now all cooperate with the Union." Civility prevailed for the first year or two, but a bitter strike in 1939 tested the limits of the relationship. The walkout ended after twelve weeks—without the closed shop demanded by the union. The Bradleys, for their part, never lost their faith in welfare capitalism. They maintained and expanded the employee amenities of previous years, convinced that Allen-Bradley was a family even when its members disagreed.

It was in the decades after World War II that a predictable pattern developed. Local 1111 and Allen-Bradley's management sat down every three years to hammer out a contract, meeting dozens of times in a typical cycle. Strikes were infrequent but serious, and the general movement was upward: in wages, benefits, and working conditions. Adding fifteen cents an hour and a week's vacation in one round of negotiations, thirty cents and paid health insurance in the next, the union pushed wages and

Strikes like this 1964 walkout strained labor-management relations but
led to a higher standard of living for thousands of Allen-Bradley workers.
MILWAUKEE JOURNAL SENTINEL

benefits to levels unimagined in the 1920s, and salaried office
workers always received what management called "a correspond-
ing increase."

The company had no shortage of cash to reward its employees for their labor. Demand for Allen-Bradley's industrial controls went through the roof after World War II, and by 1968 the
payroll had swelled to nearly seven thousand workers, most of
them union members. The Second Street plant was filled with
people twenty-four hours a day, creating some memorable
traffic jams at shift change. Factories elsewhere in Milwaukee
and across the country were experiencing the same prosperity.
For many years, in fact, Allen-Bradley's contracts were pat-
terned after those negotiated at General Electric, a much larger
competitor.

The rising tide lifted an entire fleet of blue-collar boats. Simply put, America's working class became its middle class in a single generation. Factory workers without a high school diploma could afford houses, cars, cabins, and college tuition for their children. It was economic prosperity and the unyielding pressure of labor unions that made it all possible.

That pressure, of course, made American workers among the highest paid in the world, and a countertrend eventually asserted itself. As global competition intensified, Allen-Bradley, like all of its peers, began to cut costs by shifting work to lower-wage locales in rural Wisconsin, the southern United States, Mexico, and ultimately Asia. The movement was first apparent in the 1970s. "We are trying to resist the concept of exporting jobs," said Tiny Rader, Allen-Bradley's CEO from 1970 to 1981, "but neither do we want to be buried with honors as a good corporate citizen."

The trend continued after the company was sold to Rockwell International in 1985. Saddled with an outmoded multistory building and what it considered a noncompetitive wage structure, Rockwell shifted even more production work away from Milwaukee, using both layoffs and attrition. The local shop force plummeted from 5,500 workers in 1980 to 2,500 in 1985, 1,850 in 1990, and 550 in 2006. Local 1111's membership had nowhere to go but down, and it dwindled to a mere 130 on the union's last day.

Some stark ironies were soon apparent. In 1999, even as the shop force shrank, Rockwell made the Milwaukee complex its global headquarters. In the same plant where industrial workers once turned out switches, starters, relays, and timers by the thousands, a highly trained and largely college-educated staff spent their days designing, selling, and supporting some of the most sophisticated factory automation systems in the world— systems that further reduced the need for production workers. The intellectual content is local; actual manufacturing of those systems might take place anywhere on earth.

Anywhere, that is, but Milwaukee, and Rockwell was hardly alone. By the time the lights went out at Local 1111's headquarters, production at other Milwaukee mainstays had also ended with a whimper. The list included Allis-Chalmers, A. O. Smith, Evinrude, Nordberg, Pfister & Vogel, Heil, and Louis Allis, all household names in their industries. Manufacturing is far from dead in the former Machine Shop of the World, but it is radically diminished.

Milwaukee's experience is a microcosm of what has happened all around the country. Globalization has transformed the American economy at its core, and no amount of coaxing will put the genie back in the bottle. For Rockwell and its counterparts that are still in business, the decision to move production offshore is logical, perhaps even necessary. But as manufacturing costs go down, what other kinds of costs have risen? Without an industrial base to absorb and advance our less-educated workers, what has happened to the vaunted American Dream? Without Local 1111 and thousands like it to promote their interests, how will those without college degrees find their way into the middle class?

America is growing an army of the dislocated and disaffected, and in their plight lie the seeds of a permanent underclass and a bitter foretaste of conditions in the developing world. As knowledge workers replace production workers, we have created a relatively small elite—one based largely on educational privilege—and a huge mass of Americans with lagging incomes and shrinking aspirations. That is the same structural inequity that has long prevailed south of our border. How long before the gap grows so wide that North America becomes indistinguishable, in all but language and landscape, from South America?

Putting the "Labor" in Labor Day

A Day for Workers, a Day for All of Us

We observe them as the traditional bookends of summer: Memorial Day to begin the season and Labor Day to end it. Both are occasions for cookouts and camping trips, but that's not how they began. Understandably but unfortunately, we tend to forget the war fatalities that gave rise to the first holiday and the workers' movement that created the second. Unions spare no effort to remind us. In Milwaukee, the most visible aid to memory is Laborfest, a free, all-ages event on the Summerfest grounds that features music and food, speeches and solidarity.

The Labor Day tradition is well over a century old. In the late 1800s, as America industrialized, ten-hour days and six-day workweeks were the prevailing standard. Factory hands naturally developed an intense interest in a "workingman's holiday," a day of rest and recreation for the overtaxed masses. American unions had even bigger fish to fry—the eight-hour day, an end to child labor, and workplace safety laws among them—but Labor Day was viewed as both an incremental step toward recognition of labor's true worth and a way to exercise the movement's growing muscle.

Although the origin of Labor Day is a matter of some dispute, it was first observed in New York City in 1882. The holiday's progress thereafter was slow but steady. First by custom, then by law, the first Monday in September became the generally

Labor Day parades like this one on North Third Street (now Martin Luther King Drive) were well-attended showcases for Milwaukee's trade unions. The Schlitz brewery is in the left background. MILWAUKEE COUNTY HISTORICAL SOCIETY

accepted date for the holiday, and one state after another made it official. Fifteen states had approved their own Labor Days by 1891. Wisconsin joined the crowd two years later, and the holiday went national in 1894.

Milwaukee was particularly fertile ground for the celebration. As the self-proclaimed Machine Shop of the World, the city earned its living as a manufacturing center. In 1880, industrial workers made up 45 percent of the city's labor force, one of the highest concentrations in America. Those workers had organized early and often. The first homegrown union, representing a variety of tradesmen, was founded in 1842, four years before Milwaukee received its city charter. Skilled shoemakers followed suit in 1847, organizing the Knights of St. Crispin. The Knights grew from their Milwaukee base to become a national union with a membership of fifty thousand, briefly the largest in the country.

In 1886, under the banner of the Knights of Labor, a broadly inclusive national union, Milwaukee became a center of agitation for the eight-hour day without a cut in pay. The campaign ended—temporarily—when state militia troops killed seven strikers marching on a Bay View iron mill, but the shootings gave the concept of Labor Day new and poignant relevance. With the battle lines so clearly drawn, it was imperative for local unions to demonstrate their solidarity and declare their insistence on being heard.

In the late 1880s, even before the holiday became official, a durable template for its celebration emerged. Milwaukee's Federated Trades Council was usually in charge, and its leaders arranged a parade, a picnic (complete with message-heavy speeches and lighthearted games), and an evening ball.

The parades were the most visible element of Labor Day. In the 1890s, there were often as many as five thousand workers in the line of march, with a multiple of that number watching from the curb; the processions could easily last for three hours. Many of the participating unions represented trades that are still familiar—carpenters, brewers, machinists, molders, painters—but other groups have long since faded into the mist, including the Lumber Vessel Unloaders Union, the Horse Collar Makers Union, the Typographers Union (familiarly and unfortunately known as "the Typos"), the Mattress Makers Union, and other associations representing coal heavers, hod carriers, stone pavers, coopers, cigarmakers, and horseshoers.

The most ambitious unions created floats that showcased their skills. The *Milwaukee Sentinel* praised the Seamen's Union's 1899 float, a rolling facsimile of "a three-master, square-rigged, and manned by ten sailors in navy uniforms." In 1891, 372 carpenters in blue overalls marched behind a wagon bearing "a cottage perfect in its appointments." Two years later, the cigar-makers outdid themselves with a procession of four floats. The first three depicted grim scenes of "cheap made cigars" being turned out by prison inmates, Chinese immigrants, and tenement dwellers. The final float, reported the *Milwaukee Journal*, showed a union shop where "a number of smart workmen busied themselves with their work." Piling sexism on stereotype, the union shop float featured "a beautiful blonde woman . . . surrounded by Indians and other typical national figures."

The participating groups could cut an imposing figure even without floats. In 1891, two thousand union painters in white overalls walked the route carrying palettes and brushes. Two years later, several hundred brewery workers marched in formation sporting red, white, and blue sashes; black silk caps; and walking sticks—a sight impressive enough for the *Journal* to call it "the finest part of the parade."

In the 1890s and for years thereafter, the parade's destination was always a beer garden, usually Schlitz Park on Eighth and Brown but sometimes the Milwaukee Garden on Fourteenth and State or National Park on Twenty-Seventh and National. The mood in the gardens, like the music from the bandstands, tended to be light. Revelers enjoyed picnic lunches as well as a full schedule of games, including tug-of-war and a variety of races: egg, potato, three-legged, and fat man's. In 1899, six thousand people gathered at Schlitz Park. "There was red lemonade in abundance for the girls," reported the *Milwaukee Sentinel*, "red, white and brown soda water for the boys, an abundance of foaming beer for the men and women, and happiness in large chunks all over the grounds for all."

The seriousness of labor's struggle was not forgotten in the merrymaking. Every gathering in those early years featured at least two speeches, one in English and the other in German. The rhetoric could be incendiary. The English orator in 1893 called for "industrial emancipation" from the evils of a system that had produced "an arrogant plutocracy and impoverished the common people." In 1898, the German speaker went so far as to claim that "wage slavery" was worse than the barbarous realities of the pre-emancipation South. "Workingmen are merchandise now," claimed Julius Valteich. "The old slave was at least sure of getting work and being taken care of under all circumstances."

However hyperbolic some of the rhetoric, there was a powerful political dimension to Labor Day. Both major parties were self-dealing patronage machines at the turn of the twentieth century, and their malfeasance opened the door to third parties, notably the Socialists. Even though he worked with a pen rather than his hands, Victor Berger, the movement's local leader, spoke at the 1894 event and chaired the 1895 observance. "We must have a two-armed labor movement," Berger declared, "a movement with a political arm and with an economic arm." That was the essence of his Milwaukee Idea, which called for Berger's Social-Democratic Party and the city's trade unions to form "a grand army moving on two roads for the abolition of the capitalist system." The Milwaukee Idea bore abundant fruit in the municipal election of 1910, when Socialists scored a landslide victory, and the movement developed sufficient momentum to keep a Socialist in the mayor's office until 1960, when Frank Zeidler chose not to seek a fourth term.

Labor Day was celebrated all the while, through booms and recessions, dramatic victories and crushing defeats, and it remains a fixture in American life. Just as they weathered mechanization in the nineteenth century, unions have run the gauntlet of deindustrialization in the late twentieth and political bloodletting in the twenty-first. But the holiday, like the movement it celebrates, has endured.

Milwaukee's modern Laborfests involve teachers and healthcare workers as well as painters and pipefitters, but they retain remarkable fidelity to celebrations past, with a parade, a picnic, and speeches that evoke the ideals of our ancestors. Even the location honors tradition; the Summerfest grounds are a super-sized version of a genuine nineteenth-century beer garden.

More important is the spirit of the observance. For well over 125 years, unions have added balance to our country's larger economic equation. In playing their role so well for so long, they have helped to create the American middle class, affirmed the dignity of all work, and enlarged the national conversation. The next time Labor Day rolls around on the calendar, enjoy the last long weekend of summer, but don't forget that it was brought to you, like so much else, by organized labor.

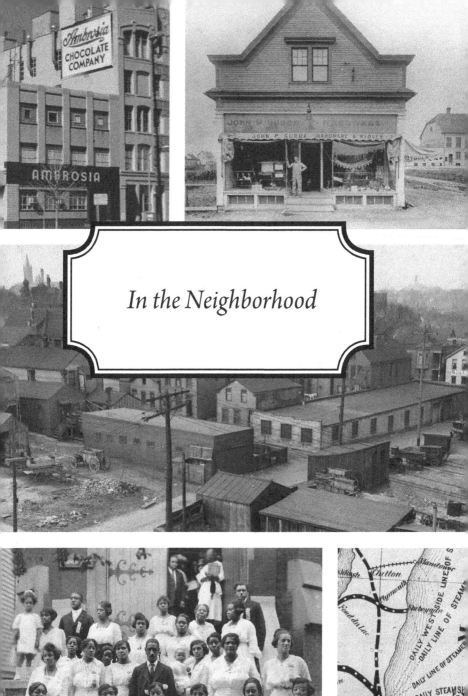

In the Neighborhood

In the Neighborhood

Witness to Change

Layton Park Neighborhood Tells an Urban Story

I've decided what I want to be when I retire. Not a teller of cautionary tales to the young, not an ache-by-ache chronicler of my ongoing deterioration, and not, heaven forbid, a golfer. What I want to be is something much simpler: an old guy on a bike who rides around looking at things. I might stop once in a while to buy a donut, raise a glass of beer, or fall into casual conversation, but I'll mainly be a witness to change, content to observe the passing scene and enjoy what the poet Wallace Stevens called "the pleasures of merely circulating."

That's something I already do fairly often, to tell the truth, and I find that change is much easier to witness as I burrow deeper into my seventies. Milwaukee landscapes I took for granted in my youth have been altered almost beyond recognition, and there is a widening gap between the city that was and the city that is.

I had an especially vivid version of that experience, likely shared by anyone with long exposure to a single place, on a recent two-wheeled tour of my first neighborhood. Until I was eight years old, my family lived on the southern edge of Layton Park, a section of Milwaukee's South Side bordered roughly by Layton Boulevard, South Thirty-Fifth Street, West Burnham Street, and the Kinnickinnic River. If you're looking for landmarks, Forest Home Cemetery is probably the best known; that gracious graveyard formed the eastern edge of my early world.

John Gurda, my grandfather, stood outside his Layton Park hardware store in 1918. Holy Ghost School, a largely German institution, is on the right. GURDA FAMILY

The reason we lived in Layton Park was generational. My Polish grandparents, John and Mary Gurda, ran a hardware store in the heart of the neighborhood, at Thirty-Second and Lincoln, from 1915 to 1965, and my father, Art, was the oldest of four children raised behind the store. When he and my mother, Clare, a farm girl from western Wisconsin, settled in Milwaukee after World War II, it was entirely natural for them to build a little house on South Thirty-Fourth Street, only eight blocks from the hardware store, and start a family of their own.

The Layton Park of Art Gurda's youth was decidedly mixed. The residents were almost entirely white, but "mixed," in those days, usually had a European connotation. Germans and Poles were almost evenly matched in the neighborhood, some transplanted from the old country and others born here but still speaking their ancestral tongues. Any businessperson who hoped to prosper had to have a working knowledge of both languages, and my grandparents were no exception.

Although Germans and Poles were Layton Park's two largest ethnic groups, a definite pecking order prevailed in the neighborhood. "There was a lot of discrimination there," my father recalled, "first because you were of Polish descent, and second because you were Catholic. The discrimination was just awful. It was almost a daily thing. They'd call you 'dumb Polack' and words to the effect that you were just like dirt, that you couldn't be considered to be on their level. I used to get beaten up once in a while by older German kids who were Lutherans. There was a very great feeling of distrust."

Given the prevailing tensions, it seems surprising that my father's parents sent him to grade school at Holy Ghost, a parish he described as "dyed-in-the-wool German." His explanation was simple: "They wanted me to have a Catholic education." It probably helped that the school was just across Thirty-Second Street from the hardware store.

Dad did well at Holy Ghost, winning a gold medal for scholarship and singing in the boys' choir, but Layton Park's Poles wanted a church of their own. In 1921, they organized St. Barbara's Parish, and three years later, they built a combination church and school precisely two blocks north of Holy Ghost. My grandfather was the first treasurer of St. Barbara's, and my great-uncle, barkeeper Tony Korpal, was a charter trustee.

Despite their mutual distrust, the Germans and Poles of Layton Park had more in common than they might have realized. Both groups had left behind the entry-level squalor of older South Side neighborhoods, trading cramped Polish flats and backyard cottages for relatively spacious duplexes and bungalows. For my grandparents and their neighbors, whatever their backgrounds, moving across Layton Boulevard was like moving to the suburbs.

That upwardly mobile character persisted for decades. When my wife, Sonja, and I were married in 1977, we rented a flat on

Latino families are
nearly as numerous in
today's Layton Park as
Germans and Poles
were a century ago.
ANDERS GURDA

South Thirty-Second Street, continuing an old family tradition.
Our apartment was next door to St. Barbara's convent and just
two blocks from the used-car lot that had replaced Gurda Hardware. Germans and Poles were still Layton Park's two dominant
ethnic groups and, after living in even older sections of town,
both of us felt that we had moved to the edge of the city.

What followed was the greatest demographic shift in the
neighborhood's history. In 1980, soon after Sonja and I left the area
for Bay View, Latino Milwaukeeans made up less than 3 percent of central Layton Park's population. By 2010, the number
had soared to 73 percent in essentially the same blocks, and that
percentage has continued to grow.

The changes go well beyond statistics. Holy Ghost and
St. Barbara's parishes merged as St. Rafael in 1999, and Sunday
Mass at my grandparents' old church is now said in Spanish.
Layton Park Lutheran, where the German boys who once tor-
mented my father attended services, is now Templo Adventista
del Septimo Dia, a Seventh-Day Adventist congregation. Tebo
and Johnson Funeral Home, where roughly half of my relatives

made their last public appearances, has become Iglesia Cristiana Palabra de Vida, or Word of Life Christian Church. El Senorial Restaurant is thriving in what I remember as La Licata's Little Italy. Taverns where my grandfather once bent an elbow now play Spanish *corridos* on the jukebox, and the occasional Mexican flag waves from the front porch of a bungalow that might have been built with nails from Gurda Hardware.

There are still names in Layton Park, and perhaps even a few faces, that my father would have recognized, but they are fewer every year. Is it unsettling to see a neighborhood so tied to my own family's history so completely transformed? Of course it is—most of us share an allergy to change. But I think it's just as important to focus on what remains the same. Layton Park looks much as it did when Sonja and I lived there, and even, in some blocks, as it did when my father was a young man. The houses are in generally good repair, and some could easily be on a tour of homes. After more than a century of change, Layton Park remains a semi-suburban community. For many of its current Latino residents, no less than for my Polish ancestors and their German neighbors, the neighborhood represents a step up and away from the poverty of their first years on the South Side.

Changing neighborhoods provide a wealth of material for meditations on impermanence, but they also underline a fundamental truth about urban life: everything is in motion. Neighborhoods are like vessels, like shells, built by one group and inhabited by a succession of others. Each group makes its own memories and then moves on. As pop singer Jewel succinctly put it, "Everything's temporary if you give it enough time."

It is those layered memories, whether fading or still forming, that constitute every neighborhood's history, and it is the histories of our neighborhoods that tell the story of the city as a whole. The memories are what matter, even when they belong to an old man on a bicycle.

History on the Scrap Heap

Foreclosures Hit Sherman Park Hard

I watched Milwaukee's history being sold by the pound one day in 2013. It arrived variously—stuffed in trash bags, piled on baby strollers, stacked in the beds of rusting pickup trucks—and it all converged on a scrapyard at 3232 West Fond du Lac Avenue. There were plenty of aluminum cans in the flow of recyclables, as well as pots and pans, box springs, bedframes, and entire bicycles, but there was also a disturbing volume of house salvage: aluminum siding, copper pipes, downspouts, loops of electrical wire, water heaters, aluminum window frames, and even bathroom sinks.

There were no architectural treasures in the mix—no pressed-tin ceilings or brass light fixtures—but the materials were historic just the same. Without plumbing, without wiring, without internal systems and some sort of external covering, even the most significant home is an uninhabitable shell.

Was I witnessing the results of a spike in home remodeling projects? A walk through the surrounding blocks suggested otherwise. The scrapyard on Fond du Lac Avenue, one of two United Milwaukee Scrap facilities open to the public, lies at the eastern edge of Sherman Park, a neighborhood bedeviled by a long-running foreclosure crisis. I'd been spending a lot of time in the community as part of the research for *Milwaukee: City of Neighborhoods*, a book that debuted in 2015. My preferred

First boarded up and then stripped of anything with salvage value, fore-closed houses are a cancer on the landscape of Sherman Park. JOHN GURDA

research mode was by bicycle. In a handlebar survey that took me down every street in Sherman Park, I saw more than two hundred boarded-up houses, some of them genuinely historic. A fair number were still relatively intact, but far too many had been picked clean by house strippers, and they fouled the landscape like roadkill carcasses.

Sherman Parkers were eager to tell me what they contended with on a daily basis, particularly in the blocks east of Sherman Boulevard. One landlord was between tenants when house strippers swept through a duplex he owns on Thirty-Third Street and ripped out every single radiator. A year later, he was still repairing the damage. A woman on Thirty-Seventh Street came home from work to find that someone had broken into the vacant house next door. What did they take? "Everything," she told me. Another homeowner on Thirty-Ninth Street woke up one morning and discovered an empty spot in the backyard where his air-conditioning unit had been. A home rehabber with years of experience in Sherman Park was trying to stay one step ahead of the house strippers. "Those [crude expletive] take it all," he complained.

The damage is obvious, but the crime can seem victimless. Many of the vandalized homes I saw in the early 2010s were city-owned, and no one had lived in them for months, even years. The city's professional junkers are careful to distinguish themselves from the criminal element. They tend to be a hard-scrabble lot, just trying to get by while staying on the right side of the law. I talked to half a dozen in the streets and several more waiting in line at the scrapyard. "It's rough out here," said one. "You gotta hustle just to keep yourself fed." He had nothing but scorn for the house strippers, grumbling that they "ruin it for all the rest of us" by increasing police scrutiny.

Nor were the scrap dealers the root cause of the problem. They're in the recycling business, and stolen property doesn't exactly announce itself. A sign at United Milwaukee Scrap contained a long list of forbidden goods, including manhole covers, railroad rails, and "any cemetery item." Every person trying to sell more than aluminum cans had to show an ID at the yard and sign a statement affirming that they owned "all of the material" being offered. Aluminum siding, said one employee, is accepted if it arrives by car or truck but rejected if someone brings it on foot. Although safeguards are in place, the system is, shall we say, permeable. "Believe me," alleged one frequent seller, "they'll take anything."

The police were acutely aware of the problem, and their presence was a real deterrent for house strippers. One junker told of an acquaintance who stole aluminum siding and found a squad car waiting for him at the scrapyard after a neighbor phoned in his description. "That's burglary," said the junker. "You got to ask yourself, is it worth doing the time?" But the police are often stymied by the generic nature of the contraband. "Is it stolen?" said one Seventh District officer. "Unless someone sees you take it, we just don't know."

The real victims of this scourge were, and are, the neighborhood's residents. The pride of Sherman Park is undoubtedly its homes. The community is huge, stretching from Thirtieth to Sixtieth Streets between North Avenue and Capitol Drive, and it took a half century—from 1900 to 1950—for the neighborhood to fill in completely. Three venerable Milwaukee house types reached their peak of development in Sherman Park: duplexes from the early 1900s, bungalows from the 1920s, and Period Revival homes (Tudor, Mediterranean, English cottage, and other styles) from the 1920–1940 period.

All three house types exist elsewhere in Milwaukee, but they are most numerous, and generally larger, in Sherman Park. Although the grandest homes are on the boulevards—Grant, Sherman, and Fifty-First—the entire neighborhood was a magnet for middle- to upper-middle-income Milwaukeeans escaping the congestion of the city's North Side in the first half of the twentieth century. For the German, Jewish, Czech, and other families who were among the early settlers, a house in Sherman Park was a conspicuous symbol of success.

That symbolism is no less powerful for the Black Milwaukeeans who constitute the neighborhood's largest ethnic group today. (All of the people I spoke to for this story were Black, including landlords, homeowners, scrapyard employees, police officers, and junkers.) Tracing their roots to the same North Side neighborhoods as their European predecessors, most of Sherman Park's Black residents view their homes as havens, hard-won and fiercely defended.

The pace may have slowed since 2013, but foreclosures remain a problem, and boarded-up houses still pose a serious threat to the neighborhood. In blocks otherwise bright with banners and filled with flowers, the casualties of foreclosure loom like sentinels of doom, and stripping them only aggravates an impending sense of defeat. "It upsets us," said a Thirty-Eighth Street homeowner. "It brings our property values down." As its history hits the scrap heap, what's most at risk is Sherman Park's future.

There is more to the story, fortunately. On every block, and I mean *every* block, someone is planting mums or painting the porch or hanging seasonal decorations—in other words, making a home. The residential neighborhoods to the east have suffered so much attrition over the years that they look like Swiss cheese, but the homes of Sherman Park are still largely intact, and an active neighborhood association with an extensive network of block clubs and block watches is working to keep them that way. That may be the most effective solution of all: a community so engaged, with so many eyes open and ears attuned, that crime simply cannot take root.

An engaged community is key, but Sherman Park and the neighborhoods nearby also need a timely infusion of cash to demolish the homes that are beyond repair and bring the sounder board-ups back to life. It's an investment worth making—one that would yield handsome dividends in preventing crime, building community, and protecting Milwaukee's architectural heritage. But first the stripping has to be brought under control. Historic preservation, after all, becomes wickedly difficult when there's nothing left to preserve.

Before the Deer District

A New Milwaukee Neighborhood Rises from One of Its Oldest

"Milwaukee's Newest Neighborhood," proclaimed the window signs on Sixth and Juneau. Banners down the street were even more insistent: "We build to live. We build to work. We build to play. We build to STAY." "We," in this case, meant the developers of the Deer District, a mixed-use project that took shape in the wake of Fiserv Forum's 2018 opening. The developers have indeed transformed a sizable swath of downtown Milwaukee's west side. The Forum itself, a metallic taco covering two square blocks, is the main event, and the surrounding area has sprouted apartments, a medical clinic, parking structures, a hotel, and enough nightspots to satisfy the thirstiest millennial. In the middle of it all is a welcome oasis of open space that has been the site of everything from a Christmas market to the Halloween-themed Fear District.

And, oh yes, the 2021 NBA Finals. As Giannis Antetokounmpo led the Milwaukee Bucks to victory over the Phoenix Suns in six games, an estimated one hundred thousand cheering fans—a crowd equivalent to the population of Green Bay—watched the action on giant screens under the open skies of the Deer District. As TV cameras scanned the masses at what seemed like every break in the action, the announcers were incredulous. Few developments anywhere have had such a notable debut on the national stage.

The future Deer District was a jumble of factories, churches, breweries, and soot-stained homes in the early 1900s. MILWAUKEE COUNTY HISTORICAL SOCIETY

I associate my own introduction to the District with a different sport. During the Milwaukee Brewers' 2018 playoff run, I was walking down Old World Third Street south of Juneau Avenue when I heard crowd noise coming from what seemed to be an alley. It turned out to be a brick-paved plaza with the biggest picnic tables this side of Munich's beer halls and a video screen the size of my backyard. Christian Yelich had just scored, and the crowd was going crazy. For a moment I didn't know where I was. I had the dreamlike sensation that I'd been transported to another city. Hadn't this been a forlorn vacant lot and a nondescript parking structure the last time I'd noticed?

Attending my first Bucks game a couple of months later felt just as otherworldly. After what seemed like an unbelievably short construction period, here was a state-of-the-art basketball venue that was both louder and more intimate than the Bradley Center it replaced. I liked the space, although I was less taken with Fiserv Forum's ten-dollar beers, and I found the barrage of "entertainment" at every time-out agitating. Why, I wondered, can't they just let us watch the game? That, I freely admit, may be the generational reaction of an older Milwaukeean more naturally attuned to the stately pace of baseball than run-and-gun basketball.

Although the Deer District may be Milwaukee's "newest neighborhood," it has a distinctive past. Every time I've visited the area, I've been struck by how many incarnations the west side of downtown has had. In the early days of European settlement, of course, there was nothing—nothing but wetland. The west side was a tamarack swamp in which stray cows would sometimes be mired up to their bellies. The area's first white settlers, including founder Byron Kilbourn, had to build their homes on the first available dry ground, which began at Juneau Avenue.

Kilbourntown prospered, first in competition and then, after the city's incorporation in 1846, in uneasy collaboration with Juneautown, its cross-river rival and the site of Solomon Juneau's original trading post. Uncounted tons of landfill created the west side's first mixed-use district. Shops and offices sprang up on both Wisconsin Avenue and Third Street, hundreds of homes were built north and west of those thoroughfares, and industry, in those pre-zoning days, was scattered liberally throughout.

The district's early accent was unmistakably German. Immigrants from the Teutonic states made up a majority of Milwaukee's population as early as 1860, and the west side became their particular stronghold. German was just as necessary in the shops on Third Street as Spanish is on Cesar Chavez Drive today. German churches abounded, including one on Fourth and Highland called St. John's Lutheran Church of the Unaltered Augsburg Confession. Nonreligious German gathering spots were just as plentiful: Liederkranz Hall, Liedertafel Hall, Freie Gemeinde Hall, the German Club Hall, and—the last one standing—Turner Hall. The yeasty smell of brewing lager wafted over the neighborhood twenty-four hours a day, coming from Schlitz to the north, Pabst to the west, and a number of smaller producers in the heart of the district.

The fondly remembered Ambrosia Chocolate plant occupied what is now practically center court at Fiserv Forum. MILWAUKEE COUNTY HISTORICAL SOCIETY

Most of the city's original German families moved north and west as their fortunes improved, and in their wake came one of the most jumbled masses of humanity Milwaukee has ever known. Between 1900 and 1930, the future Deer District provided a foothold for Greeks, Hungarians, Russian Jews, Italians, Czechs, and African Americans, sharing the same blocks and sometimes the same tenements.

The neighborhood grew both denser and more diverse as the years passed. It's easy to forget how much life can be packed into a single piece of urban real estate. I did a careful check of the 1925 city directory for every address inside the footprint of Fiserv Forum—a two-block parcel bordered by Vel Phillips Avenue (Fourth Street) and Sixth Street between Highland and Juneau Avenues. My search turned up seven soft drink parlors (Prohibition-era saloons), six restaurants, three real estate offices, two leather stores, two machine shops, two auto repair shops, a horseshoer, a tea shop, a plumber, a printer, a shirt manufacturer, a clothes presser, a carpet cleaner, a billiard hall, an undertaker, a junk dealer—and 103 households.

All that variety was packed into just two square blocks, and at the very heart of the area—practically on Fiserv Forum's center court today—was a Milwaukee institution: Ambrosia Chocolate. The Ambrosia plant's heavenly aroma was one of downtown's singular pleasures from 1894 until the plant moved to Menomonee Falls nearly a century later.

And then there was nothing again. As the district continued to age, its buildings became increasingly expendable, particularly in the post-World War II years. By 1960, the area was pocked with parking lots, and shortly thereafter its northern blocks were bulldozed completely for the Park East Freeway. Public opposition halted construction of that super-road when less than a mile had been completed. Traffic was so light that Mayor John Norquist, an ardent foe of any and all freeways, was able to lobby the state successfully for its removal. The Park East spur came down in 2002, opening twenty-six acres of prime downtown real estate to development.

Progress was relatively slow and disjointed at first, but in 2016, after the Milwaukee Bucks changed owners and the NBA practically demanded a new arena, ground was broken for what became Fiserv Forum. With Wisconsin taxpayers footing nearly half the $524 million bill, the arena gave Milwaukee a brand-new gathering place, and the larger Deer District has brought welcome new life to the heart of the city.

"Milwaukee's Newest Neighborhood"? Sure, but let's not ignore the presence of the past. Fiserv Forum takes its place in a long line of civic gathering places built west of the river: the Auditorium (now the Miller High Life Theatre) in 1909, the Arena in 1950, and the Bradley Center in 1988. When Fiserv Forum opened in 2018, it was the latest expression of a venerable Milwaukee tradition. And the Deer District surrounding it? Milwaukee's newest neighborhood rests firmly on the buried foundations of one of its oldest.

New Life in an Old Square

Near North Neighborhoods Showcase Diversity

E ven amateur naturalists know the trick. You tell the kids in your charge to drop a hula hoop over a random circle of grassland or forest floor and then have them count—and, with help, identify—every plant that falls within the circle. Even a weedy lot behind a suburban strip mall might yield a dozen different species. The idea is to give students an object lesson in the diversity of nature, a hands-on grasp of the astounding number of interdependent organisms that make up a single community.

You can do the same thing with a city. Instead of a hula hoop, however, draw a circle on a map—or, conforming to the urban grid, a square. Any square would do, but one particularly interesting section is just north of downtown Milwaukee, bordered by North Sixth Street, West North Avenue, Walnut/Pleasant Street, and on the east, the Milwaukee River and North Holton Street. Once an undifferentiated part of the Sixth Ward, this fifty-square-block area now contains three distinct neighborhoods: Brewer's Hill, Halyard Park, and Commerce Street.

Brewer's Hill, the historic core of the district, is one of Milwaukee's oldest communities. Urban settlement there began in the 1850s, not long after the city's incorporation in 1846. Milwaukee was expanding naturally, but the newcomers were also drawn to jobs along an abandoned canal that had been converted to a millrace for the region's first industrial district.

Known simply as "the water power," the riverside canal was lined with flour mills, lumber mills, and tanneries. These were joined in 1870 by the institution that would eventually give the neighborhood its name: the Schlitz brewery.

Most of the area's early residents were German immigrants, but that's about all they had in common. In the days before adequate public transportation, everyone had to live within walking distance of everything. The result was a thoroughly democratic landscape, with factory owners and factory hands sharing the same blocks. The homes they built in Brewer's Hill, most of them still standing, range from cottages to castles, and they include some of the finest Victorians in the city.

Third Street, in the meantime, was developing as the North Side's downtown. Anchored by the Schuster's department store at Garfield Avenue, the street trailed only Wisconsin (then

Calvary Baptist Church, founded in 1895, was a pillar of the Sixth Ward's Black community for decades before moving farther north in 1970.
WISCONSIN BLACK HISTORICAL SOCIETY

The Schlitz Park beer garden was a popular German institution earlier in the neighborhood's history. MILWAUKEE PUBLIC LIBRARY

Grand) Avenue in retail sales volume for decades. German was the language of commerce on Third, and even the newest immigrants felt right at home when they were buying rye bread or shopping for overalls.

West of Third Street was the area now known as Halyard Park. Its homes were slightly newer and somewhat smaller than those in Brewer's Hill, but its population was every bit as German. Local churches, including St. Francis for the area's Catholics and Mt. Olive and nearby St. Marcus for the Lutherans, met the area's religious needs. When weekly services were over, many of the faithful walked a few blocks to the Schlitz beer garden near Eighth and Walnut Streets, where they enjoyed a "continental Sunday" in the company of their Teutonic peers.

The entire Sixth Ward began to change not long after settlement was complete. The water-powered industrial district was first to be transformed. In 1885, as steam engines pushed water wheels into oblivion, the old millrace was filled in to become

Commerce Street. The Schlitz brewery remained, but most of the other riverside industries eventually closed or relocated. Their places were taken by stacks of lumber, piles of coal, and weed-covered vacant lots.

The residential areas on the high ground above the river underwent a different transformation. As the original German residents passed away or moved on to newer neighborhoods, the district developed one of the most diverse assortments of ethnic groups Milwaukee has ever known. In the early decades of the twentieth century, the blocks above North Avenue housed African Americans, Hungarians, Italians, Czechs, Slovaks, Poles, and eastern European Jews as well as holdover German families. African Americans soon outnumbered other residents. Although Third Street was still well patronized, Walnut Street emerged as the commercial center of Bronzeville—the popular name for the North Side's Black community.

The pace of change accelerated after World War II, and the long-term trends were ominous. The Sixth Ward's homes, already among the city's oldest, were showing their age. Hundreds fell to the wrecking ball, and many of the large Victorians that survived were converted to rooming houses. Between 1950 and 1970, the blocks south of Brown Street lost half their population. The epidemic of blight did not spare the commercial districts. Third Street became a commercial ghost town after the 1967 riot, and Walnut Street was denatured by a street-widening project and urban renewal. By 1970, the entire district seemed on the verge of collapse.

It was at this point that the city's innate capacity for reinvention began to assert itself. A cluster of neighborhoods, which had been developed at roughly the same time by roughly the same groups and degraded by the same forces of blight, was utterly remade, and its redevelopment took divergent paths that no one could have predicted.

The district's historic core was first to show signs of new life. In the mid-1970s, preservationists began to snap up the remaining Victorian homes in Brewer's Hill—a name adopted in 1981 to reflect the area's geography. Gay and straight, affluent and struggling, largely white but not entirely, they found common ground in their love for vintage architecture. The movement took such deep root that new houses were built to resemble the old, and the former Weyenberg shoe factory was converted to condos.

In neighboring Halyard Park—a name adopted in the 1970s to honor a pioneer African American couple—a failed urban renewal project west of North Fourth Street became the site of a conventional subdivision developed by United Realty, a Black-owned enterprise. Several blocks of blight were replaced by three-bedroom ranch homes with fireplaces in the family rooms. Suburban in everything but address, the homes of Halyard Park became a haven for Milwaukee's Black middle class.

Commercial redevelopment followed residential. The Schlitz brewery, shuttered since its 1982 sale to Stroh's, was reborn as a popular office park, and Third Street, renamed Martin Luther King Drive in 1984, regained a large measure of its original vitality. New enterprises went up alongside some of the most striking Victorian commercial buildings in Milwaukee.

Commerce Street was the last piece of the puzzle to fall into place. Milwaukeeans who knew it only as a forlorn shortcut between the East Side and downtown were amazed to witness its transformation in the early 2000s. From North Avenue to Pleasant Street, more than a mile of weed-choked empty lots gave way to some of the sleekest, priciest condos in the Milwaukee area. On a family canoe trip a few years ago, my niece amused herself by counting the grand pianos visible in the windows.

You could throw a square over any number of other areas on the Milwaukee map, but the old Sixth Ward might take the prize for both diversity and resilience. In considerably less than one square mile, you'll find the cutting-edge condos of Commerce Street, the restored Victorians of Brewer's Hill, and the Black suburban enclave of Halyard Park—joined by the resurgent commerce of King Drive and bordered by the new-old Schlitz Park. They are independent parts of an interdependent organism, as diverse as any forest, as healthy as any prairie. It is that layering of textures, and their constant interplay, that give Milwaukee's urban ecosystem its unique vitality.

A Forest in the City

Havenwoods Demonstrates the Resilience of Nature

There are state forests, and then there are state forests. Many of us have hiked, camped, or fished in the best-known units of Wisconsin's system, including Kettle Moraine, Brule River, and Northern Highland. But there is another state forest, just as official as its older, larger siblings, that lies much closer to the state's population center—within Milwaukee's city limits, in fact. Not only is this preserve nearby, but it's presumably the only state forest, in Wisconsin or anywhere else, that has been agricultural land, a county penal institution, a military prison, a missile base, and a dump before going back to nature.

I refer to Havenwoods State Forest, 237 acres of grassland and woodland just northwest of Silver Spring Drive and Sherman Boulevard. For such a large piece of land—nearly the size of Lake and Washington Parks combined—its front door is surprisingly hard to find, but if you go north on Sherman Boulevard to Douglas Avenue and turn left, you'll find yourself at the entrance.

Havenwoods, like most of Milwaukee County, was a forest before it became farmland in the mid-1800s. Located in the old Town of Granville, it attracted immigrants, many of them Germans, who grew wheat, vegetables, and livestock for the Milwaukee market.

This rural period ended in the early 1900s, when Milwaukee County began to eye the property for a new House of

With 237 acres of woodland and grassland, Havenwoods gives the resident deer plenty of room to roam. JOHN GURDA

Correction. The original institution had been a South Side landmark since 1866, filling a triangular piece of land that bordered Kosciuszko Public School on Windlake Avenue. By 1900, however, the facility was so overcrowded and underequipped that it had become a source of scandal.

When the new and improved House of Correction opened on the Granville site in 1917, its stated focus was the "safekeeping, reformation, and employment" of up to a thousand inmates. Most were short-termers, serving thirty days or less, typically for alcohol-related crimes that ranged from drunk and disorderly conduct to "running a still." Others were in for such antique offenses as sodomy, fornication, and carrying liquor on a train. The number of prisoners peaked at 1,439 in 1932, when the House was loaded with Prohibition violators. Cots filled the chapel and lined the dormitory halls, but the biggest bootleggers were said to live nearly as well as they had on the outside.

Every prisoner (including the handful of women serving time) was assigned a job. Some worked in an on-site chair factory, whose products were sold under the Granville Furniture Company trade name. (The "company" made no mention of

From 1917 to 1945, the future state forest was the home of the Milwaukee County House of Correction. MILWAUKEE JOURNAL SENTINEL

convict labor in its sales materials.) A larger number worked on the prison farm, which covered most of the property's 420 acres. Hardened urbanites became farm hands, tending a herd of registered Holsteins, collecting eggs from a flock of 1,500 chickens, harvesting fruit from a sizable orchard, and processing tons of vegetables. The yield for the 1939 canning season totaled 14,633 gallons, including 5,534 of tomatoes, 1,508 of dilled peppers, and 950 of sauerkraut. The dairy herd's 1944 output was converted to 25,000 pounds of butter, most of which went to other county institutions.

Major crops and minor criminals kept the House of Correction busy for nearly thirty years, but World War II opened a new chapter in the institution's history. As able-bodied men and women went either to war or to work in defense plants, the prison population plummeted to fewer than two hundred, but the facility was hardly idle. In 1941, a few weeks after Pearl Harbor, the federal government leased the women's barracks for the internment of "enemy aliens" whose only crime, in most cases, was the fact that they had been born in Germany. It was not only Japanese Americans who were persecuted by the federal government for having the wrong last names.

The internees left within months, and they were followed later in the conflict by German prisoners of war. There were never as many POWs in Granville as there were in the main camp at Mitchell Field, but they must have been surprised when nearby residents approached the fence to converse with them in their native tongue.

Milwaukee County's title to the land was extinguished entirely in 1945, when the US Army, over the county's objections, seized the property for use as a "disciplinary barracks"—a military jail, in other words. The House of Correction moved again, this time to Franklin, and the Army repurposed old buildings and put up new ones to create Milwaukee's own "Little Leavenworth," where deserters, mutineers, and the chronically disobedient were sent for punishment and rehabilitation.

The last court-martialed GI left in 1950, but the Army was not through with the old House of Correction just yet. Part of the land was used for military training—an Army Reserve Center still occupies the western portion of the site—and the northern edge housed a Nike antiaircraft missile base, one of eight designed to keep the Milwaukee area safe from a Soviet air strike. The introduction of long-range missiles rendered the facility obsolete in short order. The Nike site was closed in 1963, and the land that became Havenwoods was, in essence, abandoned.

It was not until 1967 that the federal government began, parcel by parcel, to declare the site surplus property. The announcement touched off a flurry of competing proposals from various public bodies and nonprofit groups. Their ideas included an industrial land bank, housing for seniors, a technical college campus, an incinerator, a postal facility, and even a comprehensive "new town in town."

As the discussions dragged on, the property became increasingly vulnerable. Vandals trashed the old prison buildings, homeless families occupied a portion of the army barracks, legal and illegal dumping went on day and night, and young people discovered the site's potential for drag racing and partying.

It was during these "wild years," as Havenwoods staff members describe them, that an alternative vision emerged. A citizens' task force suggested turning the land into an "open space and natural area" for the benefit of local residents and visitors alike. The property had already had more lives than a cat. Now it would come full circle as Havenwoods—a Custer High School student's winning entry in a naming contest.

Progress was slow until state officials began to take an interest. In 1980, after a protracted round of deal-making, Havenwoods became Wisconsin's first urban state forest. The detritus of the previous seventy years was cleared away and, season by season, the property was returned to a state of nature. In 1986, an environmental education center was built practically on the foundations of the original prison buildings. It continues as a resource for anyone who wants to know the story of the local landscape and the larger story of the planet we share.

Given Havenwoods' rich history and unique character, it sees far too little use. The forest has its ardent supporters, but I suspect that some Milwaukeeans are skeptical about the surrounding North Side neighborhoods. They needn't be. The only alert necessary here is for wild parsnip, which can blister your skin on contact, and the only bad guys are buckthorn, garlic mustard, and other invasive plants. In the heart of the property, whether it's January or June, quiet reigns.

I had my own share of quiet on a recent winter visit to Haven-woods. I skied the perimeter trail—an hour's exercise at a steady pace—and saw, even in midwinter, clear evidence of nature's amazing resilience: the calligraphic signatures of prairie plants against the snow, the purposeful tracks of a lone coyote, and a flock of robins who had apparently missed the memo about flying south.

As I was closing my loop, I encountered a herd of five young deer who regarded me intently, stock-still, for nearly a minute. As they finally bounded off into the forest, white flags flying, I marveled at how far this property had come after a century of use and abuse. The deer marked, in a very real sense, the return of the natives. Here they were, surrounded on all sides by the city, but these wild ones had found a safe haven in a most remarkable woods.

Siblings and Strangers

Chicago and Milwaukee Share a Regional "Neighborhood"

Think of them as siblings. Milwaukee and Chicago grew up on the same Great Lake in the same years with the same dreams of urban grandeur. They became, over the decades, strongholds of heavy industry attracting the same mix of industrial workers, from Germans and Poles in one period to African Americans and Latinos in the next. In the twenty-first century, both have become "majority minority" cities that boast great parks and robust cultural resources even as they struggle with entrenched poverty and ongoing deindustrialization.

For all they have in common, the relationship between Milwaukee and Chicago has been strained, even frosty, over the years. As in so many families, sibling ties devolved early into sibling rivalry, and in time the two communities became strangers to each other, familiar on the surface but completely foreign in temperament and personality.

Milwaukee had the early advantage in the intrafamily conflict. Thanks to a superior harbor and a location ninety miles closer to the East Coast by water, it was viewed by many as the more promising urban opportunity. For fifteen years, from 1835 to 1850, the two lakeshore cities had roughly equal populations. When business leader Byron Kilbourn became Milwaukee's mayor in 1848, he declared that regional dominance was the city's manifest destiny: "If New York has her Boston, so

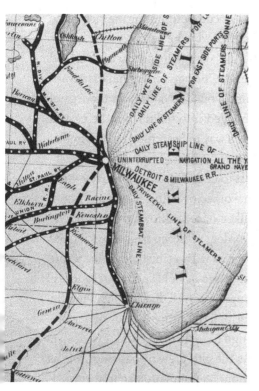

(*Left*) This circa-1870 railroad map from the Milwaukee Chamber of Commerce depicts Chicago as a minor settlement at the end of a spur line. MILWAUKEE PUBLIC LIBRARY

(*Below*) Viewed from space on a clear night, today's Milwaukee–Chicago corridor is a nearly continuous strip of light glowing on the south-western shore of Lake Michigan. IMAGE #ISS050-E-29303 COURTESY OF THE EARTH SCIENCE AND REMOTE SENSING UNIT, NASA JOHNSON SPACE CENTER

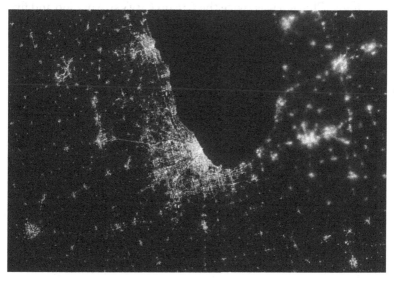

Milwaukee has her Chicago, in competition for the rich prize which nature awarded and designed to be hers."

Then came the railroads. As Lake Michigan forced overland traffic around its southern end, Chicago's marginal disadvantage in the Age of Sail became a huge advantage in the Age of Rail. After the first train chugged into town from the east in 1852, the Windy City was on its way to becoming the rail hub of the entire continent.

Milwaukee was not about to cede Chicago's primacy—not yet, at least. Byron Kilbourn worked overtime to win a Wisconsin land grant for his Milwaukee-based railroad, taking on rival rail magnates south of the border. "Chicago has always looked upon our prosperity and progress with a sinister eye," he wrote in 1857, "and she cannot bear to see us hold such equal success with her in the contest for supremacy." Kilbourn, incidentally, was explaining why he had bribed the entire Wisconsin legislature in his successful campaign to secure the grant.

Chicago won anyway. As the city grew into its new role as Freight Handler to the Nation, its population soared accordingly. Chicago was twice the Cream City's size in 1860 and five times larger in 1890—roughly the same differential that has prevailed ever since.

Chicago won, but Milwaukee was not about to wither in the deep shade of its larger neighbor. Still riding the momentum of the pioneer period, the city's leaders made two critical decisions. The first was to develop and maintain an independent rail network, known in later years as the Milwaukee Road. By expanding that network and resisting links with Chicago's carriers, the Cream City became the primary funnel for the agricultural wealth of Wisconsin and the farm districts near its borders. By the early 1860s, Milwaukee was the largest shipper of wheat on earth, surpassing, for a time, even Chicago.

The second decision—actually a multitude of individual decisions—transformed Milwaukee into a major manufacturing center. Homegrown entrepreneurs, many of them immigrants, employed immigrant workers to create global giants like Allis-Chalmers, Harnischfeger, A. O. Smith, Allen-Bradley, Falk, Chain Belt, and Harley-Davidson. Industries and immigrants were the two forces that grew in tandem to push Milwaukee's population to 204,468 in 1890, making the self-styled Machine Shop of the World the sixteenth-largest city in America.

As fast as Milwaukee was growing in the late 1800s, Chicago was growing even faster. The Windy City's 1890 population was 1,099,850—enough residents to overtake Philadelphia as the second-largest city in the country. Chicago was indisputably the Midwest's metropolis, and any lingering feelings of rivalry north of the border eventually gave way to resignation. As their relative positions hardened, Milwaukee became to Chicago what Canada was, and is, to the United States: a distinct and cohesive world of its own, but a world persistently overshadowed by its gigantic neighbor to the south. Pierre Trudeau, the colorful French Canadian who led his country in the 1970s, once compared the relationship to "sleeping with an elephant." The beast is only vaguely aware of its smaller neighbor's presence, and when it turns over, there go the covers.

Like Canada, Milwaukee has found both advantages and disadvantages to being the little brother. Chicago has long been a lucrative and reliable market for Milwaukee-made products. As early as the 1870s, "beer trains" up to twenty-five cars long chugged down to Chicago every day of the week on errands of liquid mercy. The Windy City is also a convenient moral foil; Cook County's corruption, we tell ourselves, could never take root here. And Chicago is a cultural capital for the entire region. If there's a must-see show at the Art Institute or the Field Museum, we can take it in and still be home for supper. Whenever Milwaukee begins to seem a little too quiet and we crave a shot of urban adrenaline, Amtrak's Hiawatha can get us to the Loop in 129 minutes. On so many levels, Chicago is a great town to live ninety miles away from.

Of all the influences Chicago has had on Milwaukee, the most profound is probably psychological. The fact that such a huge metropolis lies just across the state line has cultivated a modesty bordering on meekness in its northern neighbor. In the regional context, Milwaukee, like Canada, has taken on the peculiar invisibility that a younger sibling assumes in the presence of an older brother. We experience that status most acutely when we travel abroad. "Where are you from?," we're asked. "From near Chicago," we've learned to reply.

The result, depending on your point of view, is either an appealing groundedness—no one puts on airs in Brewtown—or a stubborn inferiority complex. Banker John Johnston once commented on this singular aspect of Milwaukee's character. "There is one thing we are deficient in here," Johnston wrote. "We have not the necessary blow and brag. Not only have we not that, but we daily see men standing with their hands in their pockets whining about Milwaukee being a one-horse town, and such like talk. Such men are not worthy to live here." In the very next sentence, Johnston identified what he perceived as the root cause of the local angst: "Milwaukee is not Chicago, but there are few cities like Chicago." The banker wrote those words in 1872, but his sentiments could have been expressed yesterday.

On the other hand, Chicago has long been the city that Milwaukeeans, and Wisconsinites generally, love to hate. The rivalry between the Packers and the Bears is just one expression of the prevailing attitude, and it's perhaps the only one that's truly reciprocal. Feelings north of the border go far beyond football. "Flatlander" is one name we give our neighbors to the south. "FIB" is a cruder epithet, and I need only mention that the "I" in the acronym stands for "Illinois."

For all its historic power and occasional pointed humor, the one-sided sibling rivalry between Milwaukee and Chicago has entered a new dimension in recent decades. As satisfying as it may be for the underdog to bark at the overdog on occasion, the very terms of the relationship have shifted. The increasingly global nature of the economy has both cities operating in the same weather. Overarching geographic forces have transformed the region's landscape; the chain of settlements between Milwaukee and Chicago—or between Madison and South Bend, for that matter—is fast becoming a continuous corridor of settlement, a megalopolis in the same category as the Boston-to-Washington cluster. And problems common to one—stagnant populations, inner-city blight, economic and racial inequity—are common to all.

Any Milwaukeean who wants to return to the supposed glories of past independence is bound to be disappointed, and so is any Chicagoan who wants to resurrect Sandburg's City of the Big Shoulders. For better or worse, the old order has ended: The walls are down, the world is flat, communication is instantaneous. A new order of amorphous interdependence has asserted its dominion. As borders fade and rivalries soften, it's time for the old siblings and strangers to take their places in a regional neighborhood where everyone has room to prosper.

Landmarks and Landscapes

City Hall Reborn

$150 Million Project Saves a Civic Icon

W e could have lost it. If time, gravity, and the elements had been allowed to take their course, Milwaukee's City Hall might have collapsed of its own weight, leaving a colorful pile of brick, copper, slate, and ornamental ironwork strewn across the sidewalk at 200 East Wells. The fix has been frightfully expensive, but the alternative was unthinkable. Not only is City Hall one of the most beautiful municipal buildings in America; it's also the single most important focal point of Milwaukee's identity. Imagining the city without it is like imagining Rome without St. Peter's or Washington without the US Capitol.

The building's beginnings gave no hint of future glory. In 1882, after leasing space for nearly ten years in the county courthouse on what's now Cathedral Square, city officials were notified that Milwaukee County would soon need every square inch of its building. The announcement touched off more than a decade of planning and debate. Ancient ward rivalries were rekindled, as partisans of the East, West, and South Sides advanced their own sites for a new building. The East Side won, but the site chosen in 1890 was, to say the least, difficult: a wedge-shaped sliver of reclaimed swampland on the east bank of the Milwaukee River.

An 1891 design contest generated more controversy. Eleven firms answered the Common Council's call for "a modern

City Hall was Milwaukee's first million-dollar building and a towering statement of civic pride. MILWAUKEE COUNTY HISTORICAL SOCIETY

structure, substantial, fireproof and ornamental," all of them vying for the eight-hundred-dollar first prize. A Chicago partnership appeared to have won, but the city awarded the contract to Milwaukeean Henry Koch's firm instead.

No sooner had the threat of lawsuits passed and construction

started than the Panic of 1893 cast its pall over Milwaukee. The
financial collapse jeopardized the entire project and forced the
city to drop plans for what would have been the biggest bell in the
country. Despite that subtraction and a handful of others, construction proceeded through the heart of the recession.

The travails were all forgotten on December 23, 1895, when a
bevy of local politicians followed a brass band from the old
county courthouse to their new quarters on Wells Street. Even
before the paint was dry and the pictures were hung, Milwaukee's leaders sensed that they had a world-class building on their
hands.

City Hall worked on several levels—sheer size, to begin
with. Resting on a forest of wooden pilings, incorporating eight
million bricks, and soaring 350 feet to the base of its flagpole, the
building was one of the largest in the nation. At the time of its
dedication, the only taller structures were reportedly the Washington Monument and Philadelphia's city hall. Milwaukee had
raised up a towering affirmation of its place in the top ranks of
America's cities.

City Hall was also an eloquent expression of the community's dominant ethnic tradition. Designed by a German-born
architect working with a German-born mayor (both named
Koch) at a time when most Milwaukeeans traced their roots to
Germany, the building had an unmistakable Teutonic ambience. Its graceful gables and baroque ornamentation would
have rested comfortably on any number of municipal halls in
the Old World.

The building was also a fine place to work. "Every room in it
is an outside room," wrote a local reporter in 1901, "and the large,
light and commodious offices are in great contrast to the stuffy
ones in the neighboring city of Chicago."

Milwaukee's first million-dollar building had room for every
city function, including the fire and police departments and the

entire corps of public school administrators. There was still space left over. For a year or two, students from a nearby grade school attended classes on the eighth floor while their old building was being replaced, sharing the elevators with the mayor and the police chief.

In time, of course, municipal offices filled City Hall to capacity and overflowed to other downtown buildings. As its copper roof weathered to a mellow green and decades of coal smoke gave its brickwork the patina of premature age, the building was joined by other landmarks in the heart of town. But City Hall towered over them all until 1973, when it was eclipsed by the 601-foot First Wisconsin (now US Bank) Center.

Although it was no longer Milwaukee's tallest building, City Hall lost none of its power to inspire. Recent architects, in fact, have gone out of their way to pay homage to the structure. The Wisconsin Center, 1000 North Water, the Milwaukee Center, and 100 East Wisconsin— all buildings erected since 1988—make pointed (or rounded) references to their distinguished neighbor. The result has too often been "City Hall lite," but the flattery implicit in the designs is obvious.

An open atrium with copper grillwork and marble columns is the outstanding feature of the building's interior. MILWAUKEE COUNTY HISTORICAL SOCIETY

Although it never went out of style, City Hall had a serious genetic flaw. The building had much in common with Santiago

Calatrava's 2001 addition to the Milwaukee Art Museum; both were aesthetically and technically daring designs that pushed existing technologies to their limits. Henry Koch, unfortunately, lacked the engineering expertise of his twenty-first-century counterpart. The tower he designed was simply too heavy, creating tensile stresses that threatened, over time, to completely unzip the structure.

The problem surfaced early. "City Hall Tower Becomes a Menace," reported the *Milwaukee Journal* on May 2, 1903, when the building was not even eight years old. The tower's iron supports were rusting, and the terra-cotta ornaments were on the verge of coming down. Cost estimates to remedy the defects ran as high as ten thousand dollars.

Stopgap repairs kept pedestrians below out of harm's way, but it was not until 2006 that the building's flaws were addressed in any systematic way. City Hall has been a nearly continuous construction zone ever since, as skilled workers replaced bricks, upgraded windows, installed new copper roofing, rebuilt the massive clock tower, renewed the terra cotta, and, with great difficulty, poured a new foundation. The price tag for the various projects approaches $150 million. That's a major multiple of what the building cost in the first place, even after adjusting for inflation, but allowing the landmark to crumble was simply not an option.

Conceived in controversy and born in adversity, City Hall began as a powerful statement of what a city can accomplish when vision, skill, and persistence come together. Its twenty-first-century restoration ensures that the building will remain a towering symbol of urban possibility for generations to come.

From Bogart to Beethoven

Milwaukee Symphony Finds a New Home
in an Old Movie Palace

The first impression is dazzling. Leaving behind the commercial bustle of West Wisconsin Avenue, you enter a hall of mirrors lit by massive chandeliers and set off by nickel-painted plasterwork and gleaming terrazzo floors. This grand lobby funnels you into a decidedly different space, a massive auditorium with a classically European ambience. Renaissance courtiers smile down from murals recessed in the walls, and a huge keystone cove in the ceiling bathes the interior in soft indirect light. The intended effect is grandeur, and the effect is fully achieved.

This architectural gem is the reborn home of the Milwaukee Symphony Orchestra. For most of its history, the MSO had been the anchor tenant of the Marcus Performing Arts Center—the anchor, certainly, but still a tenant. At various points in the year, particularly during the lucrative holiday season, the symphony was exiled from its home, forced to play in other venues as touring shows and that tights-and-tutus chestnut, *The Nutcracker*, took over Uihlein Hall. Those days ended when the MSO relocated to 212 West Wisconsin Avenue in October 2021. In a move that covered just three blocks, the symphony graduated from renter to owner, creating its own calendar and controlling its own destiny.

The orchestra's "new" home is actually one of the older performance venues in Milwaukee: a movie theater that opened

The Bradley Symphony Center is an elegant performance venue that was once Milwaukee's leading movie theater. SCOTT PAULUS

in 1931 as the Warner. In his book *Milwaukee Movie Palaces*, Larry Widen, the ranking authority on the subject, described the theater as "the most expensive, and the most elegant, that would ever be built in the city." The Warner had a seating capacity of 2,500 and construction costs totaling $2.5 million—close to $50 million in today's currency. A budget cinema this was not.

The new theater was the crowning glory of the movie palace era in Milwaukee. Every showhouse of the type was an elegant venue that strived to treat its patrons like royalty. Some palaces evoked specific locales far removed from the humdrum streets outside their doors—Egypt at the Egyptian, Venice at the Venetian, a Spanish courtyard at the Avalon. Others were mashups of multiple styles. The Oriental showcased Buddhist, Islamic, East Indian, and a variety of other themes, while the MSO's Warner had a dual personality: customers entered through the

When the Warner Theater premiered *The Fighting 69th* in 1940, police had to be called in to control the crowds. MILWAUKEE COUNTY HISTORICAL SOCIETY

gleaming, streamlined Art Deco grand lobby and then sat down to watch Bogart and Bacall in a Neobaroque auditorium.

Opening night in the new palace—May 1, 1931—was an event fit for a king. The *Milwaukee Sentinel* declared that it was as "vivid and tumultuous as a notable Hollywood premiere" and went on to describe the action at the Warner: "Before its flamingly lit façade bands thundered martial music, a snarl of autos honked in a vast bedlam, thousands crowded about, craning and shouting, movie cameras clicked at a furious pace, photographers' flashes created reels of lightning bolts." As an "illuminated airplane" circled overhead and "society women in gorgeous ermine" alighted from their cars, radio station WISN provided second-by-second coverage of the spectacle.

And all that was before the movie started. At the top of the opening-night bill was *Sit Tight*, a comedy starring Joe E. Brown, but patrons were also treated to a newsreel, a "sports reel" by golf legend Bobby Jones, a performance of operatic gems, a short concert on the Kimball organ, and a Mickey Mouse cartoon called *Castaways*. In the audience were 150 Warner Brothers executives who had come in from Hollywood to mark the debut of the newest addition to their empire.

The Depression was well under way by the time the Warner opened. Although consumer budgets were shrinking by the day, management felt justified in charging fifty cents for evening programs and sixty cents on Sundays—roughly eleven dollars in modern currency. Not only was the Warner the most elegant movie house in town, but it also offered valet parking and a team of forty-five ushers in powder blue and silver uniforms.

The Warner had amenities to spare, and one of the most important was its location. Without a hint of government regulation or market collusion, the east and west sides of downtown had developed distinct personalities over the decades. East of the river was Milwaukee's legal and financial district, the home of the major banks and law firms. The west bank's specialties were retail trade and entertainment. Major department stores— Gimbels, Boston Store, Espenhain's—were interspersed among theaters, many of them vaudeville houses that eventually pivoted to motion pictures. When the Warner opened in 1931, it was near the very middle of "movie row," a string of eleven showhouses extending from the Riverside on the river to the Strand on Fifth Street.

The Warner was the most lavish of the bunch, and it would prove to be the last. The west side movie district weathered the Depression, World War II, and the advent of television, but it could not survive the rise of the suburbs. As recently as the late 1960s, downtown was the place to go for first-run films, but every twin, triplex, and multiplex that opened beyond the city's edge was another nail in West Wisconsin Avenue's coffin. One by one, the marquees went dark.

All but the Warner's. In 1966, the showplace was purchased

by the Marcus Corporation, Wisconsin's largest theater chain. Proclaiming it "the landmark jewel" of their movie business, Marcus kept the Warner going for another twenty-nine years, first "twinning" it as the Centre 1 and 2 and then rebranding it as the Grand. Despite repeated attempts to revitalize the landmark, its long-term trajectory was downward. The last film was shown in 1995, and this celebrated beauty from 1931 became, for an indefinite period, a sleeping beauty.

The Milwaukee Symphony Orchestra, in the meantime, was getting increasingly restless in its Marcus Center home. Sharing the facility with other performing arts groups meant fewer available concert dates, fewer guest artist opportunities, and fewer revenue streams. Forty years after its founding, the MSO was like a plant outgrowing its pot.

The old Warner surfaced as a potential new container just a few years after it closed. In 2000, the symphony's managers built a temporary wooden stage and snuck the orchestra into the theater for a live sound check. Although it was built for sight rather than sound and opened only four years after the first "talkie," the hall's acoustics turned out to be superb, which only whetted the orchestra's appetite for a change of venue.

Although the theater was in basically sound condition, the MSO knew it would have to do more than mop up old soda spills and scrape the gum off the seat bottoms. After a timeout for the Great Recession and a lengthy quiet campaign, the orchestra went public with its plans in 2016. The MSO set a fundraising goal of $120 million (later raised to $139 million) and got to work.

Restoration was the first task. A small army of artisans and technicians repaired water damage, removed mold, replaced crumbling plaster, and wiped away decades of cigarette smoke. As the old finishes were restored, construction crews added new amenities: bars and bathrooms, improved wheelchair access, a glass-walled welcome center adjoining the theater, and a new stage created by moving the east wall—very slowly—out to the middle of Second Street. The crucial next step was to tune the instrument that is the concert hall itself, a feat accomplished by paying careful attention to both technological solutions and the room's physical configuration.

Led by David and Julia Uihlein, an all-star cast of local philanthropists underwrote the restoration project. With additional help from some timely historic preservation tax credits, the money was raised and the work completed in time for the Symphony Center's grand opening on October 1, 2021. There were no illuminated airplanes overhead this time, no high school bands on the street outside, but, ninety years after its debut, the theater reopened to thunderous applause rippling through a hall with some of the finest acoustics in the state. In a resounding victory for music and for Milwaukee, the sleeping beauty awakened to a melodious new life.

The Mansion in the Trailer Park

Future of Nunnemacher Distillery Is in Doubt

"Incongruous" would be an understatement. Where else could you find a mid-nineteenth-century Italianate mansion—of Cream City brick, no less—surrounded by the bulldozed foundations of more than two dozen mobile homes, with a strip mall to the north, a discount mattress store to the south, and a Denny's restaurant across the street? As unlikely as it sounds, that's the ensemble gathered around 3774 South Twenty-Seventh Street on Milwaukee's South Side. The mansion is a time traveler, the vestige of a vanished world marooned in the twenty-first century by the side of a busy urban highway.

The years have not been particularly kind to this South Side landmark. The imposing front windows are long gone, replaced by much smaller modern casements and crude brickwork inserts. The original front entrance has been exchanged for something cheaper—from Menard's, perhaps—and covered with a makeshift modern porch. The house has seen better days, and things are unlikely to improve in the immediate future. After years of good intentions and indifferent results, the entire property has reverted to the City of Milwaukee for back taxes. The mansion is vacant, waiting in forlorn hope for some visionary to resurrect it.

The building's current state makes its original grandeur that much harder to imagine. This survivor was once a whiskey

Once the home (far right) of a prosperous distiller and farmer . . .

. . . the Nunnemacher mansion is now a forlorn relic moldering by the side of South Twenty-Seventh Street. TOP: MILWAUKEE JOURNAL SENTINEL; BOTTOM: JOHN GURDA

baron's home perched serenely on more than six hundred acres of land three miles beyond the city limits. Its builder was Jacob Nunnemacher, a German-speaking Swiss immigrant who arrived in 1843, three years before Milwaukee incorporated. There are definite advantages to getting in on the ground floor. Nunnemacher opened a meat stall in a public market on the present site of City Hall and used his profits to buy real estate, including most of the land on East Wells Street between the

river and North Water Street. There he built, among other landmarks, the Grand Opera House, a stately predecessor of the
even more stately Pabst Theater.

The immigrant also invested in rural real estate. In 1854,
he began to assemble his farm holdings in the Town of Lake,
erecting a fine brick home and a variety of outbuildings. The
Kilbourn Road, as South Twenty-Seventh Street was known in
those days, was already a main-traveled route to Chicago, and
access to the city was easy. But Nunnemacher's farm was not a
bucolic retreat for his leisure hours. It was, in fact, the home of
two thriving and interdependent businesses. In 1856, he opened
a distillery there that became one of Milwaukee's largest, producing nearly three hundred barrels of hard liquor a month by
the 1870s. The entrepreneur also raised a herd of five hundred
cattle and fed them on the spent grain, or slops, from the distillery. Beef on the hoof became meat on the counter of his downtown market.

Nunnemacher was known as a genial and accommodating
host. "His friends were always cordially welcome," wrote one
biographer, and no one had to bring his own bottle. He was also
a major source of income for local farmers, who supplied the
distiller with wagonloads of grain that he turned into mash, as
well as massive quantities of wood he used to fire his stills. A
rampart of cordwood sometimes stretched for a quarter mile
along his front fence. Many of the farmers who brought him
wood or grain went home with slops to feed their own cattle.

The business was not without its problems. When his supply
of spent grain exceeded demand, Nunnemacher was known to
run the slops directly into the waterway behind his home, a
small creek that fed the nearby Kinnickinnic River. Complaints
from farmers downstream landed him in court more than once.
(The creek, minus the slops, is still there, confined to an ugly
concrete channel.)

Immigrant entrepreneur Jacob Nunnemacher was not reluctant to cut corners in his pursuit of profit. MILWAUKEE JOURNAL SENTINEL

Pollution suits were the least of the distiller's legal troubles. In its pursuit of revenue both during and after the Civil War, the federal government levied a stiff tax on stiff drink. Distillers were required to affix revenue stamps—each costing one dollar, then two—to every barrel of liquor they produced. Jacob Nunnemacher took a dim view of the requirement. One associate recalled him saying that "he didn't run a distillery for the Government, that he was running it for himself." Revenue agents seized his business at least three times in the 1860s and 1870s, charging that he was producing more alcohol than his license permitted, selling barrels without stamps, and colluding with other producers to evade taxes.

The culminating case went to trial in 1876. Nunnemacher was a pillar of the community by that time, a millionaire known for his public spirit as well as his business acumen. The trial, which lasted three weeks, filled the pages of local papers, and, like many trials, it yielded plenty of salacious details. The prosecutor started by calling the distillery "one continuous fraud from the time it was started." Witness after witness recounted how Nunnemacher delivered unstamped barrels to local retailers under cover of darkness and instructed his employees to remove and reuse revenue stamps.

The trial also revealed his softer side. "Jacob was exercising a paternal care over everybody and everything," testified one distillery hand. That care extended to boarding with the boss. "I took dinner with him always," said the employee. "Never paid a cent and got a good dinner." The fringe benefits, he admitted, included an extra two hundred dollars a month to look the other way when laws were being broken.

Locked in fierce competition with equally corrupt Chicago suppliers, practically every other whiskey man in town was doing the same thing. There were cries that Nunnemacher was being singled out as a scapegoat by overzealous prosecutors. The government's lead attorney did indeed resort to rhetorical overload in describing the defendant: "His name is a stench in the nostrils of every decent man in the city. . . . The example of such a distillery is infinitely more demoralizing to a community than a house of ill-fame."

Scapegoat or not, the fifty-eight-year-old immigrant was fined ten thousand dollars and sentenced to five months in the county jail—surprisingly harsh treatment for Milwaukee's "butcher millionaire." Although Nunnemacher was pardoned after serving only two months, prison broke both the spirit and the health of the whiskey magnate. Jacob Nunnemacher died on November 28, 1876, just a few months after his release.

Nunnemacher's family remained in Milwaukee, and his sons went on to distinguished careers as bankers, manufacturers, and philanthropists. The old distillery, however, soon passed into other hands, and every change in ownership took the mansion further from its original splendor. When Twenty-Seventh Street became US Highway 41 in the 1920s, the Nunnemacher homestead, much reduced by that time, was suddenly on the major road between Milwaukee and all points south. The mansion became the Evergreen Hotel, and its grounds were covered with tourist cabins.

The property's appearance changed again in 1947, when Ed Wildenberg bought the Evergreen and decided he could make more money by replacing the pint-sized cabins with mobile homes. The tourist hotel itself became a low-rent rooming house whose barroom served as a community center for all of Wildenberg's tenants, whether they had trailers outside or rooms upstairs. The main building persisted as an architectural oxymoron: an Italianate mansion in a trailer park. In my extensive and ongoing research into South Side bars—a life's work, really—I stopped at the Evergreen more than once. I recall it as a funky space, poorly lit, with a marble fireplace that was several cuts above its surroundings.

What will become of this tarnished landmark? Shortly after acquiring the property in 2014, the City of Milwaukee removed the mobile homes and sealed up the hotel, but not before declaring a portion of the building officially historic. Although the city has a strong commitment to historic preservation, years have passed with no deep-pocketed buyers stepping forward to fund a restoration. The mansion continues to molder in place, invisible to the thousands of motorists who barrel past each day. With every winter wind and summer storm, the building's fate becomes increasingly uncertain.

Architectural historians have paid it scant attention, but the Nunnemacher mansion is categorically one of Milwaukee's oldest buildings, and its ties to a pioneer family and a pioneer industry are incontestable. It's also the center point of a compelling story. The whiskey factory on the road to Chicago began as an immigrant's dream, and it ultimately led to his demise. Nearly 150 years after Jacob Nunnemacher's departure, it's high time for new spirits in the old distillery.

Wrong Turn to the Past

Trucker Blundered onto Lake Park's Historic Lion Bridges

A funny thing happened on my way to the lecture. Well, not laugh-out-loud funny, perhaps, but certainly strange. It was November 11, 2014—Veterans Day—and I was on my way to the North Point Lighthouse, one of Lake Park's high points, to give a talk about Milwaukee's water history. When I pulled up outside, the first thing I noticed was the TV trucks. *Well*, I thought, *they've really gone overboard on publicity this time.* Then I saw the police cruisers and wondered if the place was under siege. I finally detected something distinctly out of place on one of the pedestrian bridges behind the lighthouse: a full-sized semi-trailer rig. The famous Lion Bridges, it seemed, had become a truck stop.

After checking in with the lighthouse staff and making sure the projection system was working, I went back into the night air to investigate. The driver, I gathered from a couple of bystanders, had shown a little too much faith in his GPS system, which led him down a walkway past the Lake Park golf course and then onto the bridges. He barely squeezed through the first, cutting a deep groove into one of the stone balustrades, then wiped out a tree and slammed into the second span, dislodging a large piece of masonry. At that point he apparently decided that further progress was inadvisable. The driver, who may have been experiencing some sort of medical emergency, was taken to a hospital. The lions escaped injury.

I fell into conversation with a TV crew covering the incident. When they discovered that I knew something about the site, they turned on the camera, and a few hours later I was on the ten o'clock news, telling the story of Lake Park, its lions, and its lighthouse. Without realizing it for a moment, the truck driver had blundered into perhaps the most historic section of one of the most historic parks in Milwaukee County.

The lighthouse came first. Milwaukee was a major grain port during the first years of its cityhood, and lighthouses, in those low-tech days, were necessary to keep the shipping lanes safe. The community's first beacon went up at the foot of Wisconsin Avenue in 1838. The little light announced Milwaukee's presence to the passing world, but it was less than adequate as the city grew. In 1855, a new lighthouse was built at North Point, near the south end of today's Lake Park. Higher and brighter than its predecessor, the new light was visible nearly eighteen miles out to sea.

Ironically, the same storms that threatened Lake Michigan's schooners spelled the end of the beacon that was supposed to protect them. When storm waves collapsed the unprotected bluffs supporting the 1855 structure, it had to be rebuilt a hundred feet inland, out of harm's way. The new lighthouse, completed in 1888, was still well beyond the edge of settlement. "During the cold, dreary days of winter," reported the *Milwaukee Sentinel*, "the spot is deserted by all but the keeper."

The light was perched between two picturesque ravines, and Milwaukee's park planners didn't overlook such a promising site. In 1890, the city made Lake Park one of its first six major purchases. Frederick Law Olmsted's firm was hired to develop the property, and his team responded with an elegant plan thoroughly in keeping with the genteel neighborhood taking shape just inland. Its highlights included a large central meadow, pavilions, pedestrian promenades, and carriageways.

One of those carriageways spanned the ravines on either side of the North Point Lighthouse. A pair of matching steel-and-stone bridges was completed in 1898, both guarded by a pride of sandstone lions—the gift of utility magnate Henry Clay Payne. Fine carriages were soon making the rounds of Lake Park every Sunday afternoon, followed within a few years by fine motor cars. The Sunday drivers were rewarded with spectacular views of the lake, and they brought civilization to the lighthouse keeper's door. The *Milwaukee Journal*, a newspaper not normally given to hyperbole, called the Lake Park circuit "one of the most beautiful drives in the world." The extent of the reporter's travels was not disclosed.

The lake views were short-lived. Tree plantings were an essential part of Olmsted's Lake Park plan, and one of their unforeseen consequences was to render the 1888 lighthouse invisible. Within a decade or two, the trees had grown so tall that their leaves blocked the beacon during the season of navigation. The light was actually turned off in 1907 because mariners couldn't see it. The obvious solution was to raise the structure.

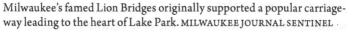

Milwaukee's famed Lion Bridges originally supported a popular carriageway leading to the heart of Lake Park. MILWAUKEE JOURNAL SENTINEL

As the park's trees grew to maturity, the North Point beacon was placed on a pedestal so that it could still be seen by passing ships. MILWAUKEE COUNTY PARKS

A new thirty-five-foot steel base was erected in 1912, and the thirty-nine-foot tower built in 1888 was hoisted atop it—a case of "additive architecture" not unlike the practice that created hundreds of Polish flats on Milwaukee's South Side.

When the North Point Lighthouse attained its present height in 1912, today's ensemble was virtually complete. There have been changes, naturally, in the century since then. The Lion Bridges were closed to all but pedestrian traffic in 1964—a memo the wayward truck driver obviously missed. The surrounding parkland has been used for everything from ice-skating to live theater to a highly acclaimed restaurant. The lighthouse itself was decommissioned in 1994; advances in navigation technology had made it obsolete. The light and its adjacent keeper's quarters were, for all practical purposes, abandoned. I vividly recall the peeling paint and water damage apparent during a "before" tour in the 1990s—we entered the main building by pulling aside a sheet of plywood—but a small band of volunteers was determined to save the complex. Passionate about Milwaukee's maritime history, they won the support of federal officials, enlisted Milwaukee County's help, and raised enough money to restore the buildings.

The landmark reopened in 2007, this time to the general public. The old residence was transformed into a nifty small museum that tells the story of the light, its keepers, and the ships they were sworn to protect. If weather and your acrophobia permit, you can crown your visit with a climb to the top of the lighthouse, which offers some of the finest views anywhere in Milwaukee.

The North Point Lighthouse has welcomed thousands of visitors since 2007, but most of them have come through the front door—until that November evening in 2014. I wonder if the misguided trucker had his GPS programmed to 1900, when Siri could have been wearing a lace bonnet and a bustle. His rig was removed without incident the next day, and observers must have noted the irony of the slogan painted on the semi's side: "We drive a fine line." The line could have been a lot finer in this case. The wrong turn produced charges of reckless driving, a seven-hundred-dollar fine, and property damages that probably exceeded the thirty-thousand-dollar cost of the original bridges, lions excluded.

I may speak at the lighthouse again. I might even show up on some future ten o'clock newscast. I seriously doubt, however, that I'll ever give a talk preceded by the spectacle of a truck perched on a bridge between the past and the present.

Civic Center or Civic Wasteland?

MacArthur Square Is Downtown's Dead Zone

It's the black hole of downtown Milwaukee. Less than two blocks north, the Pabst brewery complex has come foaming back to life. Practically across the street lies the central campus of the Milwaukee Area Technical College, home to nearly twenty thousand students in season. Immediately south are two busy and beloved cultural institutions: the Central Library and the Public Museum. Looming over it to the west is the brutally neoclassical hulk of the Milwaukee County Courthouse.

In the very middle of these familiar landmarks, sucking the energy out of its surroundings, is MacArthur Square, two square blocks of nothingness that anchors, or tries to, Milwaukee's Civic Center. If there's a deader zone in the heart of any American city, I've yet to experience it. Winter or summer, MacArthur Square is nearly as devoid of people as an Iowa cornfield, shunned even by those living without benefit of fixed address. Days after a snowfall, by far the largest number of footprints you'll see in the square belong to squirrels and rabbits, not human beings.

And why would anyone visit? Every door of every building that borders the square is locked, and a sign at what was once the central entrance of the courthouse couldn't be plainer: "Absolutely No Public Access Allowed." There are hardly even monuments in this nominally monumental space: only an obelisk

MacArthur Square, a decorative dead zone in the heart of downtown Milwaukee. MILWAUKEE COUNTY HISTORICAL SOCIETY

dedicated to fallen police officers and a lonesome statue of Mahatma Gandhi in the middle of "India-America Friendship Park," an otherwise bare terrace on the east porch of the courthouse.

How forlorn is MacArthur Square? The space is so dead that in 2014 the statue of General Douglas MacArthur, a fixture on the mall since 1979, was relocated to Milwaukee's lakefront. The general's original perch was described as "a largely inaccessible site" in a "mostly deserted square" that had "fallen into disrepair." One of the project's advocates didn't mince words in the run-up to the move. "It's such a waste to have him over there," declared Ted Hutton. "Most people don't even know the statue exists."

When conditions are so inhospitable that the military hero the space was meant to honor abandons his post, it's clear that something's radically wrong with MacArthur Square. It's not for lack of trying. Although the discussions are all but forgotten today, official Milwaukee tried for more than six decades to make the area an asset rather than an eyesore. The effort generated a minor mountain of studies, reports, plans, and newspaper stories.

The focus of all the attention was a twelve-square-block rectangle bordered by North Sixth and North Ninth Streets between State and Wells. Like most of central Milwaukee before zoning laws were adopted, the area began as a hodgepodge of land uses. Developed between 1865 and 1885 in its first incarnation, the rectangle was primarily residential, but it also housed a foundry, a coffin shop, a synagogue, a lumberyard, a livery stable, a pickle works, a trunk plant, and a "suspender manufactory." Perhaps the most unusual nineteenth-century landmark was a massive panorama painting studio on Wells Street near Sixth. When the vogue for panoramas passed, the round barn was converted to a roller-skating rink called the Hippodrome.

The area grew denser and its landscape even more jumbled after 1900. Industrial buildings multiplied and detached homes gave way to cheap hotels, boarding houses, and small apartment buildings that reflected a demand for entry-level housing near the city's heart. A number of the multifamily dwellings soon became tenements; by 1910, the early signs of blight were unmistakable.

Civic leaders, in the meantime, were beginning to think about a civic center. They drew their inspiration from the City Beautiful movement, a turn-of-the-century crusade for grandeur in the public sphere: broad boulevards, large plazas, and orderly groupings of public buildings in the neoclassical style. (The National Mall in Washington, DC, is probably the best-known example in the United States. Closer to home, downtown Kenosha has a classic City Beautiful tableau.) In 1909, Milwaukee's new Metropolitan Park Commission, headed by architect Alfred Clas, proposed a grand civic center around what would become MacArthur Square. The location was ideal, the existing buildings were increasingly expendable, and local government was running out of room elsewhere.

The focal point of the plan was a new county courthouse crowning the rise west of Ninth Street. Clas and his fellow commissioners (who included the ubiquitous Charles B. Whitnall) envisioned Kilbourn Avenue as a triumphal, tree-lined boulevard linking the courthouse and City Hall—a scaled-down version of the National Mall.

Twenty years passed before the familiar arguments about site, cost, and design were exhausted, but a piecemeal version of Clas's ode to the City Beautiful eventually began to emerge. The University of Wisconsin–Extension erected a classroom building on Sixth and State in 1928, the Safety Building opened to the west in 1929, and the county courthouse followed in 1931. Frank Lloyd Wright promptly dismissed Milwaukee's ponderous new hall of justice as "a pseudo-classic horror."

Horrific or not, the building projects came to an end with the start of the Depression, and World War II kept the steam shovels at bay. The square was named in 1945 for Douglas MacArthur, a war hero with deep local roots, but postwar development moved at a glacial pace. Progress was so slow that in 1956 city engineers proposed an interim plan for the "disorganized and unattractive" MacArthur Square area. The automobile had been tightening its grip on American cities all the while. Milwaukee's engineers proposed demolishing the handful of blighted old buildings that remained and developing five square blocks of parking lots.

Parking would be the ultimate winner, but not in the form of surface lots. In 1962, HNTB, a national consulting firm hired by the city, proposed a 1,274-car underground garage east of the courthouse, covered by four landscaped terraces stepping down to Sixth Street on the east. The basic plan was adopted with surprisingly little controversy. Through streets were closed, the hillside was leveled, and MacArthur Square was reborn in 1967 as the roof of a parking garage. No more triumphal boulevards for this space.

New buildings rose on either side of the square. After sharing space with the Central Library since 1898, the Public Museum

The Schoenleber clock tower was an ungainly lawn ornament placed on the square in 1970. When it was removed twenty years later, no one complained. MILWAUKEE COUNTY HISTORICAL SOCIETY

moved across Wells Street to its new home, one collection at a time, between 1963 and 1967, and the Police Administration Building opened on the opposite side of the square in 1971. The plaza between them sprouted one of Milwaukee's quirkiest landmarks: a three-legged clock tower featuring a five-thousand-pound timepiece and dioramas of historic Milwaukee scenes. Donated by the Schoenleber family of Ambrosia Chocolate fame and dedicated in 1970, this piece of classic kitsch was even more notable for the details that were left out, including a spotlight that would have projected seasonal messages onto low-flying clouds.

"Happy Groundhog Day" never lit up the belly of a passing cumulus, and a host of other things never happened in Mac-Arthur Square. There were sporadic concerts, rallies, and, for a time, the official city Christmas tree, but a space that one planner had envisioned in 1947 as "*the* spot which can give the populace an inspirational and emotional uplift" became instead a disengaged, disengaging civic backwater. In 1990, when the crumbling Schoenleber clock tower was judged too costly to repair, it was dismantled, and no one stepped forward to object.

Why did the square fail? To say that its surrounding buildings lack unity would be stating the obvious, but that's not the heart of the problem. In 1967, when the parking garage opened and the through streets were closed, the whole square went to sleep. Flanked by a rampart of buildings that faced outward, it became a fortress in reverse, a stronghold with nothing to protect. With the exception of the courthouse, whose main entrance was useless after Ninth Street became a tunnel, every building turned its back on MacArthur Square. Instead of the grand plaza envisioned by Alfred Clas and his colleagues, the space became an oversized alley, owned by no one, used by no one, loved by no one.

All across urban America, failed attempts at reformed landscapes are left behind like corpses on a battlefield. MacArthur Square died, for all practical purposes, more than fifty years ago, and it's been lying in state ever since. Could the square be resurrected? A community that built the Calatrava, tore down the Park East freeway, and reimagined its downtown lakefront is certainly capable of boldness. What might be done to reclaim this vacancy at the heart of things? How might we bring this municipal Sahara back to life? Reopening the through streets? Growing an urban farm? Building new landmarks?

The details await, but there are countless examples across the country of what imagination and capital working together can do. What might they accomplish with this sorriest of botched opportunities? How can Milwaukee transform its municipal black hole into a source of sustaining light?

A South Side Landmark Restored

St. Stanislaus Church Goes Back to the Past

It's not a resurrection you could have predicted. St. Stanislaus Church, one of the South Side's most familiar landmarks, had a distinguished past as a center of Polish Catholicism, but its fortunes ebbed as the surrounding neighborhood became predominantly Latino. Unable to make the demographic turn, "St. Stan's" experienced a catastrophic drop in membership. The growing tarnish on its twin steeples seemed emblematic of a more general decline.

The saviors of this historic parish turned out to be a group that was neither Polish nor Latino but Latin—as in the Latin Mass. An energetic community of traditional Catholics made the church their own in the early 2000s. Although they had few connections with the parish's past or the neighborhood's present, they brought new life to the South Side, reestablishing St. Stan's as a vital center of worship and completely restoring its landmark building.

Few parishes have played larger roles in Milwaukee's ethnic history than St. Stanislaus. When the first Polish immigrants reached the city in the 1850s, they brought their Catholic faith with them. In 1866, thirty families established a new home for that faith, buying a small brick church on Fifth and Mineral Streets from a German Lutheran congregation that had moved to larger quarters down the street. The newcomers named their

fledgling parish for St. Stanislaus, a bishop and martyr from Poland's medieval period.

Those early parishioners had no idea that they were making history, but St. Stanislaus was the first Polish church in any American city. Although Chicago's Poles organized their own St. Stan's one year later, Milwaukee was the pioneer, and the humble congregation of 1866 became the mother church of more than twenty other Polish Catholic parishes scattered around the city, particularly on the South Side.

As Poles continued to pour into Milwaukee, the original building was crammed beyond capacity every Sunday, but not for long. In 1872, the people of St. Stanislaus moved a half mile south to Fifth and Mitchell Streets, dedicating a baroque church with twin copper-clad steeples that made it an instant landmark. That building, too, was soon filled to bursting. Within a decade, there were a thousand families on the parish rolls, nearly all of them young. In 1883, the priests of St. Stan's baptized 602 children—nearly a dozen every week.

My ancestors were among those young families. When my great-grandparents, Franciszek and Apolonia Gurda, immigrated to Milwaukee with their five children in 1889, St. Stanislaus became their spiritual home. The Gurdas lived in a tiny house five blocks away from the twin spires, and their kids grew up in the parish. The older ones were all married at St. Stan's, and Franciszek and Apolonia—Frank and Pauline to their non-Polish neighbors—were eventually buried from the church, he in 1910, she in 1928.

My great-grandfather was one of the great mass of Old World farmers who became New World factory workers, a peasant who joined the proletariat. Another group of parishioners transplanted

(*Opposite*) St. Stanislaus Church is a traditional center of Polish Catholicism repurposed for devotees of the traditional Latin Mass. JOHN GURDA

their traditional way of life intact: fisherfolk from Poland's Baltic seacoast. The Kaszubs, as they were called, made Jones Island the center of commercial fishing in Milwaukee, hauling up two million pounds of trout, whitefish, and chubs in a typical year. They were faithful members of St. Stanislaus, rowing across to the mainland for Mass every Sunday. A decorative beam given by the Kaszubs in thanksgiving to God for deliverance from an 1893 storm still crowns the sanctuary.

As immigration reached flood stage, new Polish parishes—St. Hyacinth, St. Josaphat, St. Vincent de Paul, and others—relieved some of the pressure, but St. Stanislaus remained a linchpin of the South Side Polonia (Polish American community) as well as the eastern anchor of the Mitchell Street shopping district and a beehive of activity. Its grade school, established in 1868, was the first Polish Catholic school in America, and St. Stan's followed that feat by opening its own high school just north of the church in 1932. (It survives in memory as Notre Dame.) Parishioners of every age could choose from a full menu of guilds, sodalities, societies, athletic leagues, dance groups, and Polish cultural organizations.

The activity continued well into the post–World War II period, particularly under Father Raymond Punda, who came to St. Stanislaus as a young priest in 1939 and never left. Punda became such a dominant figure on the South Side that Mitchell Street was jokingly referred to as "the Pundarosa." In the 1960s, when reforms initiated by the Second Vatican Council were transforming the Catholic Church, the pastor saw an opportunity. Looking forward to St. Stan's 1966 centennial, he initiated a top-to-bottom remodeling of the church that would, according to a 1966 parish history, "embody the physical symbolism of modern Catholicism." The copper domes on the steeples were replaced with gold-leafed aluminum, and crews working under Punda's direction carpeted the floor, covered the interior walls with beige paint, and—the most unfortunate decision—replaced the original stained-glass windows with chunks of colored glass imbedded in concrete.

The remodeling was, in retrospect, too much too late. Not only did it compromise the historical integrity of the building, but the project did nothing to stem the changes engulfing the parish. As St. Stan's was celebrating its centennial, Interstate 94 ripped through the South Side, destroying hundreds of parishioners' homes and putting six lanes of concrete literally at the church's front door. The remaining Polish residents moved slowly but steadily to the south and west, and the Latino families who replaced them, although largely Catholic, gravitated to more receptive homes in other South Side parishes. By the time Monsignor Punda died in 1979, St. Stanislaus was in transition. Notre Dame High School closed in 1988, and the parish was hemorrhaging members. By the early 2000s, attendance at Sunday Mass had dwindled to a few dozen.

Enter the Institute of Christ the King, a religious order founded in France in 1990 with special devotion to "the millennial treasury of the Roman Catholic Church, particularly her liturgical tradition." Not every Catholic had embraced the reforms of Vatican II. In Milwaukee, the traditionalists basically went underground, celebrating the Latin Mass in rented quarters and then in a West Allis church that was on the verge of closing. In 2007, with St. Stanislaus about to meet the same fate, Archbishop Timothy Dolan put the Institute of Christ the King in charge of the parish. The Institute had a mission, the Latin Mass community had a passion, and the two came together on the corner of Fifth and Mitchell.

The marriage was a success from the start. Attendance at the Sunday Masses rose to 350 in 2011 and quickly doubled and doubled again. "Every week," said staff member Abbé George Baird in 2019, "I see more people, and they're sitting closer together." Baird described the reborn St. Stan's as a "commuter church," with worshipers coming from as far away as Kohler, Kenosha, and Delavan.

I experienced the elaborately choreographed ritual of High Mass at St. Stanislaus on a prepandemic Sunday. For a cradle Catholic, it was like stepping back in time. The priest faced the high altar, the women wore head coverings, everyone took communion on the tongue, and the liturgy, of course, was in Latin, both spoken and sung.

Just as striking were the physical changes in the building. With a confidence born of faith and numbers, the congregation tackled a complete restoration. The floor has new tile, the polychrome paint scheme is back after decades of beige, and the new stained-glass windows look as if they belong in a 150-year-old building. Motorists on I-94 are more likely to notice the exterior changes: a new roof, restored masonry, and spires capped with copper, just as they were in 1872. The project's total cost approached $4 million, all of it provided by parishioners.

The Latin Mass remains controversial, with strongly held opinions on both sides. Where some liberal Catholics see only pomp and patriarchy, conservatives see right reverence for God and fidelity to ancient traditions. What I see at St. Stanislaus is a landmark reborn and a heritage recovered. For that there is only one appropriate response: "Hallelujah!"

Used Cars in the Parlor

Grand Avenue Mansion Has Survived, but Barely

The building has always intrigued me. Whenever I drive down West Wisconsin Avenue, I pause at Twenty-Sixth Street to take in the singular creation on the northeast corner. Two retail businesses face the sidewalk—a Golden Chicken take-out restaurant and a check-cashing place—but these store-fronts literally encase what was once a mansion. The barnacles of modern commerce have encrusted and nearly obliterated a three-story brick edifice that must have been a real showplace in its time.

The home's glory days are long gone. No offense to Golden Chicken, but the original structure looks like a duchess who was abandoned at the ball years ago and forced to wear a scullery maid's apron for the rest of her life.

A dive into the archives confirmed that 2532 West Wisconsin Avenue was built during the street's previous incarnation as Grand Avenue, and its career is a fascinating microcosm of the surrounding area's long history. From the 1870s through the early 1900s, Grand Avenue was one of the ritziest residential districts in Milwaukee, lined with the palatial homes of the city's most prominent families. Some of the names are still familiar, including Mitchell, Pabst, Plankinton, Brumder, Johnston, and Cudahy. When Milwaukeeans wanted to show out-of-town guests the city's high points, Grand Avenue was one of their first stops.

(*Left*) The Gerhard Winner mansion was a Grand Avenue showplace when it was built in 1897 . . .

(*Below*) . . . but unsympathetic remodelings have practically erased its original lines.

TOP: *MILWAUKEE SENTINEL*, JUNE 14, 1897;
BOTTOM: JOHN GURDA

The owner of 2532 West Wisconsin is not among the names we remember today. He was Gerhard H. Winner, a German immigrant who arrived in 1858 at the age of nineteen. After brief stints as a porter and a clerk, the newcomer went into the beverage business. For most of Milwaukee's Germans, that meant beer—his father-in-law ran Cream City Brewing—but Winner gravitated to the harder side of the spirits spectrum. He became a distiller, first on Plankinton Avenue and then as owner of the Lake Side plant in Carrollville, an industrial suburb of blue-collar South Milwaukee.

Gerhard Winner was a wholesaler as well as a distiller, selling his own and others' alcoholic wares at a downtown store near the corner of Clybourn and Plankinton Avenues. By the late 1800s, he was a familiar figure in the local papers, earning praise for his opposition to the "whiskey trust," an industry cartel he blasted as "one of the worst monopolies in the country today."

Even though Winner refused to play by the trust's rules, there was still plenty of money to be made in the liquor trade. In 1897, five years after beer baron Frederick Pabst finished his mansion on Twentieth and Grand, the whiskey king built his own at Twenty-Sixth Street. Designed by local architects Crane & Barkhausen, it was described in the *Milwaukee Sentinel* as "a large and elegant residence" of brown pressed brick trimmed with sandstone and terra cotta. The dining room ceiling was decorated with panels of native oak, Italian marble was used in all the bathrooms, and the five upstairs bedrooms were finished in sycamore, gumwood, red birch, and red oak. The price tag for this magnificence: fifteen thousand dollars.

Not many Milwaukeeans of 1897 could afford a home that cost nearly five hundred thousand dollars in modern currency— a sum that didn't include the lot, the furnishings, or a three-thousand-dollar stable on the Wells Street side of the property. Gerhard Winner was one of the lucky few, but he had only a dozen years to enjoy his mansion; the distiller died in 1909 at the age of sixty-nine. After a funeral at his Grand Avenue residence, Winner was buried in Forest Home Cemetery.

By the time of the liquor magnate's death, Grand Avenue's heyday as a residential gold coast had nearly run its course. As Milwaukee grew, there was a surge in demand for housing close to the heart of town. Increasing congestion prompted the avenue's wealthy families to flee, practically en masse, to quieter pastures in communities like Washington Heights and Wauwatosa.

The mansions they left behind met a variety of fates. Some were converted to institutional uses; the Pabst home became the Catholic archbishop's residence in 1908, and Marquette University turned a number of old landmarks into classroom buildings. Other mansions were cut up into multifamily units and eventually became rooming houses. The greatest number were simply torn down to make way for apartment buildings, businesses, and hospitals.

The Winner mansion survived, but hardly in its original form. In 1920, according to building inspection records, the home was divided into a duplex, and in the 1930s it was further divided into eighteen "furnished rooms," including the servants' quarters on the third floor. The coffered ceilings, elaborate millwork, and nickel-plated bathroom fixtures were all casualties of this comprehensive "remuddling."

Although its interior was basically gutted, the exterior of the Winner home remained largely intact until 1952, when a new owner, the Jaeger Motor Car Company, slapped a two-story addition onto the south and west sides of the building. The addition became, of all things, a used-car showroom. Since selling his first Pontiac in 1926, Anthony Jaeger—like Gerhard Winner, a German immigrant—had built a dealership that was for a time Pontiac's leading outlet in the Midwest. Jaeger sold new models on Twenty-Seventh and Lisbon, but there was enough potential in used cars for him to open a second facility one mile south, on Wisconsin Avenue. The *Milwaukee Sentinel* described both showrooms as "bright and spacious" and Jaeger himself as an "energetic and enterprising" figure who routinely put in sixteen-hour days.

Used cars gave way to stereos in the next decade. By 1960, the tacked-on showroom housed Hi-Fi Fo-Fum, a fondly remembered establishment that introduced thousands of Milwaukeeans to the mysteries of subwoofers and tweeters—just in time for the musical revolution of the 1960s. Hi-Fi Fo-Fum unplugged in the mid-1970s, and since then the space has been variously used as a campaign office, a flower shop, a grocery store, a video outlet, and a succession of restaurants. The current tenants, in addition to Golden Chicken and the check-cashing business, include a barber shop and a karate studio. The twelve residential units in the original home—four on each floor—have been rented continuously while commercial tenants have come and gone.

It was only chance that kept the Winner mansion standing while those around it fell. Anthony Jaeger could just as easily have torn the place down in 1952 as tacked on an addition. Today you can count the survivors of Grand Avenue's glory years on the fingers of one hand. The only two that retain any semblance of their original form are the Mitchell mansion, still in use as the Wisconsin Club, and the Pabst mansion, which was spared the wrecking ball in 1975 to become Milwaukee's favorite house museum. The rest are long gone, leaving the oddly hybrid structure at 2532 West Wisconsin Avenue behind as a brick-and-mortar reminder that in the city, as in life, nothing lasts forever.

A Bright Idea for an Overbuilt Bridge

Hoan Bridge Spans Decades of Controversy

D an Hoan would not have been pleased. In 1971, when freeway authorities decided to put his name on the bridge taking shape over Milwaukee's harbor, they clearly had not studied
the Socialist warhorse's record. As Milwaukee's mayor from 1916
to 1940, Hoan was instrumental in leading the community out
of its corrupt past to become perhaps the best-governed big city
in the country, and he did so by following the principles of public enterprise. That meant, among many other things, reserving
Milwaukee's most important spaces for public use.

Near the top of that list was the city's magnificent lakefront.
In 1929, after years of landfill activity, Lincoln Memorial Drive
opened to the public. The official dedication on September 28 was
marred by a downpour, but Dan Hoan beamed anyway. The
completed roadway instantly became one of the most scenic
and most popular stretches of urban shoreline on the entire
Great Lakes.

Hoan's reverence for the lakefront lost none of its force
after he left the mayor's office in 1940. When the War Memorial
Center opened on the downtown shore in 1957, it was roundly
praised as an icon of modernism designed by a modern master,
Eero Saarinen. Dan Hoan begged to differ. "I think this war
memorial will be a lasting building," he said, "but it cuts off the
view of the lake. People want to see water. That lakefront . . . is

Milwaukee's showpiece. I hope it isn't ruined in the years to come by the construction of a lot of buildings that will shut off the remaining view of the lake."

A lot of buildings or, he might have added, a lot of bridge. Dan Hoan died in 1961, a decade before the Expressway Commission named the harbor span in his dubious honor. The finished bridge used 131,886 cubic yards of concrete and 30,675 tons of steel, assembled at the monumental cost of $75.1 million. That wasn't all. The bridge was the linchpin of the planned Lake Freeway, a six-lane road that would have paralleled the lakeshore from north of downtown to Mitchell Airport. Not only would the structure have obscured the view of the lake, but the attached freeway links would also have disfigured Juneau Park on the north and destroyed more than five hundred housing units on the south—all prospects that Hoan would have abhorred.

It was both fitting and ironic that a growing number of Milwaukeeans came to share Hoan's views after his death. By 1970, the freeway era was nearly over, brought to an end by a coalition

Graceful but overbuilt, the Dan Hoan Bridge links downtown Milwaukee with the city's South Shore communities. MILWAUKEE JOURNAL SENTINEL

Devoid of traffic for three long years, the Hoan was Milwaukee's "bridge to nowhere" in the mid-1970s. It was finally connected to surface streets in 1977. MILWAUKEE JOURNAL SENTINEL

of neighborhood advocates, environmentalists, and others who believed that the city was strangling in ribbons of concrete. The Lake Freeway became their particular target.

As opposition mounted on both ends, there was no one in the middle, on Jones Island, to object to the new road. Seeing an opening and unmoved by the rising tide of resistance, the Expressway Commission plowed ahead with the span itself. The result, completed in 1974, was the infamous "bridge to nowhere"—a term that residents of Bay View, St. Francis, and Cudahy actively resented. Dan Hoan's lakefront was saddled with a towering landmark that stood in useless isolation for three long years.

Proposals to make it a skateboard park or a tourist concourse failed to develop much traction. In 1977, the stub ends were finally connected to surface streets, and traffic began to flow between downtown and the South Shore. The six-lane Hoan Bridge was like an oil pipeline connected to two garden hoses.

Bay View was suddenly five minutes from downtown. Property values soared, and so did traffic congestion. The problem was largely solved and the mismatch resolved in 1999, when the Lake Parkway was completed from the south end of the bridge to Layton Avenue. Running along an old rail corridor, the parkway's four lanes did minimal damage to the surrounding communities and gave East Siders a convenient new route to the airport.

Barely a year later, just when commuters were getting used to the completed roadway, the bridge itself suffered an alarming collapse. During a cold snap in December 2000, beam supports cracked under the northbound lanes, causing them to sag toward the lake. (My wife was one of the last motorists to cross.) The damaged span was blasted to the ground a couple of weeks later, and it took most of a year to replace it and reopen the bridge to traffic.

After a $180 million reconstruction in 2015, the Hoan Bridge was pronounced good to go for another forty years. But there was one more twist in its long and convoluted story. In 2016, two young community activists, Ian Abston and Michael Hostad, were looking for a project to highlight the abundance of good things about Milwaukee. Looming over the city's eastern horizon stood the Hoan Bridge. Pursuing a suggestion from Daniel Steininger, a civic leader who happens to be Dan Hoan's grandson, the pair decided to light up the span as Milwaukee's version of San Francisco's fabled Bay Bridge.

It took four years of planning, fundraising, and jumping through bureaucratic hoops, but the project was a success. On October 22, 2020, in the darkness of a global pandemic, the Hoan Bridge debuted in a new role. Its central span was set aglow with 2,600 LED lights in a rainbow of colors and an infinite variety

The Light the Hoan project has given the bridge a bright new place in the city's landscape. JOHN GURDA

of programmable patterns, creating what Light the Hoan's leaders described as "a symbol of unity and civic pride." A transportation landmark was transformed into a kinetic sculpture.

The project helped Milwaukeeans see their lakefront span in a new light. The Hoan Bridge may be grossly overbuilt and inappropriately named, but it's iconic nonetheless. Its graceful arches, which won an industry design award in 1975, are an instantly recognizable landmark that has been used in any number of artworks and logos. Milwaukee's legendary "bridge to nowhere" is now somewhere indeed. After decades of controversy, construction, reconstruction, and reimagining, that giant buckle on the belt of Milwaukee's lakefront finally looks like it belongs there.

A City Built on Water

Paddling through History

A Memorable Day on the Milwaukee River

A river runs through it. Of all the statements you could make about Milwaukee's history, that might be the most obvious. The Milwaukee River is generally viewed as urban scenery today—an occasion for bridges, a channel for boaters— but its role in the city's development has been nothing less than formative.

At the beginning of urban time in the 1830s, long before railroads and highways, the river mouth was Milwaukee's front door, and its eighteen-foot-deep estuary provided safe anchorage for the schooners that linked the little town to the outside world. As settlers flocked to such a promising site, the river divided them into antagonistic east and west sides. As Milwaukee grew, those same settlers dammed the stream to saw their lumber and grind their flour. Their descendants eventually turned it into an open sewer, a civic embarrassment that, despite extensive cleanup efforts in recent decades, is still a work in progress.

One of my most pleasant canoe trips in recent memory was a float down this historic river with my wife and our oldest son. Using the handy Milwaukee Urban Water Trail map published by Milwaukee Riverkeeper, we put in at Villa Grove Park in Mequon and took out at the South Water Street boat ramp in Walker's Point. The trip took us seven hours and covered twenty-one river miles. I'd canoed the stream many times before, but

The Milwaukee River may be an urban stream, but this view from the Capitol Drive bridge captures its enduring wild side. EDDEE DANIEL

usually in its lower reaches; paddling such a generous swath was an eye-opening experience.

Traces of the truly distant past turned up every few miles. We began our trip among pontoon boats docked on the Thiensville mill pond, a fixture in the landscape ever since German-born John Thien dammed the river in the early 1840s. Farther downstream, in Kletzsch Park, we passed another old millrace, and just above Locust Street we scraped over the remains of an ice dam built by the Schlitz brewery to ensure a steady supply of natural refrigerant.

Almost nothing remains from the lower river's heyday as an in-town water park. The swimming schools, amusement parks, and canoe clubs are all gone, but the leisure-time tradition continues with the Estabrook Park beer garden, perched on the east bank high above the only real waterfall of the trip.

Humans love to live near water, and there are plenty of choices along the Milwaukee River, from the baronial estates of River Hills to the modest cottages that show up with surprising frequency in both Ozaukee and Milwaukee Counties. Closer to downtown, high-end apartments and condos have popped up on the faded footprints of coal docks and tannery buildings. Other signs of human presence were only temporary: fishermen in waders casting for bass, kids catching tadpoles and skipping rocks, countercultural throwbacks lounging in hammocks in Riverside Park, and a dimpling of errant golf balls on the river bottom at the Milwaukee Country Club.

Milwaukeeans have been putting their river to various uses over the past 180 years, but what impressed me most about our trip was how wild the stream still looks. Even in the city, we were graced with the presence of green herons and Baltimore orioles. Clamshells littered the bottom for miles, and we caught glimpses of mink, muskrat, deer, and snapping turtles the size of serving platters. On lengthy stretches well within the city limits, we saw nothing but broad river and green trees.

The spectacle is, to some degree, an illusion. What paddlers see along most of the river is actually a scrim—a narrow fringe of green protected from development by flood hazard, topography, and sometimes public policy. What's remarkable is the width of that fringe close to downtown. Between Port Washington Road and North Avenue, the river pitches downward toward the lake, creating fast water and a valley so deep that it's entirely wooded. That valley is now protected as the Milwaukee River Greenway, an urban wilderness less than two miles from City Hall. If the Greenway isn't unique in urban America, it's certainly close.

The river plays another interesting trick on itinerant paddlers: at any given point it was hard to know exactly where we were. Flowing at the pace of a fast walk and changing direction frequently without regard to compass points, the stream upended my sense of the local landscape. We saw the undersides of bridges I'd crossed hundreds of times, but I could detect nothing remotely familiar about them from the water. I eventually realized that we were experiencing a sort of geographic role reversal. From the solid coordinates of dry land, the river is a determinedly fluid presence; it passes us by. From the river's perspective, it's the land that's in constant motion; we pass it by. As each bend opens a new vista, getting a fix on your position is a challenge.

The result is a fresh way to see the city. Urbanites normally experience their environment as a system of transects, ruler-straight lines we follow from point to point in a grid pattern that's literally set in concrete. The river runs counter to that fixed geometry, gliding through it all with a regal inevitability that leaves us faintly disoriented.

Was there any downside to our family excursion? Although recent remediation efforts have shown dramatic results, the Milwaukee River is still miles from pristine. The day was hot, but none of us felt the slightest urge to swim, and the foam below the occasional rapids had that faintly detergent smell I associate with urban streams.

Rafters brave the falls in Estabrook Park. EDDEE DANIEL

The Milwaukee River can also be a challenge to paddle. We made our trip in late June, weeks after peak flow. The river was barely runnable in its lower reaches, and I can't imagine attempting it in July or August. Several stretches were long rock gardens that could not be maneuvered without scraping bottom—a particular hazard with three adults in one boat. We had to get out and walk occasionally, and our canoe got thoroughly hung up in the minor rapids directly beneath the Locust Street bridge, forcing me into warm, waist-deep river water to extract us. At the end of the trip, our trusty red Old Town went back into the garage with a lot more scrapes and gouges than it had sported in the morning.

We executed less-eventful portages around one falls and two dams. Not long ago, it would have been three dams, before the controversial structure in Estabrook Park was removed in 2018. Another recently dam-free stretch gave us the greatest thrill of the day. When the North Avenue barrier was removed in 1997, a genuine rapids emerged just upstream. We plowed through a standing wave at its head and shot down the chute on a wave of adrenaline. The rapids delivered us to the quiet water of downtown and a celebratory dinner at a riverside restaurant.

I'd gladly run the river again, though not so late in the season. From Mequon to the mouth, we experienced firsthand the persistence of history, the resilience of nature, and a novel perspective on our native landscape. It may lack the majesty of the Mississippi or the wilderness pedigree of the Wolf, but the Milwaukee River serves perfectly well as the major artery of a mid-sized metropolis. Nearly two centuries after the city's founding, a river still runs through it.

Lost on the *Lady Elgin*

Remembering the Worst Disaster on the Great Lakes

Lake Michigan's mood changes abruptly with the coming of fall. The sultry days and soft winds of high summer give way to gales that whip the water to a froth even inside the harbor, and any boat venturing out onto the open lake is in for a wild ride. Autumn marks the start of what early Milwaukeeans dreaded as shipwreck season. Ever since regular navigation on the Great Lakes began in the 1820s, thousands of vessels have gone down in "the gales of November"—and the gales of September and October as well.

For loss of life and broader historical significance, an 1860 shipwreck stands out from all the rest. The doomed vessel was the *Lady Elgin*, a sidewheel steamship that has achieved legendary status in our region's marine lore. Not only was the mortality on the *Lady Elgin* appalling, but most of the victims were Milwaukeeans, and their fate was tied directly to tensions that were tearing the country apart in the years before the Civil War.

The last voyage of the *Lady Elgin* was, in essence, a fundraiser gone terribly awry. Most of its passengers were affiliated with the Union Guards, an Irish militia company based in Milwaukee's Third Ward. The unit's commander was Garrett Barry, a West Point graduate who was also active in Democratic politics; local voters had made Barry their county treasurer in 1859.

More than three hundred people died when the steamer *Lady Elgin* sank in 1860, the most lives ever lost on the open waters of the Great Lakes.
MILWAUKEE COUNTY HISTORICAL SOCIETY

Wisconsin was a hotbed of antislavery sentiment at the time, particularly under Governor Alexander Randall, a "fire-breathing" abolitionist. In 1855, the Wisconsin Supreme Court had gone so far as to declare the Fugitive Slave Act of 1850, a federal law safeguarding the rights of enslavers, unconstitutional. No other state took a stand so courageous—or so potentially seditious.

Bracing for a possible confrontation with federal authorities, Governor Randall called for a declaration of loyalty from the state's militia companies. Garrett Barry, a Democrat, told Randall, a Republican, that taking sides against the United States "would render himself and his men guilty of treason." Randall promptly stripped Barry of his commission and disarmed the Union Guards.

Militia companies of the era were largely volunteer groups, typically organized along ethnic or class lines, and their activities were as much social as military. Randall might have taken their rifles away, but the Union Guards owned their own uniforms and their own band instruments. No one could keep them from meeting and marching—or even from owning guns. In June 1860, with help from a sympathetic congressman, Barry purchased eighty government-surplus muskets for two dollars each; the $160 bill would top $5,000 in current dollars. Instead of assessing themselves for the muskets, the Union Guards decided to raise the money by sponsoring an excursion to Chicago—aboard the *Lady Elgin*.

Built in Buffalo in 1851, the *Elgin* was a lavishly appointed "palace steamer," with sixty-six staterooms on its upper deck, a smoking lounge for "gentlemen," and a grand staircase to the lower deck. Although it could accommodate hundreds of passengers, the ship doubled as a freight-carrier, offering regular cargo service from Chicago (its home port) to Milwaukee and

The *Lady Elgin* with a full load of passengers. MILWAUKEE COUNTY HISTORICAL SOCIETY

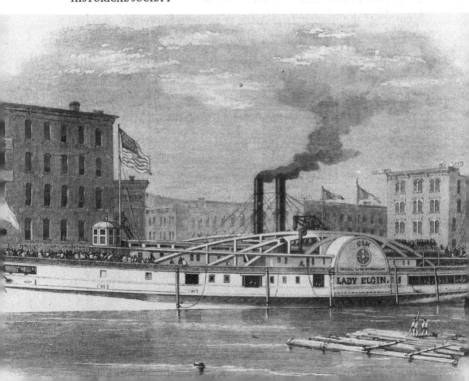

destinations on Lake Superior. It also attracted a regular stream of excursionists on the Chicago–Milwaukee run.

Even at the princely sum of a dollar each, tickets sold briskly, particularly to the Union Guards and their supporters, a number of whom decided to take along their wives and children. When the *Lady Elgin* left the Third Ward in the early-morning hours of September 7, 1860, more than three hundred Milwaukeeans were aboard, along with the company's precious new muskets.

Once in Chicago, the party paraded from the LaSalle Street dock to a downtown hotel for breakfast and then split into smaller groups for a long day of sightseeing, shopping, eating, and, for some, drinking. By the time they gathered for the voyage home, a number of passengers were so far gone that they had to be practically poured into their stateroom beds.

A stiff wind was already blowing when the *Elgin* left Chicago that night, and it quickly developed into a gale—not an unusual occurrence on the Great Lakes in autumn. The ship kept its northerly course, and some of the hardier revelers kept dancing on the upper deck.

Then, shortly after 2:00 a.m. on September 8, disaster struck. A Chicago-bound lumber schooner, the *Augusta*, was on a collision course with the *Lady Elgin*. The ships' crews could barely see each other in the heavy seas and driving rain, and neither vessel could take evasive action until it was too late. The *Augusta* hit the *Elgin* amidships—"T-boned her," modern sailors might say—leaving a hole that one passenger later described as so big "you could drive a team of horses through it."

Although the *Lady Elgin* was nearly three times larger than the schooner, it was the steamship that suffered the fatal blow; the *Augusta* fell off before the wind and limped toward Chicago.

The first reaction aboard the *Elgin* was a shocked quiet, followed quickly by pandemonium. Although Captain Jack Wilson

Heavy surf made it perilously difficult to rescue the survivors of the *Lady Elgin* shipwreck. WHI IMAGE ID 6080

was the picture of calm, considering his situation, events quickly spun out of control. As the engine room filled with water, the boilers went out within twenty minutes of the collision. The *Elgin* was dead in the water, and storm waves soon broke the ship apart.

For those who hadn't been trapped below decks or crushed by falling wreckage, hours of misery lay ahead. The *Elgin* was four miles off Winnetka when it went down. Survivors grabbed whatever they could find—cabin doors, bureau drawers, splintered beams, even a bass drum—and drifted with agonizing slowness toward shore. High waves, cold water, and pitch darkness, broken by the occasional flash of lightning, created a scene of unrelenting terror.

It was dawn before the first survivors saw land, but the view provided scant comfort. Huge breakers were crashing against the steep clay bluffs, and many who had weathered the harrowing ride to shore ended up drowning in the heavy surf.

When a determined crewman finally clambered up the bluff to civilization, word of the disaster spread like wildfire. A horde of rescuers, reporters, and gawkers flocked to the beach near Winnetka. By late afternoon, the focus had shifted from rescuing survivors to recovering bodies.

The sinking of the *Lady Elgin* made national headlines. Never before or since had so many people perished in a wreck on the open waters of the Great Lakes. In the absence of an official ship manifest, the precise number of fatalities was unknown until master researcher Carl Baehr painstakingly compiled his own list in 2009. Baehr concluded that 398 people boarded the *Lady Elgin* that stormy night in 1860, and 302, most of them Irish Milwaukeeans, never returned. The dead included Garrett Barry and his twelve-year-old son.

Swept up by currents that would remake American society, Barry and his comrades were part of a much larger story. The wreck of the *Lady Elgin* was discovered in 1989. Among the artifacts found scattered on the lake floor were the muskets of the Union Guards—mute relics of a controversy that ended in unfathomable tragedy.

In-Town Up North

Milwaukee River Was Our Ancestors' Wisconsin Dells

Pity our ancestors in the dog days of summer. When temperatures climbed past eighty and stayed there, Milwaukeeans of the 1800s had little choice but to swelter and sweat, without air-conditioning, without screens, without car windows to roll down, without even antiperspirants. The city's streetcars must have smelled like locker rooms when the day shift went home.

Add to their plight the fact that most workers put in at least ten-hour days six days a week, with Sunday as their sole day of rest. Even the minority who could afford to get out of town couldn't have gone far, and Lake Michigan, cool as it was, offered little respite; the city had no public beaches on the lakefront until the end of the century. Even then, the water was generally too cold and too rough for all but the hardiest to enjoy.

Milwaukee did, however, have a welcoming oasis near the very heart of the city, one that was not just refreshing but also accessible to everyone. When our overheated ancestors sought relief on the water, they found it, more often than not, on the Milwaukee River, particularly the stretch between North Avenue and Capitol Drive. From the 1870s through the early decades of the twentieth century—long before Wisconsin Dells caught the wave—the upper river was a nearly continuous water park.

This wonderland was the serendipitous byproduct of a dam. As part of a canal he planned between Milwaukee and the Rock

(*Left*) In 1896, a water toboggan called Shoot the Chutes gave the Milwaukee River an attraction worthy of Wisconsin Dells. Note the "water bicycles" in the foreground.

(*Right*) Rohn's was one of three swimming schools that used the deep pool just above the North Avenue dam. BOTH PHOTOS: MILWAUKEE COUNTY HISTORICAL SOCIETY

River, Byron Kilbourn, the West Side's founder, built the first North Avenue dam in 1843 to ensure himself a dependable volume of water. Political opponents scuttled his project, but the first mile of Kilbourn's ditch became a millrace that powered Milwaukee's pioneer industrial district. By the 1860s, the west bank of the river below North Avenue was lined with flour mills, sawmills, and various other enterprises. We know that old millrace today in its more solid form—as Commerce Street.

The industrial zone below the barrier was twinned, yin for yang, by a recreational corridor upstream; the North Avenue dam was a hinge that joined business and pleasure, work and leisure.

The structure created an irresistible urban lake, long and narrow but deep enough to support every type of recreation.

The main attractions were largely in place by 1900. Three swimming schools, two run by Germans, provided docks and diving boards near the dam. A water toboggan called Shoot the Chutes crowned the east bank at North Avenue. Canoe clubs, boathouses, and beer gardens dotted the upstream banks; on a hot Sunday afternoon, you could practically walk across the river by stepping from one canoe into the next. An amusement park with the requisite roller coaster, carousel, and water slide— admission ten cents—occupied the site of Hubbard Park. Water taxis plied the upper river, stopping at all points of interest for a fifteen-cent fare—less than five dollars in today's currency.

Although the admission fees could add up, there was room for penny-pinchers as well. The ravines of Riverside Park were open to everyone for free, and the public swimming beaches at Gordon and Estabrook Parks attracted crowds of young people. The ruins of the Gordon Park bathhouse are still plainly visible from the Locust Street bridge.

At the other end of the economic spectrum, wealthy German families—including the Kerns, Uihleins, Meineckes, and Puelichers—claimed some of the choicest spots on the upper river for their lavish summer homes. They moved out to this idyllic rural district when the school year ended and came back to the big city in autumn—never traveling more than three miles from downtown Milwaukee.

From North Avenue to Capitol Drive, the upper river was Milwaukee's "in-town Up North" for decades, but it could not remain rural forever. Urban development transformed the surrounding bluffs in the early decades of the twentieth century, and some of the riverside retreats entered the public domain. The Kern family's summer farm became Kern Park, and the Blatz beer garden followed suit as Pleasant Valley Park. A horrendous pollution problem made the rest of the river unappealing and finally unsafe; the last swimming school closed for good in 1940. Milwaukeeans in search of recreation on the water turned to inland alternatives, and the automobile got them there.

For the next fifty years, the upper river was nearly forgotten. A new, more hopeful chapter began in 1990, when the North Avenue dam was opened to facilitate reconstruction of the North Avenue bridge. As the mudflats dried out and vegetation returned, the upper river was viewed as a golden green opportunity, and its rebirth gathered momentum when the dam was removed in 1997.

A coalition of nonprofit groups and governmental agencies turned that opportunity into the Milwaukee River Greenway, an urban wilderness that encompasses eight miles of shoreline and nearly nine hundred acres of land. Protected by ownership, easements, and zoning regulations, the Greenway features hiking trails (both formal and improvised), an arboretum filled with native plants, canoe and kayak launches, and an outdoor classroom maintained by the Urban Ecology Center. Even more impressive is what's *not* there: buildings, parking lots, roads, and all the other fixtures of urban development.

The survival of this sylvan corridor, starting just a mile and a half from City Hall, is a happy anomaly, one that few other cities in America can match. Just as the downtown Riverwalk focuses attention on the Milwaukee River as an urban, even urbane, amenity, the Greenway serves us all as an easily accessible wild space.

Our ancestors once turned to the river for respite from the summer heat, and today we seek a different kind of respite on its shores: respite from the city itself. The swimming schools and the rowboats may be gone, along with the beer gardens and the water slides, but the river remains, a living link that connects both past and present with the natural world around us.

"Low Bridge, Everybody Down"

Erie Canal Carries Bicyclists Back to Milwaukee's Roots

I've got a mule and her name is Sal,
Fifteen miles on the Erie Canal.
She's a good old worker and a good old pal,
Fifteen miles on the Erie Canal.

Low bridge, everybody down.
Low bridge, we're coming to a town.

Millions of baby boomers can still sing that old American standard from memory. It was a staple in the music classes of the 1950s, and the tune still rests, dusty and disused, in the folds of our aging brains. For younger Americans, the song, mules and all, is as forgotten as the canal it celebrated.

In the summer of 2019, a group of Milwaukee boomers refreshed our memories. For a week and a day in early June, seven of us bicycled along the Erie Canal from Buffalo to Albany, a distance of 363 miles. It was a great trip, marked by agreeable terrain, interesting towns, and the occasional chorus of "Low bridge, everybody down."

Although we were biking in New York State, our trip took us back to Milwaukee's beginnings as a city. In the 1820s, when the little trading post on Lake Michigan was just starting to emerge as an urban possibility, Milwaukee was separated from the East

The intricate locks at Lockport, New York, were one of the Erie Canal's most celebrated feats of engineering. JOHN GURDA

Coast by a thousand miles of wilderness. Getting there was possible, but only for the most intrepid.

The Erie Canal changed all that. It was the missing link in the all-water route between the Great Lakes and the Atlantic Ocean, and it released a torrent of people and goods flowing in both directions.

Although other visionaries had floated the same idea, one man is credited with carrying the canal to completion: DeWitt Clinton, governor of New York between 1817 and 1828. Not a man allergic to hyperbole, Clinton saw the project as "a work more stupendous, more magnificent, and more beneficial than has hitherto been achieved by the human race." It would become, he declared, "a bond of union between the Atlantic and Western states [that] will create the greatest inland trade ever witnessed." When the federal government declined to fund the fabulous waterway, Clinton convinced his fellow New Yorkers to pay for it themselves.

The Erie Canal was the most American of projects, built on a scale proportionate to the dreams of the young republic. The technical hurdles its creators faced were formidable: climbing the falls and rapids of the Mohawk River on one end, scaling the Niagara escarpment on the other, and, in between, holding water as level as a board for stretches of fifty miles or more. Impossible? Clinton and his engineers proved otherwise.

The wonder is that the canal was completed in just eight years and on budget. As many as three thousand men were at work on any given day, a motley crew of immigrants, local farmers, and at least a few convicts who chose labor on the canal over prison time. Starting on July 4, 1817, they cut down trees, pulled stumps, blasted rock, moved dirt, cut stone, mixed cement, and redirected existing streams to keep "Clinton's ditch" full from end to end.

When they were done, on October 26, 1825, New York could boast one of the longest canals ever built, a custom-made waterway 4 feet deep and 40 feet wide, with 83 locks that descended like a staircase from 570 feet above sea level at Lake Erie in Buffalo to tidewater on the Hudson River at Albany. The project's total cost was $7,143,789.86—nearly $200 million in today's dollars.

That proved to be a bargain. The Erie Canal was an engineering marvel immediately hailed as the eighth wonder of the world, but its economic impact was even more impressive. Practically overnight, the canal cut freight costs in half and reduced the travel time across New York State from six weeks by wagon to as little as six days by boat—two fewer days than we spent on our bikes. Heavier cargoes could travel longer distances and suffer far less damage than ever before. Syracuse brewers could stop worrying about their barrels exploding on the axle-cracking roads of the day.

Although New Yorkers benefited most directly, the Erie Canal transformed the entire nation north of the Mason-Dixon line. Schooners and then steamships carried the natural wealth of the developing Midwest—wheat, flour, lumber, coal, ore, even live pigs—across the upper Great Lakes, down the St. Clair and Detroit Rivers, then up Lake Erie to Buffalo. There the cargoes were transferred to canal boats and pulled by three-mule teams all the way to Albany—on towpaths that are now bike trails. Albany's harbor basin could hold a thousand canal vessels, which were towed in groups by steam-powered tugs down the Hudson to New York City.

The Erie Canal's return cargoes included Eastern-made products—plows, furniture, nails, carpets, boots, stoves, books, harnesses, paint—and Eastern-born people. The new waterway shifted the flow of Midwestern migration from the Ohio River Valley to the Great Lakes, and as a result Wisconsin became, to an important degree, New York once removed. New York led the list of states sending their sons and daughters to Wisconsin, and a healthy majority of delegates to the territory's first constitutional convention in 1846 were tied to New York by birth, education, or business background. Whole sections of the document finally adopted two years later were lifted verbatim from New York's constitution.

The Erie Canal had a specifically urban impact. As traffic swelled, it was dubbed the "Mother of Cities"; Albany, Utica,

Three bikers from Milwaukee enjoyed a just-opened section of the Canalway Trail. JOHN GURDA

Syracuse, Rochester, and Buffalo all grew magically at the touch of the canal. My friends and I also biked through a succession of small inland towns with improbably wet names: Lockport, Middleport, Eagle Harbor, Brockport, Adams Basin, Fairport, and a dozen others—all offspring of the liquid lifeline that stretched across New York State.

The canal's magic touch reached well beyond its actual route. It was canal trade that cemented New York City's status as the commercial capital of America. On the Great Lakes, Cleveland, Toledo, Detroit, Milwaukee, Chicago, and scores of smaller settlements owed much of their early economic size to the canal. Beer may have made Milwaukee famous, but it was the Erie Canal that helped make Milwaukee in the first place.

By 1850, a quarter-century after the first locks opened, railroads had captured the bulk of the passenger trade, but the Erie Canal continued to prosper as a long-haul freight corridor, carrying nearly six million tons every year in the 1880s. It was so popular, in fact—and such a moneymaker for New York State—that the waterway was rebuilt not once but twice, each iteration wider, deeper, and straighter than the last. The latest version, completed in 1918, could accommodate barges with capacities of a thousand tons.

The Erie Canal was revolutionary in its day, but two newer transportation breakthroughs doomed it commercially. The interstate highway system, launched in 1956, became America's leading carrier of both people and goods, and the St. Lawrence Seaway, completed three years later, siphoned off the inland marine trade. The Erie Canal was reduced to what it is today: a recreational corridor, used primarily by cabin cruisers, tour boats, kayaks—and bicycles.

The Canalway Trail we traveled has nearly as many layers as the area's history. Roughly 80 percent of the route runs on dedicated pathways whose surfaces range from blacktop to packed gravel and, in a few places, dirt. The trail can be wide or narrow, open or wooded, and the canal it parallels is a dried-up ditch in some places and a broad linear lake in others. The landscape, too, is a study in contrasts. We encountered bucolic scenery reminiscent of Wisconsin, cows included, but also standout Victorian hamlets like Medina and Little Falls and inner-city scenes in Buffalo and Rochester.

Eight days after we started, the Milwaukee crew pedaled into downtown Albany as the trail's newest End-to-Enders. Early promoters heralded the canal as an open door to "the immense treasures of the illimitable and prolific West." We found an open door to other riches. Nearly two hundred years after its completion, the Erie Canal is a pathway to the past that illuminates the story of our entire region.

Condo Canyon Echoes with History

A New Chapter in the Milwaukee River's Story

There's a relatively new feature in Milwaukee's landscape. It's not as wide as the Menomonee Valley, not as high as the Rockwell Automation clock, and nowhere near as striking as our lakefront, but it makes an impression nonetheless.

My wife and I first made its acquaintance on a 2007 canoe trip up the Milwaukee River. After putting in at the South Water Street boat launch, we paddled slowly toward downtown. Within a few minutes, we found ourselves running a gauntlet of sleek new housing that extended along both banks for nearly half a mile. There, in the very heart of the city, we had discovered Condo Canyon.

The canyon is a recent addition to the landscape that, like all additions to the landscape, erases, or at least obscures, everything that came before. It occurred to me that here was a new chapter in a very old book, one that comes close to telling the story of the city itself.

It was the river, first of all, that put Milwaukee on the map. Clear to a depth of eighteen feet, its lower reaches could float anything on the Great Lakes—a fact that was not lost on the speculators who began to size up the region in the 1830s. At a time when the only practical route to the interior was by water, the deep river and broad bay practically screamed "Harbor!"

Boaters run a gauntlet of condos on the lower Milwaukee River. JOHN GURDA

Settlers streamed into the tiny trading post, determined to make it a metropolis.

After undergoing a few judicious improvements, the river opened for business. Year by year, the city's European settlers turned the soft green riverbanks familiar to the Potawatomi and their neighbors into rigid walls lined with docks, piers, and pilings. Milwaukee was soon earning its living as a point of exchange between farm goods from the west and finished goods from the east. There was no outer harbor to speak of; most of the exchange took place along the lower river. Virtually every railroad in the region had a freight depot on the stream, and their docks were piled high with incoming cargoes that ranged from barreled whiskey to barbed wire to Bibles.

Entrepreneurs built grain elevators at the water's edge to fill the holds of outbound ships. Two of the largest were located on the south bank of the river just east of Broadway. Built in the

1870s by wheat kingpin Angus Smith, they towered 135 feet above the surrounding blocks and held nearly two million bushels of grain.

As the wheat trade faded, the next stage in the river's development was manufacturing. Easy access to both rail and water transport attracted scores of would-be industrialists in the late 1800s and early 1900s. Most of the riverside freight terminals stayed in business, but they were joined by factories that turned out paper bags, gas stoves, bedsprings, horse collars, soap (the predecessor of Palmolive, in fact), loose-leaf binders, ink, furniture, knitwear, and a host of other products.

Industrial development reached a peak of sorts just after World War I. The Marine Terminal and its look-alike, the Terminal Building, were built on either side of Broadway in 1918 and 1920. Designed as industrial incubators, each covered nearly a block of Third Ward waterfront. Some of their tenants graduated to much greater things; a little lock washer business in the Terminal Building became, in time, Charter Manufacturing, a Mequon-based firm that now plays a prominent role in the American steel industry. Charter's early home has become a different sort of incubator; the Terminal Building now houses the Milwaukee Institute of Art and Design.

The river's next chapter was neglect. As the twentieth century progressed, Milwaukee, with the rest of the nation, moved steadily from water and rail transport at the city's heart to rubber tires on the city's edge. Although business was still done along the lower river even after World War II, by then it had become a polluted urban canal lined with dingy, underutilized industrial buildings and rotting wharves.

It took years to emerge, but a new spirit was apparent by the late 1970s. Homeseekers and businesspeople discovered a taste for vintage buildings in historic neighborhoods, and the Third Ward filled the bill. The old warehouse and manufacturing district came alive again, and the energy eventually spilled across the river to Walker's Point, a.k.a. the Fifth Ward.

It was only after 2000 that the riverbank itself became a focus of revitalization efforts. One condo project after another rose at the water's edge, usually after older structures had been removed, and new buildings continue to sprout. They have not completely erased the past. There's still a moldering warehouse or two on the south bank of the river, and the old fireboat station at the Water Street bridge is still standing.

There's also an unexpected historical tribute at the Harborfront, the project closest to the lake. Developer Peter Renner has turned his riverside boardwalk into a horizontal timeline that highlights important events in the history of the world, the nation, and Milwaukee. It's not the easiest to read, but the timeline is probably the longest one-page book in Wisconsin.

The downtown river is where Milwaukee's work was done in the nineteenth century. MILWAUKEE PUBLIC LIBRARY

For all its cutting-edge appeal, Condo Canyon can be a little forbidding. Particularly where the canyon is deepest—on both sides of Water Street—the unrelieved hardness of the surfaces and near-total lack of green space can make the condo projects look like upscale versions of Soviet-era apartment blocks. The Riverwalk—a stroke of civic genius—provides essential public access, but I'd prefer strips of parkland that remind visitors as well as residents that they're on a river rather than a canal.

Its shortcomings aside, Condo Canyon brings a new sheen and a healthy shift in perspective to the heart of Milwaukee. Its residents have come in pursuit of the city's vitality, and in doing so, they have created a more vital city. The result is a round of self-generating energy that continues to transform a resource that was Milwaukee's original reason for being.

The years turn like pages in a book, presenting one new look after another. Condo Canyon may not be the grandest gorge I've ever seen, but it's a welcome addition to our landscape. As development continues, it serves as both symbol and substance of Milwaukee's continuing capacity to reinvent itself.

A Yuletide Tragedy

"Christmas Tree Ship" Is a Great Lakes Legend

The custom must seem bizarre to outsiders. We pay good money for dead trees, prop them up in our living rooms, cover their carcasses with electric lights and assorted baubles, then proceed to practically venerate them for weeks on end. "Really?" someone from another culture might ask.

As with all customs, only the insider's view makes sense. For those of us who grew up with Christmas trees, they evoke the magical side of childhood, of course, but the annual rite draws its power from even deeper roots. During the darkest days of the year, when the sun and our spirits both sink to their low points, Christmas trees provide the antidote. They bring light and life into our homes—green in a season of white—and their symbolism rhymes perfectly with the Christian message.

I remember being surprised to learn, as a child, that the date of Christmas was arbitrary. Augustus Caesar may have ordered the census that brought Mary and Joseph to Bethlehem, but he didn't issue birth certificates. We have no idea when Jesus Christ was actually born, and early church leaders showed great psychological insight when they grafted the celebration of his birth onto the pagan celebration of solstice. God's sun and God's son, they were saying, would rise together.

It is that power—psychological, cultural, and religious— that gives the story of the *Rouse Simmons* its enduring appeal.

The schooner *Rouse Simmons* at a lumber dock with all its canvas up.
MILWAUKEE PUBLIC LIBRARY

The *Simmons* was a Lake Michigan schooner like hundreds of others, but its last cargo was Christmas trees. Bound for Chicago, the vessel went down with all hands off Two Rivers, Wisconsin, in 1912, and it has since found a hallowed place in Great Lakes lore as the Christmas Tree Ship.

The story of the *Rouse Simmons* begins in Milwaukee, where the ship was launched in 1868. Built as a bulk carrier, it was 132 feet long and 27 feet wide—nearly the same dimensions as the *Denis Sullivan*, Wisconsin's twenty-first-century tall ship. Its owners were Kenosha businessmen who named the craft for one of their lead investors, a prominent Kenoshan whose family would give the world the Simmons Beautyrest mattress. Whether Rouse Simmons ever sailed, or slept, on his namesake ship is unrecorded.

The *Simmons* did not look much different from its sisters on the Great Lakes, which is to say it was gorgeous—a three-masted seabird whose white sails seemed the essence of freedom to certain land-bound admirers. The schooner sailed under different owners from different home ports over the years—Milwaukee, Muskegon, Beaver Island, Chicago—but its specialty was always lumber. Over an exceptionally long career, the *Simmons* carried millions of board feet, either stowed in its hold or stacked on its deck, from ports near the pineries of northern Michigan and Wisconsin to lumber-starved cities on the southern lakeshore, particularly Chicago. The Windy City was forced to virtually start over after the fire of 1871, and the *Rouse Simmons* was an integral part of the supply chain that made rebuilding possible.

Like most vessels in the freshwater fleet, the *Simmons* had its share of close calls. Perhaps the closest came in the autumn of 1905, when it was dismasted in a gale off Two Rivers. Without sails, the *Simmons* drifted clear across the lake before a car ferry spotted the ship and towed it into port.

Twenty years was the life expectancy of a typical Great Lakes schooner of that era. With the help of some timely repairs and refittings, the *Rouse Simmons* more than doubled that span. In 1910, at the advanced age of forty-two, the ship began its sailing season under a new captain: Herman Schuenemann. Born in Algoma, Wisconsin, Schuenemann was the product of a maritime family and a veteran of the lakes. He continued in the lumber trade, but the captain also took on an end-of-season cargo that was significantly more profitable, foot for foot, than cut lumber. Weeks after other skippers had called it a year, he carried Christmas trees from the Upper Peninsula to market in Chicago. The *Simmons* was the last of several schooners Schuenemann sailed in the holiday trade.

The captain's favorite sales spot in Chicago was the Clark Street bridge, just east of today's Merchandise Mart. With boughs in its rigging and trees lining its rails, the *Simmons* was a picturesque symbol of Christmas for countless Chicagoans. These

Captain Herman Schuenemann (center) and crew with a load of Christmas trees at Chicago's Clark Street dock. DN-0006926, CHICAGO DAILY NEWS COLLECTION, CHICAGO HISTORY MUSEUM

were open-grown forest trees, not the pruned and pampered products of today's tree farms. Although they were scrawny by modern standards, the choicest living-room specimens sold for one dollar—nearly thirty dollars in current currency—and the ceiling-scrapers ended up in churches or hospitals.

Although the tradition was romantic, maintaining it was hazardous. The Great Lakes are notoriously rough late in the year, and the *Rouse Simmons* was a working antique by the time Herman Schuenemann took the wheel. The schooner fleet had been pushed to the margins of the lake trade, replaced by faster, larger, more durable steamships. Schuenemann's own brother, August, had perished in a late-season gale in 1898, and the number of schooners in service had declined steadily since his death.

On November 22, 1912, the *Rouse Simmons* left Thompson, Michigan, a tiny town up the coastline from Escanaba, carrying three hundred to four hundred tons of trees and greens bound for Chicago. A gale was soon blowing, and the *Simmons* found itself in trouble. At midafternoon on November 23, the crew of the Kewaunee life-saving station observed a schooner flying a distress signal. A lifeboat was dispatched from Two Rivers, but even the sharpest eyes could see nothing but waves.

When the weather cleared with no sign of the *Simmons*, the ship was presumed lost. The news was received with palpable sadness in Chicago. "The Christmas season didn't really arrive," wrote one of Captain Schuenemann's contemporaries, "until the Christmas Tree Ship tied up at Clark Street." The 1912 holiday was muted for hundreds of Chicagoans and somber indeed for the families of those who had lost their lives.

Tangible evidence of the tragedy materialized during the following season, when local fishermen began to haul up Christmas trees in their nets. The wreck's precise location remained a mystery until 1971. After a long search, master diver Kent Bellrichard discovered a sunken schooner that proved to be the *Rouse Simmons*. It was lying on a nearly even keel in 165 feet of water six miles northeast of Two Rivers.

Hundreds, perhaps thousands, of recreational divers have visited the wreck since 1971, and they have practically picked it clean of artifacts: clay pipes, dinner plates, the jawbone of a pet dog, and, yes, the bare bones of Christmas trees that never reached their destination.

It was not until 2006 that the Wisconsin Historical Society completed a thorough survey of the *Simmons*. Using forensic clues from the wreck itself, underwater archaeologists concluded that the crew had dropped anchor in a desperate attempt to remain stable and then taken on so much water through the ship's leaky decks that it sank. "New research," the experts wrote, "will give insights into why some sailors challenged the odds and sailed their schooners long after it was viable, or wise, to do so."

Unwise or not, Captain Schuenemann became a legend on the lakes. By the time the archaeological study was published, his ship had been talked about, argued about, and sung about for so many years that only one casualty of the gales of November was more famous: the *Edmund Fitzgerald*.

It was the ship's cargo that set the *Rouse Simmons* apart. The three-masted workhorse carried Christmas trees for only three years, but that was enough. In a dark and dangerous season, the *Simmons* brought light and life to a people in need of both. The message still resonates more than a century later, particularly in the season when we welcome, as we may, a child of light and life.

Stream of Memories

Kinnickinnic River Is Ripe for Rebirth

My memory has started to feel suspiciously like my father's. He grew fond, in his later years, of describing a Milwaukee that no longer existed. He could talk at length about the German-speaking nuns at Holy Ghost grade school, the Polish businesses on Mitchell Street, and—my favorite image—the babushka-clad women who rode horse-drawn carts to work every day in the celery fields west of his family's hardware store on South Thirty-Second and Lincoln.

Past seventy now, I find myself revisiting my own vanished Milwaukee, and at the center of the scene is the Kinnickinnic River. I spent the first eight years of my life in a postwar prefab on South Thirty-Fourth Street, a block north of the river. Although it is by far the smallest of the three streams that converge to form Milwaukee's harbor, the Kinnickinnic was the Mississippi of my early years.

The stream had a decidedly rural character in those days. One of my first memories is of a group of much older boys swinging from a rope into a deep pool in the river just west of Thirty-Fifth Street. To a kid of four or five, they seemed heroically daring.

My siblings and I crossed the Kinnickinnic hundreds of times on a graceful Lannon-stone footbridge west of Thirty-Fifth, walking to Manitoba School for kindergarten and then to Blessed Sacrament for the primary grades. (Yes, parents

The Kinnickinnic River was once a South Side showplace, particularly the "rockery" created by WPA crews just east of Twenty-Seventh Street.
MILWAUKEE PUBLIC LIBRARY

once allowed their four-year-olds to walk a half-mile to school unattended.)

Another of my favorite destinations was the home of our Uncle Paul, a retired police captain who lived across the river on South Thirty-Eighth Street. Actually our great-uncle, he was a hero to our father and therefore a hero to us. It was a point of family pride that Paul Gurda was the first Polish captain to lead the Sixth Precinct. I crossed the bridge to visit him nearly every day in summer, and our father, who lacked his own garage on Thirty-Fourth Street, parked his precious Chevrolet in Uncle Paul's every night. I can still vividly recall the long shadows we cast walking home across the Kinnickinnic parkway under a full summer moon.

I can also remember the time a cousin and I tried to break up the river ice with our feet one frigid afternoon and nearly fell in. When a shelf gave way unexpectedly, my leg plunged in past the knee, and my pants were as stiff as a board within seconds. My mother was not pleased.

Downstream, near St. Luke's Hospital at Twenty-Seventh Street, was the neighborhood's showpiece: an artfully constructed waterfall cascading into the Kinnickinnic River from an artificial pond perched on the south bank. The authors of a 1947 WPA guide to Milwaukee called the scene "one of the most attractive in the city."

I had no way of knowing it at the time, but I was experiencing the Kinnickinnic River at its peak. Earlier in the 1900s, the stream had been, like most other local waterways, denatured beyond recognition. Stripped of its vegetation, contaminated by urban runoff, and used as a dumping ground by nearby residents, the Kinnickinnic was a stagnant, smelly eyesore—particularly the stretch east of South Sixteenth Street. Its condition was so repulsive that in 1930 the local alderman proposed turning the river into an underground sewer and covering it with grass.

Not everyone was ready to give up on the Kinnickinnic. I was delighted to learn, many years later, that the riverscape of my early years was largely the work of one of my favorite Milwaukeeans: Charles B. Whitnall, the Socialist urban planner who exercised a dominant influence on local land use for the first half of the twentieth century. In 1923, Whitnall unveiled a master park plan that called for eighty-four miles of green space along the county's waterways, including the Kinnickinnic.

When he ran into opposition from Alderman Max Galasinski, Whitnall published a highly persuasive pamphlet in 1931 called "How the Kinnickinnic Should Look." The South Side's crowded Polish quarter, Whitnall argued, was "in greater need of park influences than almost any part of the city." Why not start, he asked, by turning the "filthy and fetid" Kinnickinnic into a model of "naturalized landscaping"?

That's precisely what happened. Parcel by parcel, the city acquired land along the Kinnickinnic and, with major help from Depression-era work relief programs, turned it into the verdant parkway of my childhood.

One problem remained. Although the parkway itself acted like a sponge, development in the rest of the Kinnickinnic watershed accelerated runoff after every storm, causing some memorable floods. Charles Whitnall might have suggested planting more trees to fix the problem, but he died in 1949, and the chief architect of our park system was not succeeded by leaders of comparable vision. In 1960, city engineer Raymond Leary declared that it was high time to "correct conditions that slow down the flow of flood waters in the main branch of the Kinnickinnic between S. 35th St. and Chase Ave."

Leary's plan required ripping out the riverside trees and the stone bridges, the rope swings and the waterfalls, and all the other "natural obstructions" so painstakingly created in the 1930s. The rocky streambed was replaced by a barren concrete raceway—an exercise in Soviet-style brutalism. My family had moved to Hales Corners by then, but I recall a feeling of anger and betrayal every time we crossed the Kinnickinnic on the way into town.

I'd like to trust engineers—my father was a proud member of the profession—but the channelization of the Kinnickinnic was one of the Milwaukee contingent's low points. The concrete ditches did move more water, but they moved it so fast that the section east of South Sixteenth Street was overwhelmed. The bridges there acted as dams during heavy rains, forcing the water into adjacent residential areas. I returned to the Kinnickinnic in the 1970s, renting an apartment on South Twelfth Street, and some of my neighbors' basements were filled to overflowing each spring.

The city engineers' solution to the new flooding problem? Remove most of the bridges—an expedient that divided the

(*Left*) Flooding along the Kinnickinnic was a persistent problem in spring.

(*Right*) Channelizing the stream in the 1960s destroyed its natural beauty without putting an end to floods.
BOTH PHOTOS:
MILWAUKEE COUNTY PARKS

neighborhood, impeded traffic, and still did nothing to alleviate the drowning hazard. Every year, it seemed, children were swept to their deaths when the Kinnickinnic reached flood stage.

Only since the early 2000s has there been a concerted attempt to undo the damage of the 1960s. The Milwaukee Metropolitan Sewerage District and its partners have launched an effort to renature the Kinnickinnic by removing houses, opening the floodplain, restoring the stream's natural flow, and re-creating the green landscape of my youth.

In case you're keeping score, that's the fourth transformation of the Kinnickinnic River since the early 1900s. Urbanization soiled it, Charles Whitnall saved it, city engineers denatured it, and now we're returning to Whitnall's vision. As salmon spawn, children play, and the Kinnickinnic gurgles again, this latest approach is showing dramatic results. Mile by mile, the river of my past is flowing cleaner and clearer into Milwaukee's future.

Summertime

A "Breathing Place" for the Masses

National Park Offered Both Thrills and Quiet Close to Home

When the weather heats up, Wisconsinites cool down. Some of us head to family cabins Up North, others to nearby lakes, but tens of thousands opt for more highly developed amusements. Great America and Wisconsin Dells attract hordes of urbanites seeking a few thrills during their time off and willing to pay dearly for them. They wait patiently in line for their turns on King Chaos, Howlin' Tornado, Raging Bull, Screaming Hyena, Poseidon's Rage, and a roller coaster named Goliath—all names suggesting more than a hint of menace.

Call us bad parents if you like, but my wife and I managed to raise three kids to adulthood without a single pilgrimage to Gurnee or the Dells. I have nothing against theme parks—aside from the crowds, the expense, and the noise—but our family vacations were usually spent outdoors, near water, and in tents—trips lighter on adrenaline than the thrill rides but longer on relaxation, and a good deal cheaper.

Our ancestors split the difference. They looked for excitement where they could find it but also sought the peace and quiet of the countryside, at a time when the countryside started at the city limits. Keep in mind that no one had paid vacations until well into the twentieth century, and that one-day weekends were the rule; most wage earners worked six days a week.

NATIONAL PARK, CORNER NATIONAL AND WASHINGTON AVES.

National Park offered a winning combination of civilized amusement and unspoiled natural surroundings. MILWAUKEE PUBLIC LIBRARY

That limited their choice of Sunday amusements to how far they could travel by streetcar or on foot.

Milwaukeeans had plenty of choices nonetheless. Privately operated beer gardens and picnic groves were sprinkled generously throughout the county, and the first adequate public parks began to appear in the 1890s. There were even rides: a Ferris wheel at Pabst's Whitefish Bay resort, a water slide called Shoot the Chutes on the Milwaukee River near North Avenue, and a cluster of amusements at Shorewood's Hubbard Park when it was still called Wonderland.

The largest of the city's embryonic theme parks, in area if not attractions, was on the South Side. In the late 1800s, as the blocks south of the Menomonee Valley filled in with the homes of industrial workers, there was an obvious need for green spaces where factory hands could relax after a week of ten- to twelve-hour days. On July 4, 1883, two local promoters opened just such a retreat. It was bordered by National Avenue, Green-field Avenue, Layton Boulevard, and South Thirty-First Street—a sprawling tract of forty-four acres just two blocks south of today's Mitchell Park Domes.

Naming it was easy. In 1867, the federal government had opened the National Soldiers Home for disabled Union veterans just west of town, and the old Mukwonago plank road on its southern margin was rechristened National Avenue. Milwaukee's freshest summer garden debuted in 1883 as National Park. Local papers hailed it as "the new breathing place on the South Side."

Much of the property was covered with trees, and the owners wisely chose to leave the forest intact. Although it was barely two miles from downtown, National Park was wooded enough to support both fox hunts and trapshooting tournaments—with live foxes and live pigeons. (The Humane Society's objections were ignored.) But the park's managers also tried to improve on nature, adding a half-mile racetrack, a small artificial lake, a two-story pavilion (with its own ballroom and bowling alley), extensive playing fields, and, of course, beer.

With city streetcars running directly to its gates, National Park was an overnight success. Nearly ten thousand people—a large portion of Milwaukee's work force—came out for a labor picnic on the Fourth of July in 1888. Not long after, local Scots moved their annual Highland Games to the park, drawing eight thousand spectators and participants in a typical year. When William Jennings Bryan stopped during his presidential campaign in 1896, six thousand people turned out in a downpour to hear the orator.

The racetrack was a perennial draw. Some of the finest trotting horses in the Midwest pranced around the oval at National Park, and bicycle contests were added when two-wheeler fever swept the nation in the 1890s; one early race drew cyclists from four states. In 1898, the proprietors struck a pioneering blow for feminism by hosting a women's cycling event—a move that prompted the League of American Wheelmen to blacklist the park. Just one year later, Milwaukee's first motorcycle race was held on the grounds. Harley-Davidson didn't compete because Harley-Davidson didn't yet exist.

The playfields, too, broke new ground in the world of sport. Scottish and English teams faced off in occasional cricket matches. In 1889, Milwaukee's first intercollegiate football practice was held at National Park. A game between the University of Wisconsin and Northwestern University followed one year later. There were also less conventional gridiron duels. The most unlikely pitted Northwestern Mutual Life Insurance against East (now Riverside) High School; the actuaries beat the adolescents, 10–4.

A variety of other events attracted notice in the local press: a "grand balloon ascension" in 1883, an appearance by Barnum & Bailey's Circus in 1895, and periodic "monster fireworks displays" that included portraits of the governor and the mayor in outline. The city's volunteer militia companies held an annual encampment at National Park that featured plenty of drilling and rifle practice. Although the summer months were busiest, the lake was cleared for ice-skating in winter, creating a rink described as "the finest and largest in the city."

National Park's attractions may seem sedate by modern standards, but its managers took a revolutionary step forward in 1885—just two years after opening—when they erected Milwaukee's very first roller coaster. It was a classic wooden structure that must have towered above the surrounding trees. The cars traveled a five-hundred-foot circuit that took thirteen seconds to complete, and thrill-seekers paid a nickel for two rides. An intrepid *Milwaukee Sentinel* reporter experienced a definite adrenaline rush: "The sensation produced by the first ride is 'goneness,' and when the car reaches the last dip in the track, it attains a fearful velocity which sends it to the starting-point again." Not the American Eagle, perhaps, but pretty impressive for 1885.

National Park's reign as a center of summer fun lasted for sixteen years. As working-class families pushed west from the Walker's Point and Clarke Square neighborhoods, balloon ascensions and bicycle races inevitably gave way to houses on such a large piece of prime real estate. In 1899, two East Side developers bought the park for a reported $275,000 and announced that it would be "cut up into building lots." The pavilion was torn down, the lake filled in, the coaster dismantled, and the racetrack plowed under. Stripped of its amenities, the land was sold, piece by piece, for what would become a solidly middle-class neighborhood.

"The closing of National park will mark the passing of one of the best-known pleasure grounds in the Northwest," reported the *Sentinel* matter-of-factly. Today, there is absolutely nothing to indicate that such a large and well-patronized "breathing place" ever existed. National Park has become a ghost in the landscape, but it's one worth remembering at a time when we travel much farther afield for summertime amusement.

Generations of Oohs! and Aaahs!

Milwaukee Has Always Been Crazy about Fireworks

Milwaukee, I'm convinced, suffers from a case of collective pyromania. Is there any city in America that takes more delight in watching stuff blow up? Any place where "Oohs!" and "Aaahs!" are heard more often? From June to September, summer in the community can feel like one continuous explosion.

The downtown lakefront is Milwaukee's flash point for fireworks, particularly during Summerfest, the ethnic festivals, and on July 3, when the Big Bang touches off the celebration of America's birthday. Even in Bay View, miles from the action, we can see the bursts and, when the wind is right, hear the booms of artificial thunder. It's gotten so we barely look up when the shows start.

You don't have to dig very far in the old newspaper files to find evidence of Milwaukee's historic obsession with fireworks. With the exception of the periodic war years, when different forms of firepower took precedence, pyrotechnics have been a vital part of virtually every summer celebration. The Fourth of July was always the big one, when every beer garden, picnic grove, public park, and private club in the area did its best to light up the sky.

But July 4 was just one day among many. In September 1892, Milwaukeeans enjoyed a triple bill that may have been the pyrotechnic pinnacle of the city's first century. The Wisconsin State

Pyrotechnics lit up the sky on Milwaukee's lakefront in 1953. MILWAUKEE
JOURNAL SENTINEL

Fair opened for the first time in its present location with elaborate fireworks displays. The Industrial Exposition, an annual showcase held in a glass palace at North Sixth Street and West Kilbourn Avenue, began its run at the same time with a show that lasted for nearly an hour. The *Sentinel* reporter strained for words to describe the Exposition fireworks: "Now a skyrocket going seemingly away up among the stars, then multiplying into dozens of varicolored balls, darting serpents and dangling balloons, then a genuine cannonade, filling the air with mystifying forms of fire, in a rain of golden-hued splendor. It was a magnificent display."

The State Fair and the Industrial Exposition would have had enough bangs and booms for all of September in 1892, but they were outshone in the same month by a third extravaganza: The Last Days of Pompeii. The traveling show's producers rented Athletic Park, a baseball stadium at North Eighth and West Chambers Streets (later known as Borchert Field), and proceeded to bury the village of Pompeii in lava from Mt. Vesuvius every night for two weeks running.

Billed as the "Most Costly and Magnificent Pyrotechnic Production Ever Produced," the Pompeii show featured three hundred actors and extras dressed in Roman costumes. They fought with swords and raced their chariots around the diamond, but the real star of the show was Mt. Vesuvius. "The sleeping volcano begins to smoke," reported the *Sentinel*, "and in a few moments it is belching forth fire and smoke in such torrents that the people sit absolutely awe-stricken."

That wasn't even the finale. "The sky gleams with darting rockets," the *Sentinel* continued, "and the crater pours forth its fiery stream. There is a panic and actors and spectators rush through the streets pursued by an unrelenting molten mass. Houses fall and the great temple of Isis crumbles to a shapeless ruin."

Patrons who wanted to see Vesuvius in all its glory had to pay for the privilege—one dollar for box seats and fifty cents for the bleachers—but the eruption was followed by a "gorgeous fireworks spectacle" that could be seen all over the North Side. By what secrets of stagecraft such wonders came to pass is unrecorded, but the show was clearly a hit. "Words hardly describe the grandeur of the spectacle," gushed the *Sentinel*, proclaiming the Pompeii pageant "one of magnificence never before equaled by any amusement in this city."

There were other contenders after the turn of the century. In 1902, Niagara Falls was the headliner at National Park, the private amusement grounds near what is now South Layton Boulevard and West National Avenue. "It is a realistic, vivid and marvelous representation," declared the *Sentinel*, "in seething white and blue flames of the massive flow of the world's greatest cataract." Thousands turned out for the spectacle, which included a portrait of Mayor David Rose rendered "in lines of fire."

Five years later, Mitchell Park, famed for its conservatory and gardens, was the scene of a Venetian night that attracted five thousand people. "Adding to the beauty and weirdness of the night," reported the *Sentinel*, "were the flashes of red and green fire continually blazing up from all sections of the park." Visitors were spellbound by "red fire from the top of the flower house, first burning brightly, dying down and almost disappearing, then blenching forth again even more vividly . . . quickly followed by the flashes of green and red from other parts of the great south side garden."

Even during the Depression, when Milwaukee presumably had better things to do with its tax dollars, fireworks were featured attractions, particularly at the annual Midsummer Festival, an event cosponsored by the city and the county. Held on the downtown lakefront from 1933 to 1941, the free festival was one of that dark time's brightest spots, and I mean that literally.

Ten tons of fireworks went up in smoke during a typical festival week, delivering "the very last word in evening entertainment." The Midsummer Festival was particularly famous for its themed ground displays, which included, over the years, the 1892 Third Ward fire, the end of Prohibition in 1933, and even the Civil War battle of the ironclads *Monitor* and *Merrimack*, which was re-created in Milwaukee Bay. In 1938, an entire mile of the outer breakwater was lit up with Roman candles and flares.

Generations later, we're still at it. Every year brings fresh magnificence to our summer skies—new colors, more complicated designs—and we never seem to tire of it. I attend a couple of fireworks shows each season, and I always spend at least some time watching the crowd. With every flash, the faces of my neighbors are illuminated as if by daylight. Nearly to a person, they are utterly transfixed: the adults absorbed and the children rapt, terrified, or some combination of both.

Why is Milwaukee so passionate about its pyrotechnics? Some argue that it's the historical presence of the homegrown Bartolotta Fireworks Company, but the Bartolottas didn't enter the field until 1977. I suspect that something more basic is at work. Human beings have always been fascinated by things that go boom in the night, and Milwaukeeans seem to have a special affinity for them—a reflection, I would argue, of our legendary thrift. In a community that has always appreciated a good value, fireworks are unbeatable entertainment. We sit mesmerized as the summer sky above us explodes with flowers of bright fire that bloom and fade and bloom again: beautiful, dangerous, and absolutely free.

Where Have All the Odors Gone (Long Time Passing)?

Milwaukee's Air Is Thinner than It Used to Be

M y wife thinks I'm part dog. Whether we're walking in the woods or just ambling around the neighborhood, I have an apparent need to smell things. Not everything, mind you; unlike a full-blooded canine, I stop well short of roadkill and scat. But I've learned that smell can add a potent, even pungent, dimension to my experience of the world, especially in summer.

Flowers are just the entry level. I like the spicy notes of petunias and the slightly cloying, maiden-aunt odor of lilacs, but why, I wonder, do wild roses smell so much better, and so much more powerful, than the fussy hybrids that are their direct descendants? And how do much smaller flowers, like lily of the valley, pack so much punch into such tiny packages?

In general, I'd rather sniff wild plants than the domesticated variety. Smell, I've been taught, can be an aid to identification as well as a sensory rush. The inner bark of cherry twigs smells like almonds, prickly ash leaves smell like lemons, catnip like mint, and skunk cabbage like, well, an angry skunk, but notably less intense. Every conifer needle has its own aroma, with cedar the sweetest.

The wild rose is far more aromatic than its hybrid cousins. PIXY.ORG

It's entirely possible to be misled, of course. A few summers ago, I was walking in Seminary Woods, near my Bay View home, when I got wind of a new smell that seemed too strong for my surroundings. It was definitely floral, with overtones of lilac, but hard to identify precisely. Was I on the verge of finding a new plant? My excitement growing, I walked upwind until I reached a soccer field at the edge of the woods. The smell, I discovered, was the industrial-strength deodorizer wafting downwind from a Porta-Potty. I haven't quite trusted my nose ever since.

Smells are powerfully associated with memories, including that one. The scent of new-mown hay, or even cow manure, takes me right back to my Uncle Laurence's farm in Coon Valley, Wisconsin. A whiff of lemon meringue pie brings back my mother in an instant. Old-house attic smells, with their amalgam of dust, lumber, and age, recall my grandparents' hardware store on Lincoln Avenue.

Smells can also be associated with entire cities. Every community has its olfactory signatures, and Milwaukee's were once bolder than most. Who can forget the heavenly scent of Ambrosia chocolate drifting out from the company's old plant on Fifth and Highland? I can recall standing on a downtown street corner and practically drinking the air. When the wind blew from another direction, downtown enjoyed the hoppy, yeasty smell of beer brewing in the kettles at Pabst or Schlitz. A few miles away, on South Forty-Third Street (now Miller Park Way), were the plants that supplied that beer's key ingredient. A phalanx of towering elevators—owned by the Kurth, Krause, and Froedtert firms—formed a "malt belt" of national importance. When the maltsters were drying and roasting their sprouted barley, a smell like unbuttered popcorn permeated the surrounding neighborhoods.

Other odors were an acquired taste—or smell. From 1882 until the start of Prohibition in 1919, a distillery on the north rim of the Menomonee Valley made whiskey, gin, and an abundant byproduct—yeast—that was sold under the Red Star label. Yeast was the company's only product after Prohibition. When Interstate 94 opened just behind the plant in the mid-1960s, thousands of motorists were treated to the smell of Red Star's emissions every day: a heady, organic aroma of yeast in the making, reminiscent of bread dough but many times stronger. The plant at Twenty-Eighth Street was shut down in 2005 and torn down seven years later, but it lingers in memory. If there is one smell that ex-Milwaukeeans associate with their former home, it's probably Red Star Yeast.

Other historic smells were downright offensive. Alewives, an invasive species of ocean herring, died off by the millions in the 1960s, and their carcasses littered the perimeter of Lake Michigan. There they rotted in windrows knee-deep and even higher, producing a stench so overpowering that Milwaukee's most popular beaches were practically deserted even on the hottest days of summer. There was a less-noxious reprise of the pestilence in the early 2000s, when thick blooms of cladophora algae drifted ashore, usually attached to invasive zebra mussels that had died when more aggressive quagga mussels displaced them.

Neither dead alewives nor dead algae could compare with the smell of the Milwaukee River in the late 1800s. The city had

The stench from dead alewives effectively closed Milwaukee's most popular beaches for weeks at a time in the 1960s. MILWAUKEE JOURNAL SENTINEL

turned its major stream into an open-air commode, and during hot spells, in particular, a revolting slurry of human and animal waste created an odor that one 1878 observer described as "simply unendurable." The *Milwaukee Sentinel* upped the rhetorical ante a year later: "The bad smells of Chicago are as the perfume of violets in comparison with the odors of the deadly gases of Milwaukee's open sewer."

It was not until the Jones Island sewage treatment plant opened in 1925 that Milwaukee finally got a handle on its waste problem. The plant is hardly a cologne factory, as anyone who's been on the Hoan Bridge with a west wind blowing will tell you, but it smells infinitely better than the Milwaukee River in its odoriferous heyday.

The "river nuisance" is gone, thank goodness, along with a host of other historic smells—good, bad, and neutral. It's no longer possible to experience the acrid scent of coal smoke from a thousand factory stacks, the barnyard odor of the stockyards, or the stench from the Menomonee Valley rendering plant. All have succumbed to progress, broadly defined.

There's still something in the air over Milwaukee. A south wind brings the smell of bacon from Cudahy Packing. Seasoned woodsmoke fills the air around the Usinger and Klement sausage plants. You can still smell beer being brewed at a growing number of craft breweries as well as at giant Molson Coors. And there are new smells our ancestors wouldn't have recognized: the pungent scent of curry downwind from any Indian restaurant, the sharp chili smells from the taquerias in Walker's Point, and the tangy char of barbecue from backyard barrels on the North Side.

There's still life in the wind, but no one can deny that Milwaukee has fewer smells than it once did. That's good, in most ways. Who could possibly desire a return to the days of sooty skies and stinking rivers? But something's been lost along the way. Milwaukee's air is cleaner these days—cleaner and emptier.

Summerfest's Prehistory

Lakefront Site Has Seen Trains, Planes, and Guided Missiles

What began as an embryonic notion has become a middle-aged institution. In 2020, to the amazement of doddering baby boomers who were there at the start, Summerfest marked its fiftieth anniversary on Milwaukee's lakefront. No one was there to celebrate—yet another casualty of the COVID-19 pandemic—but the event has since resumed with its traditional vigor.

Although the site is familiar to millions, its prehistory is, in a word, obscure. Summerfest has been a Milwaukee staple for so long that most of us can't remember what occupied the grounds before it existed. Hasn't there always been a Maier Festival Park on the lakefront?

Well, of course not. The Summerfest site, in fact, is a classic example of how much one parcel of urban real estate can change over the decades. Each phase is like a chapter in a book, and together they illuminate the story of the community as a whole.

The first chapter for which we have a written record began nearly two centuries ago, in the waning days of the fur trade, when Milwaukee's central lakefront was a modest strip of sand separating Lake Michigan from the wetlands that covered most of today's Third Ward. The beach was packed hard enough for the young men from a nearby Potawatomi village to stage bareback pony races that enthralled spectators. Those races, in

Summerfest moved to the lakefront in 1970 and became the world's largest music festival. MILWAUKEE JOURNAL SENTINEL

Solomon Juneau's opinion, "surpassed in horsemanship and physical training anything he had ever seen or read of."

But the lakefront of Juneau's time was actually a couple of blocks inland from today's. If Summerfest had been held in the 1800s, it might as well have been called Swimmerfest, because the entire site was underwater. It was not until the 1870s that landfill activity began in earnest, and the focus then was on transportation, not entertainment. Transportation, in fact—by rail, water, and air—was the dominant theme on the Summerfest site for most of its existence.

The Chicago & North Western Railroad was first on the scene. Beginning in the early 1870s, the C&NW covered the entire lakefront with tracks, stretching from a roundhouse on Polk Street to a depot at the foot of Wisconsin Avenue and continuing up the lakeshore to Lafayette Place. After repeated batterings from northeast storms, the North Western decided to shore up its shoreline. Land east of the tracks was filled in and an eight-foot bulkhead was constructed to ward off the waves. Milwaukeeans were effectively blocked from their most important natural resource for generations.

Ships were supposed to come next. Although the Socialists who took over City Hall in 1910 wanted to turn the "north harbor tract" into a park, local authorities ultimately decided to build a port facility on the site. The Milwaukee River had been the city's commercial waterfront from the very beginning, but the advent of larger ships and the maddening frequency of downtown bridge openings sparked a campaign for docks in the outer harbor. Jones Island, which the city condemned in 1914, was the project's focal point, but the north tract—today's Summerfest grounds—was slated for "piers and warehouses to be devoted to the passenger and freight business of the port."

It was during the projected port phase of its history that the lakefront site assumed roughly its present dimensions. In 1917, work crews built a stone breakwater nearly seven hundred feet east of the old C&NW bulkhead and proceeded to make the water between the walls disappear. The city wasn't too picky about what went into its landfill. Although cinders and ash from local industries were used in huge quantities, much of the fill was just plain garbage.

Before the "made land" could be lined with docks, an emerging technology prompted a change in direction. America developed a mania for aviation in the 1920s, and no city worth its salt was without an airport of its own, including a place to land downtown. The north harbor tract seemed to fill the bill. In 1927, one year after Milwaukee County began to develop today's Mitchell International Airport, the city opened Maitland Field on the present Summerfest grounds. The strip was named for Lester Maitland, a Milwaukee-born aviator who had completed the world's first transpacific flight earlier that year.

Originally slated for port development, the filled-in lakefront site became a municipal airport in 1927. MILWAUKEE PUBLIC LIBRARY

Maitland Field was one of the first downtown airports in America, and the adjacent waters supported an even more novel venture. In 1929, Kohler Aviation began regularly scheduled seaplane service between Milwaukee's lakefront and Grand Rapids, Michigan. Kohler's aircraft were promoted as "The Bridge across Lake Michigan," bypassing Chicago and providing easy connections with eastbound trains. Each "amphibian" held six passengers, and the one-way fare was eighteen dollars—nearly three hundred dollars in today's currency.

The Depression practically grounded commercial aviation for most of the next decade. The only sign of life on the lakefront was Milwaukee's Midsummer Festival, a low-budget precursor of Summerfest that was held every year from 1933 through 1941.

Development of the lakefront site finally resumed after World War II. On October 24, 1945, following a modest upgrade, Maitland Field reopened to the flying public. "Great possibilities

exist for Maitland Field in the coming air age," declared Mayor
John Bohn. Great deficiencies soon became just as apparent.
Pilots prefer to take off and land into the wind, and Maitland's
three-thousand-foot runway was at right angles to the prevailing
westerlies. Lake fog and air pollution posed frequent visibility
problems. The proximity of tall buildings tended to discourage
faint-hearted fliers, and the original landfill presented hazards of
its own. Broken glass and nails kept poking up through the cin-
der airstrip, causing frequent flat tires.

Covering the runway with concrete in 1948 solved the tire
problem, but Maitland Field never lived up to its supposed
potential. Looking back in 1961, port director Harry Brockel,
whose agency oversaw the strip, summarized it as "a colossal
flop" that averaged only seven planes a day and "ran three operators out of business."

The Cold War determined the next chapter in the site's history. In 1956, without serious objections from local officials, the
US Army claimed Maitland Field for a Nike antiaircraft missile
base—one of eight designed to protect the Milwaukee area
from a Soviet bomber attack.

I can recall regular field trips to "the Nike site" as a Cub
Scout and then a Boy Scout in the late 1950s. The drill was the
same every time. As we watched in awe, the doors of the underground bunker opened, a sleek missile rose from the gloom, and
the launcher raised it to a fully erect position, ready to fire. For
boys on the cusp of adolescence, it was always a stimulating
experience.

By the late 1960s, long-range missiles had supplanted long-
range bombers as the chief threat to America's security, and the
Nike antiaircraft bases faded into obsolescence. The lakefront site
was once again ripe for redevelopment. In 1970, after two years
without a permanent home, Summerfest moved in, establishing
its headquarters in a building handed down from the Army.

Poised to bring down attacking Soviet bombers, Nike antiaircraft missiles
dominated the site in the 1950s and 1960s. MILWAUKEE JOURNAL SENTINEL

The Nike-era administration building is still in use, but
every other sign of the site's earlier history has long since vanished: the racing ponies, the steam locomotives, the small airplanes, and the guided missiles. In their place has emerged the
world's largest music festival. After decades in other roles, the
lakefront site finally found its best and highest use as a festival
park. Cruising into middle age from an unusually fluid prehistory, Summerfest today is clearly on solid ground.

Our Rocky Road to the Big Leagues

From Grays to Brewers to Braves to Brewers Again

You don't have to win games to fill stadiums. It helps, of course, but some teams draw fans almost regardless of their records. Milwaukee is definitely in that category. Although recent squads have been competitive, the Milwaukee Brewers endured some long dry spells before the Christian Yelich era. For too many years, the tying run was in the minors and the winning run still in high school, and yet attendance never flagged. In 2015, for instance, the Brewers finished thirty-two games out of first place with a 68–94 record and still averaged 31,390 fans per home game. Cleveland and Tampa Bay had much better records, but the Indians (now the Guardians) averaged fewer than 18,000 fans per game and the Rays a paltry 15,403.

The numbers indicate that Milwaukee is a good baseball town, fair weather or foul, and we've been earning that reputation for more than 150 years. Ever since the first game on a local diamond was played in 1859, America's pastime has also been Milwaukee's pastime.

It was a different sport in those early years. Pitchers threw underhand, players fielded without gloves, and the bats were so big that they were sometimes called "wagon tongues." Players wore woolen uniforms even on the hottest days, and they could really work up a sweat; it was not unusual for scores to soar into the triple digits.

By the late 1800s, improving play and a growing fan base had transformed what began as a gentleman's hobby into a professional sport. As recounted by historian Harry Anderson, however, Milwaukee's road to the majors was rocky indeed, a decades-long series of dead ends and false starts broken by short winning streaks.

Milwaukee's first professional team, minor-league by modern standards, was the Grays, who took the field in 1878. Competing in the six-team National League, the local squad finished in the cellar with a dismal 15–44 record—a performance that led to its unceremonious dismissal from the league. The franchise was transferred to St. Louis, not the last time that city would prevail over its northern neighbor.

It took a while to recover from the Grays debacle, but in 1884 Milwaukee joined the minor-level Northwestern League. The club drew up to two thousand fans per game and was good enough to spend the last month of its inaugural season in the major-league Union Association, an upstart rival to the National League and the American Association that lasted only one year.

Milwaukee was bypassed in the National-American wars that followed, but minor-league play continued against other Midwestern clubs. In 1891, the local team moved up to the American Association when Cincinnati dropped out with a third of its schedule remaining.

We were finally in the bigs, but not for long. The American Association folded after the 1891 season, and Milwaukee was once again shut out. The city's prospects brightened in 1901, when the Brewers competed as a charter member of the American League. The league, in fact, was organized in Milwaukee's Republican Hotel, a vanished landmark whose site is now occupied by a parking lot on King Drive and Kilbourn Avenue. That foray, too, proved to be short-lived. After a single unsuccessful season, the franchise moved to St. Louis, repeating the insult of 1878.

A new club with the old Brewers name took the field in 1902, competing in the reorganized American Association, a minor-league circuit that would define baseball in the city for the next half-century. The Brewers spent the final years of their long tenure in the minors as a farm team for the Boston Braves, and that connection would prove to be the city's true entry into the big leagues. If you're keeping score at home, Milwaukee had seventy-five years, from 1878 to 1953, of professional baseball under its belt by the time the Braves moved to the city from Boston, but only three seasons, two of them partial, in the majors.

Still the fans turned out. Milwaukee was a minor-league city with a big-league appetite for baseball and remained so for generations. And where did our ancestors watch their baggy-pantsed heroes chase down fly balls and turn double plays? At a series of diamonds on the near North Side, the undisputed (and unsung) cradle of professional baseball in our town. There is

The Milwaukee Brewers—in their minor-league incarnation—posed with flannel uniforms and "cake box" caps in 1905, three years after the team was organized. MILWAUKEE COUNTY HISTORICAL SOCIETY

absolutely nothing in the modern landscape that would indicate a tie to the nation's pastime, but the venerable streets of the central city were once packed with eager fans on game days.

First came the field at Eleventh and Wright Streets, a site currently occupied by houses. More rudimentary than many of today's public park diamonds, the Wright Street grounds opened for play in 1884. According to the *Milwaukee Sentinel*, not everyone paid to watch; the fences were so porous that the field was known for "the wholesale amount of peeping through the cracks that was indulged in by economical persons."

A more imposing ballpark on Seventeenth Street between North Avenue and Lloyd Street hosted minor-leaguers from 1895 to 1903. Known for its covered wooden grandstand, the Lloyd Street park's site is now occupied by the orchards, gardens, and community-building activities of the Walnut Way Conservation Corporation.

The most durable of the North Side diamonds was Borchert Field. Built in 1888 for thirty-five thousand dollars, the field was crammed, bleachers and all, into the single city block bordered by Seventh and Eighth Streets between Burleigh and Chambers— a site vaporized when Interstate 43 came through in the 1960s. "Borchert's Orchard" was the home of the American Association Brewers for their entire stay in Milwaukee. For fifty years, from 1902 to 1952, fans took the streetcar to watch players variously nicknamed Hot Potato, Specs, Cuckoo, Dinty, Kewpie, Jersey, Tink, Ski, and Wee Willie take on the Toledo Mud Hens, the St. Paul Saints, the Louisville Colonels, and other regional powers. The team brought home eight pennants during its half-century run.

It was the minor-league Brewers' success, both on the field and at the turnstiles, that gave Milwaukee the confidence to build County Stadium in 1953. We built it, and they came. The former Boston Braves moved in as soon as the stadium was

The Brewers played their home games at Borchert Field, a ballpark crammed into a single square block at Eighth and Burleigh. MILWAUKEE JOURNAL SENTINEL

finished, certifying our pedigree as a major-league city. In the decades that followed that first opening day, Milwaukee has lived through the intoxicating success of the Braves, the heartbreak of their defection to Atlanta, the soporific slumps of the early Brewers, the glory years of the Yount-Molitor era, and the ups and downs of the Miller Park/American Family Field period.

I vividly recall the dear dead days of the 1970s, the era of George "Boomer" Scott, Don Money, and Darrell Porter, when the Brewers rarely poked their heads out of the cellar. Milwaukeeans came to County Stadium anyway. Attendance passed the million mark for the first time in 1973, when the team finished twenty-three games out of first place. Four years later, when the Brewers ended their season a whopping thirty-three games back, there were even more people in the stands.

I have my own fond memories of sitting in the upper deck on summer evenings, with the big red Johnston's cookie factory sign shining over the center-field bleachers and nighthawks flittering about in the lights. There was something magical, even slightly psychedelic, about the glow of County Stadium during a night game; all those lights created a cocoon of brightness so intense that the surrounding city seemed dark by comparison. And every so often you got to see something spectacular, like the night José Cardenal, during his one year with the Brewers, tried to steal home. Cardenal was thrown out by a mile, but more than forty years later, I still recall his attempt as the single most outrageous athletic feat I've ever witnessed.

Like thousands of my fellow Wisconsinites, I find my pulse quickening with the return of baseball each spring, and I'll head out to American Family Field whether the Brewers are surging toward a pennant or slumping toward the cellar. Whatever the final score, the ballpark still glows with a magical brightness, and the spectacle I found so enchanting as a boy retains much of its power as I round third base and head toward home. A tradition started in 1859 is still vital. Win or lose, the long streak continues.

Personalities

Hank, Meet Gertie

Milwaukee's First Community Pet Was a Duck

They wouldn't have gotten along. He, being a dog, would have chased her. She, being a duck, would have flapped away, quacking indignantly. Their turns in the spotlight were also separated by nearly seventy years, but the stories of Hank and Gertie are so closely matched that the pair might have been siblings beneath their fur and feathers. Both emerged from total obscurity to win Milwaukee's heart, and both gave us something else to think about when good news was as scarce as ducks' teeth.

Most residents of Brewerland will recall the saga of Hank the Dog. In the spring of 2014, the plucky stray was wandering alone down the mean streets of west Phoenix, Arizona, friendless and forsaken, with fur more gray than white and what appeared to be a tire mark down his back. But getting run over didn't slow him down—not our hero. He began to hang around the Brewers' ballpark in Maryvale during spring training, where his winning personality earned him a nonplaying spot on the roster and a brand-new name: Hank, after perhaps the greatest Brewer of all time, Henry Aaron.

The media promptly picked up the story and ran with it. Rags to riches! Dirty fur to snow-white fame! A no-trade clause and all the kibble he could eat! Frequent news reports chronicled the doings of "the biggest star on four paws": Hank receiving his very own "K9" jersey, Hank being greeted at the

Facing off across the decades, (*above*) Gertie the Duck and (*opposite*) Hank the Dog were civic mascots who lightened the community's mood during uncertain times. BOTH PHOTOS: MILWAUKEE JOURNAL SENTINEL

Milwaukee airport by the mayor and the county executive, Hank posing for photos with fans who had waited in line for hours, Hank chilling in his custom condo. He was dogged by reporters and hounded by panting "puparazzi" wherever he went, never letting it go to his fluffy white head.

Hank did spend some time on the disabled list after being neutered—no bases on balls for our little buddy—but pain is often the price of fame. He was honored with his own bobble-head, or maybe bobbletail, late in the season, and there was even talk of a Hank the Dog baseball card. (Shakes: Right. Scratches: Left. Runs: Right, Left, Right, Left.)

Hank was presumed to be a cross between a bichon frise and a Lhasa apso. You might think that professional ballplayers would prefer their mascot to be a bit more, well, manly than a curly-haired lapdog, but Hank is probably a good choice for these metrosexual times. When my own kids were younger, we had a bichon frise—or, as my brother-in-law insisted, a bitchin'

frizzy. He was hypoallergenic and didn't shed, which was fine, but we ran across a troubling news story about doggie IQs soon after bringing him home. Bichons were way down the list, light-years behind border collies and the other Einsteins of the canine universe. Our cuddly pet was, comparatively speaking, a box of rocks with fur—a washout at obedience school and a young dog who never began to learn even the oldest tricks. I could only hope that Hank had more brains than our dear departed Elmo.

Whether Gertie the Duck was first in her class is unknown, but her story, like Hank's, begins with an inspired geographic choice. Just as Hank decided to hang around a major-league ballpark, Gertie opted to build her nest near the busiest bridge in Milwaukee. On April 25, 1945, a mallard hen began to lay her eggs on a piling just south of the Wisconsin Avenue span. One of the bridgetenders—it was a full-time job in those days—brought her to the attention of Gordon MacQuarrie, a *Milwaukee Journal* outdoor writer, and the anthropomorphic follies were on.

MacQuarrie named the duck Gertie and began the same wall-to-wall coverage that Hank the Dog enjoyed in his rookie season. There were breathless reports about Gertie's exploits, which, to be honest, were more dramatic than Hank's. When a careless smoker threw a cigarette onto her piling, firefighters raced to put out the little blaze. When Gertie's first-hatched duckling (whom MacQuarrie named Black Bill) fell into the river, he was rescued, twice, by a pair of bridgetenders in a rowboat. When two ships with cargoes to deliver had the audacity to demand that the bridge be raised, the tenders inched it open with the greatest of care.

Milwaukee's maternal instincts were thoroughly aroused. As soon as Gertie's eggs began to hatch, the bridgetenders doubled as round-the-clock guards, and uniformed Boy Scouts kept watch over the crowds, eyes peeled for any thoughtless smokers. The gigantic pump in the lakefront flushing station (now Colectivo Coffee) was turned on to purge the filthy river and make it clean enough for ducklings. On Mother's Day, Gertie received (through MacQuarrie) hundreds of cards and, from someone not quite clear on the concept, diapers. At the peak of Gertie-mania, more than two thousand fans jostled for space at the railings—to watch a duck.

The heroine and her young brood were ultimately relocated to the Juneau Park lagoon, where they promptly melted into the web-footed crowd. But Gertie was not forgotten. She became the heroine of a children's book that was translated into several languages, and in 1997, she and her ducklings were immortalized in bronze on the very bridge where they had enjoyed such adulation.

Gertie, it must be understood, gave Milwaukee a rare moment of levity in an extraordinarily heavy time. Like the rest of America, the city had not experienced normalcy since before the stock market crash of 1929. The Depression lingered through the 1930s, and it was followed immediately by the pressures and privations of World War II. President Franklin Roosevelt died less than two weeks before Gertie made her debut, and American casualties were still piling up on battlefronts around the world. People were absolutely starved for a feel-good story, and Gertie, so to speak, filled the bill.

The problems facing Milwaukee in 2014 paled in comparison with those plaguing our ancestors in 1945, but Hank played much the same role as his feathered predecessor. Mired in toxic political partisanship and a less-than-robust economy after a brutally long winter—not to mention a so-so Packers season and a 15–67 record for the Bucks—Milwaukeeans were ready to embrace a ball of fluff that had weathered some hard times.

Hank the Dog has since padded off into semiretirement, living a life of ease with a Brewers executive and her family, but the legend lives on. Will Hank someday have his own children's book and a bronze statue next to Bob Uecker's at American Family Field? I'd call it a long shot—once you get past the cuteness, there's not much drama in a house pet's life—but never underestimate the power of a good public relations team. In the meantime, Brewers fans can fondly recall how Hank helped us all hit the paws button at the uncertain start of another new season.

Beulah Brinton of Bay View

Neighborhood Activist of 1800s Is Still a Role Model

She was the uncrowned queen of an entire neighborhood. By the time Beulah Brinton died in 1928, as a ninety-two-year-old dowager slowed by a stroke, the people of Bay View had named a street, a park, and a community center in her honor. Few Milwaukeeans have ever received such tangible recognition, and fewer still during their lifetimes.

The street and the park bear different names today, but a newer and much larger community center still honors Beulah. Even more fittingly, her old house on Superior Street is now the home of the Bay View Historical Society. Extensively restored in recent years, the landmark celebrates this singular figure's impact on the surrounding neighborhood.

Who was this civic saint? The answer is more complicated than you might expect. Beulah Brinton was born Bulah Tobey in upstate New York in 1836. She was raised in modest circumstances, but her fortunes improved in 1854, when she married a Connecticut Yankee named Warren Brinton. Twelve years her senior, Warren was rising through the ranks of America's fledgling iron industry. In about 1870, he became the superintendent of blast furnaces for the Milwaukee Iron Company, and the couple moved west from Michigan.

The furnaces were only two years old when Warren took charge. Sprawled across the lakefront at what is now the foot of the Dan Hoan Bridge, Bay View's new rolling mill quickly became the second-largest producer of railroad rails in America and the largest employer in Milwaukee, providing work for nearly fifteen hundred men at peak periods, many of them immigrants.

Bay View came to life as a compact company town built around the iron mill, and one of its earmarks was an unusually democratic streetscape, a quality that persists today. In such a small community, mill executives and smoke-blackened mill workers lived on the same streets, often on the same

Beulah Brinton was a one-woman improvement committee for the industrial suburb of Bay View.
BAY VIEW HISTORICAL SOCIETY

blocks. In 1873, Warren and Beulah built a striking Gothic Revival home at 2590 South Superior Street. It stood just down the street from a row of tiny houses still known as "puddler's cottages" after one of the mill's skilled trades.

The lady of the house quickly became a pillar of the community. Beulah Brinton was in some ways a conventional Victorian—a giver of teas, a presenter of silver spoons, a fixture in the society pages of the local papers. She was also a devout Methodist, leading the local Women's Foreign Missionary Society and even serving as a lay preacher on occasion.

Like other proper Protestant women of her time and station, Brinton was a staunch advocate of temperance, a nineteenth-century euphemism for total abstinence from alcohol. In 1883,

Beulah's home became an informal social center for her working-class neighbors. Her portrait graced the front lawn in 2010. JOHN GURDA

according to the *Milwaukee Sentinel*, she called on one of Bay View's female barkeepers "to try to persuade her that her forte was in the coffee and eating house line instead of the saloon." The response was a hearty "Get out now."

She didn't always succeed, but such direct action was typical of Beulah Brinton. An older generation would have called her redoubtable—a woman with scant tolerance for obstruction and delays.

That was particularly true of her work in the Bay View community, and it was her community work that earned Brinton a lasting reputation. Since they were some of her nearest neighbors, she naturally focused on the problems of the immigrant workers. Laboring long hours for modest wages at hot and hazardous jobs, the mill hands led lives of unrelieved brutality, and their families suffered under the same shadow. "Man was not made to be a mule, or a machine," Brinton wrote. "Many of us are compelled to work so hard that we be more like beasts of burden than like Sons and Daughters of a King."

True to form, Beulah Brinton resolved to do something about it. Although she was raising three children of her own, Brinton launched a concerted effort to raise both the mental and the moral standing of the mill workers and their families. In about 1874, she started a small lending library in her own home, and a few years later she organized a mass meeting to rally support for "a library and reading room for the use of the public." The result, in time, was the Bay View branch of the Milwaukee Public Library.

Long before that branch opened, Beulah Brinton began to hold periodic "children's hours" in her home. She read stories to neighborhood youngsters and, as one of her listeners later remembered, Brinton sometimes looked up from the page "to tell about the wonderful things she believed would come about in the world of science in our lifetime."

Adults were not forgotten. Beulah Brinton was an accomplished writer—her Civil War novel, *Man Is Love*, still holds the reader's interest—and she became the guiding light of the Bay View Literary Society. It was not a circle of soft-handed aesthetes. Brinton let it be known that her society had "no class interest to subserve, being strictly cosmopolitan and free to all who feel any interest in advancing the moral and thoughtful welfare of the community, irrespective of sect or station." The Literary Society was open, in other words, to mill workers, and its meetings were held in Puddler's Hall, a union headquarters on St. Clair Street. In 1892, Brinton herself presented a lecture on "Ingersoll's Voltaire" designed for "the workmen in the rolling mill."

This one-woman improvement committee also organized some less-cerebral activities for her neighbors. She installed a tennis court in her side yard on Superior Street that was open to anyone, with a box of rackets at the ready on her porch. She also reportedly played the piano for her young guests as they danced—a definite breach of Methodist protocol—and served as a midwife for the community's new mothers.

These were not tasks that the average business executive's wife tackled in the 1800s—or in any century, for that matter. But Brinton was hardly an average executive's wife. She saw herself as a representative type of the "new woman" working to bring forth a "new world" from the squalor of the old.

There was a bit of the mystic as well as the moralizer in Beulah Brinton. When Bay View was racked by labor trouble in 1886, she had a solution that sounded more like a New Age guru's than a proper Victorian's. Beulah urged her neighbors to simply put their minds together. "If all would concentrate their mind force every day at 2 P.M.," she wrote, "in a persistent, determined effort to bring the children and the All-Parent into a closer union, where the life of the Infinite could flow into and stimulate the less life of the child, many more would be able to rejoice in God and rest in the Arms of Peace and Love."

Her "working people's prayer test" failed to produce labor peace, but Bay View was clearly a better place for her presence. It would be too much to call 2590 South Superior Street a settlement house, or to compare Beulah Brinton to Jane Addams. Brinton was known in her time as a literary figure, not a social worker, and her residence remained a private home. But there is no mistaking her generosity of spirit, her penchant for organization, and her determination to improve the lot of the people around her.

When Bay View's first official community center, a remodeled firehouse on St. Clair Street, opened in 1924, it was named in her honor. The center's director, Henry Otjen, whose father had once been Beulah Brinton's debating partner, called her "a noble woman, a true mother and the first community worker in Bay View." That's a legacy worth celebrating—and worth emulating—as the neighborhood and the city around it confront new challenges in a different century.

A Bouquet for Mr. Whitnall

Honoring the Father of Milwaukee County's Parks

I practically grew up in his park. When my family moved from the old South Side to Hales Corners in 1955, it didn't take us long to discover Whitnall Park and its tributary green space, Root River Parkway. Whenever aunts and uncles came to visit, Whitnall's centerpiece—the Boerner Botanical Gardens—was a mandatory stop. (My father loved to compare his chrysanthemums with the work of the pros at Boerner.) In winter we skated on Whitnall's frozen lagoon—the smell of woolen mittens drying on the warming shack's stove has lasted a lifetime—and in summer, my friends and I spent hours under the Forest Home Avenue bridge, trying to coax crayfish out of beer cans motorists had tossed into the Root River.

When I was old enough to bike across busy Forest Home, Whitnall Park was our after-school destination practically every day in spring and fall. We knew the trails nearly as well as the resident deer, and our two-wheeled forays continued into adolescence. As eighth-graders, we gathered to smoke cigarettes and utter forbidden words in a creekside spot we called Rubber River, just downstream from a bridge where the older teens parked.

My greaser period was mercifully short-lived. Even though my gang broke up after grade school, I remained a Whitnall Park regular, and my visits have continued to the present. Even as a kid, I knew that the park wasn't really Whitnall's, whoever

Charles Whitnall, a visionary planner and the father of Milwaukee's renowned park system. MILWAUKEE JOURNAL SENTINEL

that might have been; this square mile of green space obviously belonged to all of us. But I have developed, over the years, a deep appreciation for the man whose name it bears.

Charles B. Whitnall was hailed as the father of Milwaukee County's world-class park system even during his lifetime. He merits, in my opinion, a place of honor in Wisconsin's proud environmental tradition, for it was Whitnall's vision and, just as important, his tenacity that made the state's metropolis such a capital of green space. At a time when Milwaukee's parks are under duress after years of starvation budgets, a look back at the founder's vision might help us reestablish our priorities.

Charles Whitnall's biography is fairly straightforward. He was born in 1859 in what is now the Riverwest neighborhood, the son of an English immigrant and a Milwaukee schoolteacher. After a brief foray into sign-painting, the elder Whitnall became a power in the local flower trade, developing a phalanx of greenhouses behind his home on the west bluff of the Milwaukee River near Locust Street.

Charles followed his father into the flower business, but he soon developed interests that went far beyond petals and stems.

Whitnall paused for a rare look back at his career in 1931, when he led a reporter and a photographer from the *Milwaukee Journal* on a day-long, seventy-five-mile tour of the county's emerging park system. (Their story appeared on June 21, 1931.) Whitnall recalled that his family had nearly cornered the market on wedding and graduation arrangements by the time he was a young man:

> At first, I enjoyed the decorating work immensely, but gradually it began to impress me with its futility. I saw that I was not creating real beauty. "This," I said to myself, "is like making a stage setting. There is nothing real about it." So I abandoned decorating and went into landscaping. There I could create an effect that would not be faded and limp the morning after. For a little while landscaping satisfied me . . . but in 1900 I was all caught up on that work too. My satisfaction in it had lasted only ten years before I had a sense of incompleteness. One home might be made beautiful, but it would not fit in with the next. I came to realize that landscaping ought to be done on a larger scale. "The only way to take care of a few homes is to take care of all of them," I said to myself. That is how I came to be interested in city planning.

Planning would be Whitnall's passion for the rest of his life, but it was not the only one. After leaving the plant business, he became a walking oxymoron, earning his livelihood as the officer of a local trust company and at the same time rising to prominence in Milwaukee's newly organized Socialist party. Whitnall's trust experience prompted him to found the cooperatively owned Commonwealth Mutual Savings Bank in 1912; his political ties led to his election as city treasurer (for one term) in the Socialist landslide of 1910.

Charles Whitnall's unusual combination of business acumen and political skills provided a solid foundation for his third and most fruitful career: as Milwaukee's chief planner for nearly forty years. He was appointed to the city's Public Land Commission and the county's Park Commission in 1907, eventually becoming secretary of both. Although the posts were generally uncompensated, they enabled him to leave a permanent imprint on Milwaukee's landscape.

Largely self-taught, Whitnall was a voracious reader and a rigorous thinker. He developed a planning philosophy that proceeded organically from humanity's relationship with nature. "Nature is more than a city ordinance," he told the *Journal* reporter during their 1931 tour. "Natural landscape exerts an important influence. . . . I am convinced that most physical ills and a good portion of our economic ills are due to the crowding out of natural influences."

Whitnall believed that it was the particular role of local government to restore the influences of nature and, even though the Depression was nearing its low point, he expressed high hopes. "No one in the city of the future," he predicted in 1931, "will be more than five or six blocks from a beautiful recreation ground." But Whitnall had no interest in placing parks just anywhere; the framework for all his plans was the local watershed. "Remember," he told his journalistic companions, "the valley is the proper unit in the development of any territory."

Whitnall's ideas found mature expression in his 1923 master plan for Milwaukee County's parks. The plan featured a double loop of parkways following the county's rivers, creeks, and lakeshore, with individual parks strung along the loop like pearls on a necklace. The resemblance between Whitnall's plan and today's system is uncanny. "We are seeking," he wrote, "to conserve not only God's country but Humanity."

It goes without saying that Charles Whitnall would be aghast at the current state of the county's parks. Despite the best efforts of an overworked and underfunded staff, the backlog of deferred-maintenance projects is so huge that no one knows its exact dimensions, and signs of decay are unmistakable. Whitnall would view the system's steep decline as a form of civic suicide. The parks, he would say, are everyone's birthright, part of our common wealth, and we neglect them at the peril of our collective soul.

There is no better guide to a sustainable solution than Charles Whitnall himself. Making his grand vision a reality was the work of decades, and reclaiming it will take just as long. The planner encountered spirited opposition and frequent defeats throughout his career, but he never retreated to an airy elitism or a frosty despair. Whitnall stayed in the game whatever the weather and regardless of the score, and that persistence may have been his greatest strength. Every setback inspired one more speech, one more article, one more attempt to rally public support. If that required spending an entire day with a reporter on his own time, Whitnall was glad to oblige.

One of the highlights of that marathon 1931 tour was a stop at Hales Corners Park, a six-hundred-acre tract in the southwestern corner of the county that had been acquired only the year before. "Today," wrote the *Journal* reporter, "it is a beautiful, wild section of land where little springs bubble up and with watercress and mint along a trickling stream."

In the very next year, that park, which is still the county's largest, was renamed in Whitnall's honor. The naming was a clear recognition of his towering role in the system's development, but Whitnall was far more interested in public use than personal glory. Just as he would have wished, I still think of it as my park after all these years—mine, yours, and above all ours, an inheritance from past generations that is here for us to use, appreciate, and draw inspiration from as we work to recapture the vision that brought it to life.

Jay Scriba's Milwaukee

Remembering a Journalistic Legend

How quickly we forget the good ones. When Jay Scriba, one of the finest writers ever to enliven the pages of the old *Milwaukee Journal*, died in 2014, his passing was barely noticed in the community he chronicled so well for so long. His former employer published an obituary, but only in its online edition—perhaps the last place his devoted (and increasingly aged) readers would have looked for it.

The dearth of attention may have something to do with the fact that Scriba, eighty-eight at his final birthday, had retired in 1981 and never lived in Milwaukee again. It also reflects the evanescent nature of the news business. Journalists prepare their famous "first draft of history" one day and move on to the next day's draft, rarely pausing to look back. Scriba's collected works exist only online and in the musty volumes of old papers at the Central Library, sandwiched between stories about the Vietnam War and ads for $2,695 Buick Electras.

That seems a shame at a time when the newspaper business is in such dire straits. Jay Scriba was a member of a select *Milwaukee Journal* fraternity that included Robert Wells, Gerald Kloss, and Mel Ellis—writers whose work readers looked forward to and savored. They demonstrated what was possible in a daily paper, and presumably what still is.

Scriba, who pronounced his name with a long "i" (as in "scribe," appropriately), may have been the best of the bunch. Raised near Gary, Indiana, and educated at Notre Dame, he came to the *Journal* in 1960 as a features writer for the editorial page. Week in and week out, he produced thousand-word essays on topics as diverse as Mohandas Gandhi, German POW camps, and Hollywood stuntmen, generally relying on recently published books for his information.

His features were accomplished, even erudite, but Scriba really hit his stride in

Jay Scriba, a master wordsmith and connoisseur of the ordinary. MILWAUKEE JOURNAL SENTINEL

the 1970s with a series of columns that reflected the true breadth of his interests. "Where the Streetcar Bends" was his food and drink column, covering Croatian picnics, Jewish delis, and Milwaukee saloons by the dozen. "Nature in the City" recounted his forays as a "city naturalist, searching everywhere for all that is still green, wild and free living" within Milwaukee's borders. "Jay Scriba's Milwaukee" was the longest-running and most elastic of his efforts. If *Seinfeld* was a show about nothing, "Jay Scriba's Milwaukee" was a column about everything.

He was a particular hero of mine both for what he wrote about and for how he wrote about it. Jay Scriba was a connoisseur of the ordinary. He loved to scrutinize an underlit fragment

of the world and find within it something wondrous he could
share with the rest of us. Scriba's attention was drawn to sub-
jects as mundane as sidewalk ice and house sparrows, as taken
for granted as factory whistles and fish markets, as random as
which zoo animals were the most dangerous and what it felt
like to ride the school bus with a crew of forty fourth-graders—
"bundled, sniffling, lunch bucketed gnomes who hop and tussle
at windy crossroads or squish through clay-hole housing developments to join our tribe."

Scriba turned such apparent dross to gold on a regular
basis. Patient with detail, wary of shortcuts, he could pack
more information into a single paragraph than some writers
use to fill a page. He might have interviewed twenty people for
a single column, and he carried a tape recorder to make sure
he got their words right. When he finally sat down to write, his
words had an elegance, a long-legged grace that commanded
attention and yet remained completely natural, as unforced as
breathing.

A downtown jeweler Scriba visited for one column was "a
true courtly gentleman whose precise voice, wavy white hair
and manicured manners would credit a senior ambassador."
Describing his farewell to a South Side Latino man whose icon-
covered car he had admired, Scriba wrote, "Augustine's face
widened in a slow, sunburnt grin. Wordlessly he waved his hand,
offering the carefree, Acapulco-breeze beauty of his fluttering
blue saint and diaphanous fiesta kerchief."

On one occasion, Scriba test-drove a sixty-five-thousand-
dollar Rolls-Royce: "As we motor sedately, peasant pickups and
nouveau riffraff Caddies ease up to gape upon the polished marble sheen of our Ivory top and Highland Green flanks, the result
of 14 to 20 coats of hand rubbed paint. Too bad they can't get a
whiff of a new car that smells of beeswax and cowhide instead
of polyvinyl chloride."

For another column, the bald-pated reporter paid a visit to a purveyor of men's hairpieces: "Like any customer off the street, I begin my visit in a carpeted office rich with the Miami Renaissance décor common to branch banks and suburban dental offices. While putting me at ease with kindly graciousness, the partners study my desolate dome and mousey friar's fringe like plastic surgeons appraising a botched nose job."

Even the humble knotweed that grows in sidewalk cracks caught Scriba's eye:

> Why is it that bards, poets and city street crews panic at the sight of a tuft of wild greenery amidst all that concrete? Their fear probably lingers from the days when great forests loomed hungrily over tiny villages. Let them be assured then that the knotweed has no territorial ambitions except as a modest niche filler: Release it from its strangling sidewalk crack and it wilts for lack of a challenge. Fertilize its favorite compost of motor oil, coal dust, broken glass and rusty bottle caps and it advances only timidly, a few clumps from the trampled curb. I am now convinced that, for reasons known only to itself, it likes being stepped on.

Like a lot of writers who make it look easy, Scriba worked hard to bring his words to life. Dan Stefanich, a friend and neighbor in Shorewood, recalled his weekly rhythm: "Friday night he would come home from work rather calm and cool, pulling off his tie, walking in his garden. Saturday was still pretty good, but by Sunday night Jay was almost a basket case sometimes, because the next day was work again. For a guy who wrote so marvelously, he really suffered with anxiety about what he was writing and what to write next."

The cure for that anxiety turned out to be early retirement. By the late 1970s, Scriba was so highly regarded that his editors gave him summers off—with pay, no less. In 1981, at noon on his fifty-fifth birthday, he quit completely. For the rest of his life, he and his wife, Mona, divided the year between his boyhood home in Hobart, Indiana, and a tarpaper shack they had purchased on Lake Superior, across the bay from Marquette, Michigan. Scriba turned in a handful of postretirement columns with a Lake Superior dateline. "The fragrance of crushed wild raspberries in one's pail is an annual summer miracle," one dispatch began, "a thrust of nostalgia for times and places too deep for remembrance." He was capable of a rare lyricism, but this gifted wordsmith never wrote for regular publication again.

What he left was a solid body of work that is wickedly difficult to access. (The best portal is the Milwaukee *Journal Sentinel*'s historical database on the Milwaukee Public Library's website.) Jay Scriba's Milwaukee was different from the town we know today, but a searching curiosity and a healthy sense of wonder are perennially in season. "Looking. Really looking," he wrote in 1972. "This is the secret." Thanks for honoring our world with such lovingly close attention, Jay. We'll keep our eyes open.

A Green Pantheon

Five Legendary Wisconsin Conservationists

If Wisconsin had its own Mount Rushmore, whose faces would you carve into the rock? Not that we have a surplus of promising locations. Although you can find Mount Pleasant, Mount Horeb, and Mount Sterling on the state map, none are mountains that any Coloradan would recognize, or even a South Dakotan. But who would you choose? Someone from the sports world, perhaps Henry Aaron or Vince Lombardi? How about political legends like Robert La Follette or George Kennan? Candidates from the cultural sphere might include Harry Houdini, Laura Ingalls Wilder, and Spencer Tracy, or, on the artistic side, Frank Lloyd Wright and Georgia O'Keeffe.

My own choice would be a distinguished fraternity of Wisconsin conservationists. I would one-up the Rushmore quartet and pick five individuals: Increase Lapham, John Muir, Charles Whitnall, Aldo Leopold, and Gaylord Nelson. Their work was spread across more than 150 years of Wisconsin's history, but the five shared an intimate familiarity with the state's landscape and a fervent desire to preserve it in its natural state.

It is that landscape, after all, that makes our state unique. Sheer luck and sharp politics gave us borders that enclose a landscape of uncommon diversity and undeniable beauty, starting well below our feet. Wisconsin's bedrock ranges from the hard granites of the Canadian Shield to the softer sea rocks of

A

B

A quintet of famous conservationists made Wisconsin a capital of the environmental movement.
(A) Increase Lapham. WHI IMAGE ID 99875
(B) John Muir. WHI IMAGE ID 1946
(C) Charles Whitnall. MILWAUKEE *JOURNAL SENTINEL*
(D) Aldo Leopold. WHI IMAGE ID 34893
(E) Gaylord Nelson. WHI IMAGE ID 2844

C

D

E

the American heartland. The soils perched on that bedrock support the famous (among botanists) "tension zone," with the long-needled Northwoods on one side and broad-leaved oaks and maples on the other. Wisconsin has freshwater seas on two of its borders, America's largest river on a third, and fifteen thousand inland lakes between them. Prairies and wetlands, ridges and valleys, black earth and white sands—we've got it all, and the Driftless Area preserves a gorgeous remnant of Wisconsin in its preglacial state.

Small wonder that this midsized state has played an outsized role in the American conservation movement. Wisconsin's smorgasbord of natural bounty inspired a quintet whose impact has extended far beyond the borders of the state. Let me call the roll.

Increase Lapham, a New York–born Quaker with a scientific turn of mind, came to Wisconsin in 1836 and promptly fell in love. He singled out the state's lakes: "Many of them are the most beautiful that can be imagined—the water deep and of crystal clearness and purity, surrounded by sloping hills and promontories covered with scattered groves and clumps of trees." But Lapham was a generalist who studied every dimension of his adopted state, from shells to grasses to Indian mounds. He was also a conservationist—Wisconsin's first— who denounced the wanton destruction of our forests and urged systematic replanting to restore the natural hydrologic cycle. Lapham's fervent belief in applied science was a major factor in the establishment of the US Weather Service.

John Muir came from Scotland to a Marquette County farm as a boy in 1849, and he, too, fell in love: "This sudden plash into pure wildness—baptism in Nature's warm heart—how utterly happy it made us! Nature streaming into us, wooingly teaching her wonderful glowing lessons, so unlike the dismal grammar ashes and cinders so long thrashed into us. Here without

knowing it we were still at school; every wild lesson a love lesson
not whipped but charmed into us. Oh, that glorious Wisconsin
wilderness!" Muir's enduring fame came after his move to California at the age of thirty. With the lessons he first learned in
Wisconsin as a foundation, he embarked on a largely unpaid
career as America's leading conservationist and a founder of
both the national park system and the Sierra Club.

Charles Whitnall worked closer to home. The Milwaukee-
born Socialist was the dominant influence on local land-use
planning for an entire generation before World War II. Railing
against the "civilized vandalism" that bulldozed native ecosys-
tems in the name of progress, he sought to "make the best use of
this earth with the least possible blemish to desirable landscapes," and the unifying principle in his planning philosophy
was the watershed. "Every home," Whitnall wrote, "should feel
the environmental influence of natural shores with the essential
forest support." His lasting legacy is Milwaukee County's park
system, an outstanding resource by any measure and the green
embodiment of Whitnall's ideals.

Aldo Leopold enjoyed a larger stage. He didn't move to Wisconsin until 1924, when he was thirty-seven, but it was in this
state that his ideas came to maturity, particularly at the Sauk
County "shack" that served as his family's retreat. Leopold's mus-
ings there, collected in *A Sand County Almanac*, have become a
bible of the environmental movement, not only for the grace
and subtlety of his writing but also for his articulation of the
land ethic as a way to live. "We abuse land," he maintained,
"because we regard it as a commodity belonging to us. When
we see land as a community to which we belong, we may begin
to use it with love and respect."

Gaylord Nelson was one of Leopold's most avid readers.
Born in the Polk County hamlet of Clear Lake, Nelson was
shaped profoundly by his exposure to the woods and waters of

northern Wisconsin. As the state's governor from 1959 to 1963 and a US senator for eighteen years thereafter, Nelson made the environment his signature cause. "The fate of the living planet is the most important issue facing mankind," he wrote, and he maintained that the planet's welfare should trump purely economic concerns. "The economy," Nelson insisted, "is a wholly owned subsidiary of the environment, not the other way around." His most visible legacy is Earth Day, which he started in 1970.

Lapham, Muir, Whitnall, Leopold, and Nelson. If any state has a comparable pantheon of environmental all-stars, I'm not aware of it. They rose from the soil of Wisconsin as organically as a grove of burr oaks or a patch of trout lilies. This state shaped each of them in decisive ways, creating inner landscapes that corresponded to the polychrome patchwork of physical landscapes that framed their days. From Wisconsin, their influence rippled out to the world. Yes, they're all dead white men, but the quintet's influence is undeniable. They would also, to a person, have abhorred the idea of defacing a perfectly good mountain with anyone's face, including their own.

In recent years, there have been repeated attempts to overturn their legacy. Wisconsin legislators have passed some measures and proposed even more to weaken environmental regulations, open more resources to development, and eliminate funding for public land acquisition. In contrast with the fabled figures of our past, they are, in my view, short-sighted, small-minded cynics who literally can't see the forest for the trees. The best property, in their view, is private property, and nature is fine as long as it can be taxed, sold, or used for profit.

That utilitarian attitude puts them radically at odds with a core Wisconsin tradition. Regardless of their party ties, state residents have always had an appreciation for the exceptional natural riches that surround us here, whether they hunt, fish, camp, hike, or simply enjoy the beauty of the passing scene through their windshields.

"Harmony with land," wrote Aldo Leopold, "is like harmony with a friend; you cannot cherish his right hand and chop off his left." In the spirit of the quintet who did so much to preserve Wisconsin's native bounty, let's not sever the hand that has been feeding us so abundantly from the very beginning.

City Hall, Northwoods Style

Mayor Dan Hoan's "Shack" Was His Summer Retreat

The lot is huge, the pines are tall, and the house is, well, cozy. Set on the shore of a clearwater lake not far from Eagle River, the cabin is practically indistinguishable from thousands of others in northern Wisconsin, but this one's important because its owner was important: Daniel Webster Hoan, mayor of Milwaukee from 1916 to 1940.

Hoan called his Northwoods home "the shack"—a claim of unpretentiousness befitting a Socialist—but he was a towering figure in the political landscape of Milwaukee and far beyond. Not only was he one of America's longest-serving mayors, holding his city's top office for twenty-four years, but he was also, in my opinion, the best mayor Milwaukee has ever had. Hoan guided the community through the tumult of World War I, the Roaring Twenties, and the Depression, and he was at the helm as the city sailed away from a prolonged period of malfeasance and corruption to become a paragon of civic virtue. In 1936, *Time* magazine put Dan Hoan on its cover, calling the mayor "one of the nation's ablest public servants."

It's a wonder that Hoan had any time at all to spend at his cottage. He led a city whose population climbed from roughly four hundred thousand to nearly six hundred thousand during his tenure, and yet he usually managed to spend *two full months* Up North each summer. He never downplayed the demands of his post; Hoan once claimed that only the president of the United States had a harder job than a big-city mayor, simply because the tasks involved were so numerous and often so minute. But his time off was sacred. In these days of nonstop news cycles, such prolonged absences from City Hall would be both unthinkable and politically suicidal.

Hoan's time away was made all the richer by the remoteness of his location. When he bought the little

Mayor Daniel Hoan relaxed and recharged at his Vilas County cabin for two full months each summer. HOAN FAMILY

cottage on Carpenter Lake in 1918, it took two days to drive there from Milwaukee. There were no telephones, and he went into Eagle River, nine miles west, only twice a week. Visitors were received but hardly courted. Even the most persistent had a hard time finding the place because there was, by design, no mailbox. In 1926, the mayor issued a tongue-in-cheek invitation to President Calvin Coolidge, America's most laconic commander-in-chief. "Coolidge is a man after my own heart in one respect," said Hoan. "He doesn't talk much. And I go up into the dense forest to commune with myself alone, to talk to myself, and only occasionally to a squirrel."

And what did His Honor do when he wasn't communing with Vilas County's squirrels? He spent time with his wife and two kids, of course, but mostly he worked, and not always on pending legislation or policy initiatives. In 1928, the *Milwaukee*

Journal sent Richard Davis, one of its star reporters, Up North
to interview Hoan. Davis found his subject in overalls, working through a long list of projects, including a screen porch, a
partial basement, an open-air garage, a dove house, a smoke-
house, and concrete sidewalks. "Keep busy?," the mayor asked
rhetorically. "I should say so." When Davis rose to leave, Hoan
insisted that the reporter examine his hands. "Just look at these
calluses," he said. "Hammers and saws and what not always do
that to a man."

The mayor could not escape his official duties completely.
He received one newspaper and a briefing letter from his secretary every day, and there were occasional emergencies. In 1928,
the Common Council, dominated by non-Socialists at the
time, staged a minor insurrection during his summer sojourn,
voting to strip the mayor of his power to fill aldermanic vacan-
cies between elections. Hoan rushed home—"rushed" being a
relative term in those days—to veto that measure and several
others, then motored north again to finish his vacation.

Dan Hoan was by no means the only public official to seek
the solace of the Northwoods. Edward Kelly, the political boss
who became Chicago's mayor in 1933, owned a lavish home on
Catfish Lake, just a few miles from Hoan's. "The Milwaukee
mayor," the *Milwaukee Journal* assured its readers, "has a much
more modest and secluded retreat." Other Milwaukeeans were
nearby. Jacob Laubenheimer, the city's police chief, vacationed
at an Eagle River resort every summer until he died there in
1936. Laubenheimer lived across the alley from Hoan in Milwaukee's Concordia neighborhood, and the pair were practically neighbors Up North as well.

The summer exodus became so general that Milwaukee
experienced an occasional leadership vacuum. On August 24,
1937, the *Milwaukee Journal* described the city as "a ship without a skipper." Mayor Hoan was Up North, and the next

Hoan called his unassuming Carpenter Lake home "the shack."
JOHN GURDA

officials in the line of succession—the Common Council president and the Finance Committee chair—were out of town as well. The *Journal* reported no panic in the halls of power: "Several aldermen, not eligible for the mayorship, loitered about the city hall, but nothing was stirring sufficiently to necessitate mayoral action."

The exodus is more understandable when you realize that air-conditioning was an unaffordable luxury until well after World War II. Electric fans were available to move air around during the dog days, but many offices, not to mention all factories, must have felt like saunas in late summer. Vilas County was a comparative heaven.

Not that summer cottages lacked hazards. In 1939, Dan Hoan was banging away on a chisel when a splinter of steel pierced his eyelid and lodged in his eyeball. He lost the sight in that eye permanently—an infirmity that took an emotional as well as a physical toll.

Hazards aside, it's clear that the mayor relished his time on Carpenter Lake. After two months of solitude and exertion in the Northwoods, Hoan generally came back to City Hall recharged and refreshed. After his 1927 break, he pronounced himself "physically fit for the winter's work."

The sojourns continued after he lost the 1940 mayoral race to a vigorous young city attorney named Carl Zeidler. Retired to civilian life, Dan Hoan outlived two wives, weathered eight strokes, and witnessed the collapse of his own party as an electoral force. He died in 1961 at the age of eighty. For years before his death, Hoan was the patriarch of family gatherings at Carpenter Lake, and he remains the presiding spirit of the place.

True to his Socialist ideals, Hoan decided to share the wealth. His will dictates that the property, which includes forty acres and a quarter mile of lake frontage, be sold following the death of his last grandchild. (The youngest is now in her sixties, and there are family jokes about putting her on life support when the time comes.) One-third of the sale proceeds will go to his great-grandchildren, one-third to the Milwaukee County Historical Society, and the final third to a foundation Hoan established to continue his legacy.

Whatever its ultimate fate—a public park would be ideal—Dan Hoan's "shack" stands as a testament to his vision and a tangible expression of his values. "It's a great summer resort I have," the mayor said in 1927, "and silence is its predominating factor." That's something we could use a great deal more of in our public life.

Frank P. Zeidler, 1912–2006

Former Mayor Was a Model Milwaukeean

W e thought he'd live forever. Frank Zeidler was such a vital presence in the Milwaukee community for so many years that mortality seemed to be just one more convention he'd defy. That wasn't to be, of course. Zeidler died on July 7, 2006, at the age of ninety-three—far later than he ever expected and far sooner than any of us would have wished.

With his passing, we lost an authentic American hero. He was certainly a hero to me. I was well into middle age by the time I could bring myself to call him "Frank." For years he was "Mr. Zeidler," a mark of earnest respect he tolerated with good grace.

Frank was certainly a hero for all he accomplished as mayor. His tasks between 1948 and 1960 ranged from rebuilding Milwaukee's infrastructure after years of neglect to doubling the city's land area. But it's easy to forget that Zeidler spent the last forty-six years of his life *not* being mayor. What makes him a hero to me is the unique role he played in this community for nearly half a century—as our memory, our conscience, and our teacher.

Frank Zeidler was, first of all, our collective memory—our griot, if you will. No one knew more about Milwaukee's history. His grasp of both the major themes and the minor details was

---

A eulogy delivered at Frank Zeidler's funeral, Redeemer Lutheran Church, Milwaukee, July 12, 2006.

Frank Zeidler spent twelve years as the city's mayor and the next half-century as Milwaukee's memory, conscience, and teacher, always with a twinkle in his eye. MILWAUKEE JOURNAL SENTINEL

encyclopedic, and no one was more willing to share what he knew. Frank gave thousands of talks to a comprehensive range of audiences. One of my great pleasures in the last decade of his life was presenting tag-team history programs with Frank for the University of Wisconsin–Milwaukee's School of Continuing Education. I would speak from laboriously prepared notes, Frank would speak from memory, and I guarantee you that no one could tell the difference. He was one of those rare individuals who communicated in complete paragraphs.

But it wasn't just public programs. Frank never drove a car, and hundreds of colleagues and friends had the pleasure of taking him where he needed to go. Along the way, he'd generally present a traveling history lesson, telling stories about who lived in this house or what happened on that corner. I think he considered those stories his cab fare, and we were all richly paid.

Frank Zeidler was our memory, but he was also our conscience. Frank never had to find the higher moral ground, because he lived there. He was a tireless voice for social justice and world peace, and his causes were as local as the Central North Community Council—a neighborhood group he chaired until the day he died—and as global as the United Nations Association. Zeidler encouraged all people to assert their rights, but he was just as adamant that they accept their responsibilities. The two were inseparable in his mind. By the power of his presence, he called everyone around him to a higher moral standard.

Finally and most emphatically, Frank Zeidler was our teacher. His first lesson was how we should treat each other, and that is with absolute respect. Respect for others was instinctive to Frank. He was unfailingly courteous, even courtly, in conversation, and he was a tireless letter-writer, quick to share thanks, congratulations, suggestions, or sympathy with a daunting list of correspondents. Such gestures reflected Frank's abiding concern for others and his deft human touch. Although he was hardly a typical public figure, anyone who thought Frank Zeidler wasn't a politician never saw him work a crowd. He'd have a hearty handshake, a tip of the fedora, or a personal word for everyone—often about members of their families or details of their neighborhoods— and always with that familiar twinkle in his eye.

Zeidler also taught us about the importance of curiosity. The world, in his view, could be dangerous and disappointing at times, but it was never anything less than fascinating. There was nothing that did not interest this man; I don't think he spent a bored minute in his life. At ninety, he plowed through a nine-hundred-page tome on Islamic history and pronounced it riveting.

But he needed more than books. The last time I saw him, about three weeks before his death, Frank was lamenting that he could no longer read a newspaper. I suggested that he might enjoy audiobooks from the public library. "Sure," he said, "but by the time something gets into a book, it's out of date." How many ninety-three-year-olds have such a burning desire to stay informed? How many thirty-year-olds?

Frank taught us one last lesson, and that is how to grow old. He had the great foresight to stay around long enough to outlive all his enemies and earn a whole new generation of admirers. But one thing is often missed about Frank Zeidler: he refused to let himself be a legend. Someone else in his position might have long ago lapsed into the role of elder statesman, content to rest on his laurels and dispense his hard-won wisdom to the young. Not Frank. He was always self-critical, always self-correcting, and never *too* sure of himself. Frank may have been the most intellectually honest person I've ever known. And so he deflected praise the way some people deflect criticism; he refused to be anything more—or less—than a human being, and one who viewed the world around him with a keen sense of informed wonder.

So how do you grow old? You don't retreat into a shell of memory. You don't polish your plaques. You don't rehash your war stories. You ignore the diminishments of age as best you can. You rise above its constraints to stay engaged with the world as it is—changing, imperfect, and all we have.

Frank was our memory, our conscience, and our teacher, but underlying all those roles was a simple, unshakable belief. If Frank had one precept, it was this: we are connected, each to each. We are not solitary sparks in an endless void, but individual threads in a wondrously complex fabric. That fabric may fray at times, and the colors may clash, but we are woven inseparably together. It was that belief that informed his spirituality, that shaped his concept of history, and that underpinned his view of our common wealth. Frank believed with all his heart that government, in the end, is all of us, and we have lost that vision at our extreme peril.

We could mourn Frank Zeidler as the last of his breed, as a paragon of civic virtue whose like won't come again. But that's the last thing Frank would have wanted. He would say, and I can almost hear him, that the model of citizenship he chose is a choice open to every one of us, and what are we waiting for?

We'll miss you, Frank, but your legacy endures. May the marvelous depth of your memory encourage us to cultivate our own. May the clarity of your conscience lead us to redouble our efforts for justice and peace. And may the lessons you taught us find new light in our lives, as we work to build a better world from the materials at hand.

PREVENT INFLUENZA!

With the present shortage of doctors and trained nurses, it behooves the citizens of Milwaukee to unite in the fight to prevent the spread of Influenza.

Consider your near and dear ones and elect yourself as a special health officer to see that the dangerous Influenza germs do not menace your home and the homes of your neighbors.

With cool head and common health-sense observe the simple rules of health and fight this danger to a finish.

Adopt the Following Precautionary Measures! Help Wage the War Against the Flu!

Walk to work if possible. Avoid persons who cough or sneeze.
Should you cough or sneeze, cover nose and mouth with a handkerchief.
Wash your hands before eating. Get plenty of fresh air, night and day.
Do not use common towel—it spreads disease.
Keep out of crowded places. Eat good, plain food, plenty of it.

GE C. RUHLAND, M. D.

The Common Good

Socialist Citadel

Milwaukee Was Land of the Free, Home of the Left

O n April 5, 1910, Milwaukee launched one of the most fascinating periods in the political history of any city in America. After a fiercely contested race, voters made their community
the first (and only) major city in the nation to elect a Socialist
mayor, and they kept doing it for most of the next fifty years. A
former patternmaker named Emil Seidel won a decisive victory
that April, the first in a string of Socialist wins that would continue until Frank Zeidler stepped down in 1960.

To many observers outside the city, Seidel's win seemed
positively revolutionary, a bold and abrupt departure from the
American norm. The truth is that municipal Socialism had been
germinating in Wisconsin's metropolis for generations, and its
success reflected a blend of global influences and purely local
conditions.

It mattered, first of all, that Milwaukee was the most German
city in America. German immigrants and their children made up
a majority of the populace as early as 1860, and in their number
were assorted radicals who had fled the failed revolution of 1848.
These fabled "Forty-Eighters" continued to publish, debate, and
agitate in their new home, founding Turner societies and free-
thinker congregations that nurtured leftists of all stripes.

If German intellectuals brought the seeds, a huge working class furnished the soil. As Milwaukee became a center of

Milwaukee Welcoming the Sunrise

The party press greeted the Socialist sweep of 1910 as the dawn of a new era.
MILWAUKEE PUBLIC LIBRARY

industry in the late 1800s, the city attracted legions of blue-collar immigrants who worked ten to twelve hours for a dollar or two a day, without a dime in benefits. They were understandably open to the Socialist argument that workers deserved a greater share of the wealth they created. Their receptiveness peaked after May 5, 1886, when the state militia opened fire on a group of strikers who were marching for the eight-hour day. Seven people died, including a thirteen-year-old schoolboy. The shootings radicalized thousands of workers and inspired a movement for revenge at the polls.

A thoroughly corrupt city administration provided a different kind of motivation. Under Mayor David Rose, a dandified scamp known to his cronies as "All the Time Rosy," a red-light district flourished in the shadow of City Hall, and five dollars was the going price for an alderman's vote. In an era of easy virtue across the nation, Milwaukee was every bit as crooked as Chicago on a bad day.

Milwaukee Socialism, finally, had superb leadership. The movement's standard-bearer was Victor Berger, an Austrian-born newspaper editor with a gift, rare on the left, for seeing beyond the ideological trees to the electoral forest. Berger forged an alliance with organized labor (the Milwaukee Idea, he called it) and went to work on real-world reforms. Although he believed firmly in the "cooperative commonwealth" envisioned by his comrades, Berger wanted to succeed in the here and now rather than wait for the sweet by-and-by.

His goal was to educate by governing, and you could govern only by winning elections. Berger's party began to field candidates in 1898, and one of their most potent weapons was the "bundle brigade," a small army of workers, many of them union members, who could reach any household in the city with literature on any issue in any of several languages within forty-eight hours.

The party's first successes, not surprisingly, came in the working-class wards of the German North Side. The aldermen elected from those neighborhoods showed a diligence and a creativity that made their regular-party counterparts look like hacks by comparison. Honesty in office, said Victor Berger, marked the pinnacle of virtue for the capitalist parties. "With us," he crowed, "this is the first and smallest requirement." Voters soon learned to trust the Socialists and, despite some shameless redbaiting by both Republicans and Democrats, a rising tide of popular support lifted the party higher with each election.

There was, in short, a constellation of forces that aligned to make Milwaukee a Socialist citadel. The party's desire for a new social order gave its members a motive. Disaffected industrial workers gave them the means. The open corruption of the Rose era provided an opportunity. Victor Berger developed a strategy, and his comrades on the Common Council set an example. It all came together on April 5, 1910. Not only did Emil Seidel win the mayor's race, but Socialists took a large majority of seats on both the Common Council and the County Board. Victor Berger himself went to Washington as the lone Socialist in Congress.

The landslide of 1910 proved to be no fluke. Seidel served as mayor until 1912, Daniel Hoan from 1916 to 1940, and Frank Zeidler from 1948 to 1960. No other big city in America entrusted its government to the Socialists, much less kept them in office for most of fifty years. That record makes Milwaukee unique in the nation.

And what did they do in office? The key to understanding Milwaukee's Socialists is the concept of public enterprise. They didn't just manage, and they didn't just enforce laws and regulations. They pushed a program of public necessities that had a tangible impact on the average citizen's quality of life: public parks, public libraries, public schools, public health, public works, public port facilities, public housing, public vocational education, and even public natatoria.

The Socialists' emphasis on practical reforms prompted a telling sobriquet from their more doctrinaire comrades in places like New York. "Some eastern smarties," wrote Emil Seidel in his memoir, "called ours a Sewer Socialism. Yes, we wanted sewers in the workers' homes; but we wanted much, oh, so very much more than sewers. We wanted our workers to have pure air; we wanted them to have sunshine; we wanted planned homes; we wanted living wages; we wanted recreation for young and old; we wanted vocational education; we wanted a chance for every human being to be strong and live a life of happiness."

THE SOCIALIST.

AS HE IS DEPICTED.   AS HE IS. (over)

Milwaukee Socialists countered the prevailing stereotype of their movement by governing ethically, economically, and effectively. MILWAUKEE COUNTY HISTORICAL SOCIETY

It's hard to detect even a whiff of Karl Marx in that passage. If their pragmatic idealism placed them on the right flank of a left-wing movement, Milwaukee's Socialists cared not at all.

Underlying their notion of public enterprise was an abiding faith, curiously antique by modern standards, in the goodness of government, especially local government. The Socialists believed that government was the locus of our common wealth—the resources that belong to all of us and to each of us—and they worked to build a community of interest around a deeply shared belief in the common good.

The results were plain to see. After years in the political sewer, Milwaukee became, under "Sewer Socialists" Seidel, Hoan, and Zeidler, a model of civic virtue. *Time* magazine put Dan Hoan on its cover in 1936 and called Milwaukee "perhaps the best-governed city in the U.S." The community won trophy after trophy for public health, traffic safety, and fire prevention, taking home the health prize so often that Milwaukee had to be retired from competition to give other municipalities a chance.

Even the most potent political movements eventually run their course. By the time Frank Zeidler left City Hall in 1960, Democrats had long since captured the Socialist Party's labor base, appropriated much of its rhetoric, and even enacted some of its pet programs, notably Social Security. The party of Seidel and Hoan became a dwindling core of the faithful who stuck to their ideological guns but were no longer a credible threat at election time.

Although the party's days of electoral glory are long gone, the Socialist imprint on Milwaukee is practically indelible. Not only did the movement create lasting amenities like a stellar park system, but it also spawned a political culture that retains much of its original power. Although they worked for real-world reforms, the Socialists didn't stop there. They called their fellow citizens to a higher conception of our life in common, one that placed cooperation above competition and mutualism above bare self-interest. The Socialist movement had a moral gravity and a passion for results that still resonate in the community's civic life.

At a time when Socialism has become the "S-word" in American politics, even a cursory look at Milwaukee's experience is instructive. During their long political tutelage, the city's residents learned that Socialist principles need not be identified with a stultifying statism. Milwaukee's Socialists were compassionate, competent, and every bit as frugal as the most penny-pinching German hausfrau. Their party may not have created a working-class Camelot, but the Socialists made a difference. They turned a boss-ridden city into a model of sound government, and Milwaukee, thank goodness, has never been the same.

The Power of Work

CCC Crews Remade Milwaukee's Landscape

Nick Zielinski loved to talk about the CCC. When I was in my twenties and Nick was in his sixties, we were both regulars at Big John's Tap, a twelve-stool tavern on South Twelfth Street that served as our block's communal living room. During a lull in a sheepshead game or while bending an elbow at the bar, this gentle, grandfatherly man would put down his cigar and drift back in time to the 1930s, when his parents, like so many other Americans, were struggling to put food on the table.

Nick was determined not to be a burden. Soon after finishing high school, he volunteered for the Civilian Conservation Corps, a New Deal work relief program designed for young men between the ages of seventeen and twenty-five. He was assigned to a camp in northern Wisconsin—near the Brule River, if memory serves—where he planted trees, trees, and more trees. The CCC allowed Nick to keep only five dollars of his thirty-dollar monthly stipend; the rest was sent home to his parents. Although the pay was modest and the work was hard, he remembered only the good things: fresh air, plenty of food, and the spirited company of other young men on the same adventure. Looking back from the safe haven of retirement, Nick Zielinski considered the CCC one of the high points of his life.

Most of Wisconsin's volunteers were, like Nick Zielinski, assigned to conservation projects Up North, planting trees,

Shovels at the ready, the young men of the Estabrook Park CCC camp prepared to go out and remake the landscape. MILWAUKEE COUNTY HISTORICAL SOCIETY

riprapping streambanks, and fighting forest fires. But the program had a significant urban component as well, and few communities in America were better prepared to use it than Milwaukee. Under the guidance of Charles B. Whitnall, the Socialist visionary who led the charge for public green space in both the city and the county, land-use planners had spent the 1920s filling drawer after drawer with detailed blueprints for park development. When CCC crews became available in July 1933, Milwaukee County knew exactly where to put them.

There were ultimately six camps within the county's borders: in Whitnall, Estabrook, Sheridan, and Kletzsch Parks, with two more along what is now Honey Creek Parkway. Each accommodated roughly two hundred young men who lived under the authority of regular Army officers and worked under the direction of trained foremen on highly specific tasks. The improvements they made to our parks and parkways have proven remarkably durable. CCC crews built the jetties in Grant and Sheridan Parks that still trap sand and prevent the erosion of the bluffs overlooking Lake Michigan. They reshaped the bed

of the Milwaukee River in Lincoln Park. They erected the graceful suspension bridge that crosses the Menomonee River near
Hoyt Park, and they built miles of walkways and retaining walls
with dolomite from a quarry in Currie Park. The waterfall on
the Milwaukee River in Kletzsch Park—a popular fishing spot
during the fall salmon run—is actually a concrete dam faced
with local dolomite. CCC crews worked day and night to finish
the structure before the spring floods of 1936 could wash it away.

The Civilian Conservation Corps left its mark all over the
county, but its work in and around Whitnall Park is especially
noteworthy. Not only did the "lads" of the CCC grade, pave, and
landscape more than four miles of parkway along the Root
River, but they also developed a network of lagoons in the park
itself, each held in place by a picturesque stone dam. The largest lagoon, just north of Whitnall Park's golf course, covers
fifteen acres and required the removal of more than thirty thousand cubic yards of earth. Muskrats and mallards still find it a

The Milwaukee River waterfall in Kletzsch Park was a particularly ambitious
CCC project. MILWAUKEE COUNTY HISTORICAL SOCIETY

congenial place to live. Given the program's impact on the area, it seems appropriate that the last remaining CCC camp building in Milwaukee County—a humble service garage—was located in Whitnall Park, just south of the Boerner Botanical Gardens parking lot.

As the CCC began to wind down in the spring of 1940, county officials calculated that the twelve hundred young men they had put to work were directly responsible for park improvements worth $2,347,800—nearly $35 million in current dollars. The Corps had clearly been good for the county, but it did just as much for its volunteers. The Park Commission noted in 1936 that many CCC workers had become "so proficient in construction work that with the termination of their enlistment period, contractors were glad to employ them."

Contractors may have come calling, but Uncle Sam was not far behind. When the United States entered World War II in 1941, thousands of young recruits benefited enormously from the discipline and maturity they had developed in CCC camps.

The role of the Corps in fighting the Depression is self-evident, but it was neither the only nor the largest of the New Deal's work programs. From the Works Progress Administration (WPA) to the National Youth Administration (NYA), federal authorities concocted an alphabet soup that spelled R-E-L-I-E-F. The various programs were a creative response to a catastrophic downturn in the economy, and they channeled the energy of the unemployed toward projects that were popular, constructive, and impressively permanent. It's a safe bet that most of us pass New Deal landmarks every day without having a clue about their origin.

No one would wish a return to the conditions that made the CCC and its counterparts necessary, but America does face two crises that seem unrelated at first. A long period of economic upheaval, including a drastic decline in entry-level

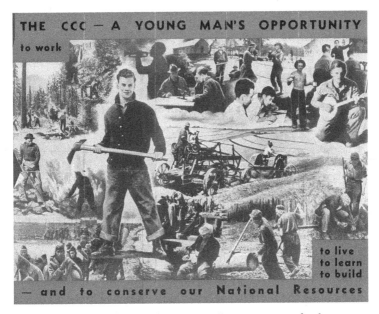

A CCC brochure promised adventure as well as opportunity for the young men of America. WHI IMAGE ID 5762

factory jobs, has created stubborn unemployment, particularly in the nation's low-income communities. At the same time, our infrastructure—roads, bridges, parks, public buildings—shows unmistakable signs of decay. Might the first problem be used to solve the second? Might the army of the unemployed be enlisted to shore up our infrastructure? That approach, curiously missing from the Biden administration's otherwise ambitious plan, worked in the 1930s, for both the nation and legions of Nick Zielinskis, and there's no reason it can't succeed again. Good ideas are always in season. As the CCC so amply demonstrated, a belief in the power of work can move mountains.

A Pioneering Approach to Poverty

Elizabeth Kander's Settlement Served "the Ghetto"

The neighborhood, such as it was, has been urban-renewed out of existence. You'd be hard-pressed to find, in the scrambled landscape north of Fiserv Forum, any evidence of an earlier community. Appearances notwithstanding, this was once among the most densely settled sections of Milwaukee—and one of the poorest. It was also the home of a pioneering social service agency that became a local legend. At a time when poverty threatens the fabric of too many neighborhoods, it's worth looking back to an era when reformers were sure they had answers for some of society's most pressing problems.

The neighborhood's focal point was an open-air market at Fifth and Vliet Streets. Farmers from rural Milwaukee County and beyond gathered there to sell the products of their fields, particularly hay for hungry urban horses. That led to its designation as "the haymarket," and Haymarket eventually became the name for the entire neighborhood extending from Third to Eighth Streets between Juneau Avenue and Walnut Street. The community's bookends were today's Hillside Terrace housing project on the west and the former Schlitz brewery on the east.

There were no planners on duty when the Haymarket neighborhood developed. It looked as if someone had filled a dice cup with houses, factories, saloons, stores, breweries, and grain elevators, shaken it vigorously, and then spilled the contents across the ground. In those pre-zoning days, churches, foundries, meat markets, and houses might well have been next-door neighbors, and frequently were.

The first residents of this urban hodgepodge were nearly all Germans, a group that had been settling on Milwaukee's North Side since the 1830s. They were replaced in the late 1800s by Jewish immigrants fleeing intolerable living conditions in eastern Europe. The newcomers quickly transformed the Haymarket neighborhood, swelling its population to nearly five thousand and sprinkling its residential blocks with kosher butcher shops, peddler's stores, and nearly a dozen synagogues, all of them Orthodox.

Some refugees who had known even bleaker surroundings in Europe found their new neighborhood luxurious by comparison, but Milwaukeeans of longer standing felt differently. The Haymarket was frequently referred to as "the Ghetto," Milwaukee's worst specimen of blight, poverty, and public health hazards. "In the Ghetto," reported a city official, "in one building live seventy-one people, representing seventeen families. The toilets in the yard freeze in winter and are clogged in summer. The overcrowding here is fearful and the filth defies description."

A hardy handful of Milwaukee-born Jews, most of them women, decided to do something about the Haymarket's squalor. Their leader was Elizabeth Black Kander, a formidable figure who founded a remarkable institution. Lizzie Kander was firmly entrenched in the city's German-Jewish aristocracy, a group that had arrived early and grown with the city, but she never let her own privileged status blind her to harsher realities.

Kander had made the neighborhood's acquaintance as a volunteer with the Ladies' Relief Sewing Society, whose members provided warm clothing for the children of the Haymarket. She found herself spellbound by "the unwritten living Drama that is being daily enacted in the Ghetto, or Jewish Quarter of our own

(*Left*) Elizabeth Kander outgrew her privileged background to become a pioneering social worker. (*Below*) The Settlement offered something for everyone in Milwaukee's Jewish immigrant quarter. BOTH PHOTOS: JEWISH MUSEUM MILWAUKEE

Very Truly Yours
Mrs. Simon Kander

City," seeing in its residents a cast of characters worthy of a Dickens novel or a Shakespeare play. Kander urged other women "to enter its unique atmosphere, ramble through its dirty alleys, climb its rickety stairs, descend to its dark, damp basements." Her paternalism, or perhaps maternalism, was showing, but Lizzie would eventually outgrow it.

The first fruit of the ladies' "friendly visiting" was the Keep Clean Mission. Founded in 1895 at Temple B'ne Jeshurun, a Reform synagogue on Tenth and Kilbourn, the Mission hosted the neighborhood's children once a week for games, songs, arts and crafts, sewing and cooking classes, and lessons in what Kander called "the Gospel of order and cleanliness."

Gaining courage as they gained experience, Kander and her intrepid society women left the safe confines of the synagogue in 1900 and took over a spacious old home on Fifth Street south of Galena—the very heart of the Haymarket. Known simply as the

Settlement, their new agency offered something for everyone in the neighborhood. The Settlement was busy from 9:00 a.m. to 11:00 p.m. nearly every day of the week, serving thousands of local residents with manual training and sewing classes, a public library branch, debating societies, cooking classes, social clubs, a penny savings bank, a night school, a reading room filled with Yiddish newspapers, and a variety of literary and dramatic entertainments.

Perhaps the most novel addition to the program came in 1904, when the Settlement moved to a larger home just down the block. Its nearest neighbor was the Jung Brewery, whose owners kindly piped hot water from their bottle-sterilizing machines to a battery of showers and baths in the Settlement next door. In a neighborhood where indoor plumbing was a rarity, this public bathhouse was an instant success, drawing 23,582 patrons in 1906 alone.

As the Settlement's programs grew, so did its financial needs. In a stroke of marketing genius, Kander decided to bind the best recipes from her cooking classes into a single book, featuring precise measurements and easy-to-follow instructions. Published in 1901, *The Settlement Cookbook* became as much a fixture in America's kitchens as flour and lard, selling well over a million copies in its first fifty years and generating vital revenue for Milwaukee's Jewish charities.

The point of the Settlement's programs, including the cooking classes, was what Kander called "preventive philanthropy." Her goal was "to help, by example and precept, to improve the home conditions of the neighboring community." The Settlement, in Kander's view, was the beating heart of the entire neighborhood—"not a big, cumbersome, cold institution, but a mother house, a community home, where people come with their joys and sorrows." But Kander was hardly a conventional do-gooder. Showing great capacity for growth, she evolved from a society matron who wanted to "uplift the downtrodden" to a social activist who took a systemic view of the problems she encountered. "We do not claim to uplift people," she wrote, "neither do we seek to reform them. All we ask is justice toward every one." Decades after her death in 1940, it's easy to imagine Kander walking a picket line or attending a Black Lives Matter rally.

Since outgrowing its home on Fifth Street, the Settlement has had a number of incarnations in a variety of locations, each version somewhat different from the last. Its successors were the Abraham Lincoln House on Vine Street, which opened in 1911; the Jewish Center on Milwaukee Street (1931); and the Jewish Community Center on Prospect Avenue (1955). The founding idea lives on, however modified, at the sprawling Jewish Community Campus in Whitefish Bay.

The neighborhood where the community idea was born has changed almost beyond recognition. The Settlement is long gone, as are nearly all of the adjacent buildings, but there is surprising continuity as well. The Hillside Terrace housing project, which covers the western portion of the former Haymarket area, is much less densely populated than the old neighborhood, but its residents, nearly all of them Black, face similar challenges.

On Sixth Street, barely a block from the original Settlement, you will find the Hillside Family Resource Center, a multiprogram facility that includes a Boys and Girls Club, a Milwaukee Area Technical College satellite, a health clinic, an employment program, and a day care center. The resource center's resemblance to the Settlement is by no means intentional, but it's impossible to miss. Both institutions were founded not to reform but to empower, providing impoverished Milwaukeeans with the tools they need to move from the margins of society to the mainstream. It's been more than a century since she tackled similar problems in the same neighborhood, but Lizzie Kander would undoubtedly approve.

Turning on the "Lighted Schoolhouse"

Milwaukee Recreation Division Was America's Pioneer

When things work, we tend to take them for granted, whether they're car engines or search engines. When things work in the public sector, we tend, these days, to be surprised. When they work in the Milwaukee Public Schools, we're incredulous. MPS has been the target of so much criticism in recent years that words like "failing" and "troubled" seem to attach themselves to the system like barnacles to a fishing tug.

The problems are real, but, as the father of three MPS graduates and the spouse of a longtime MPS employee, I can tell you that there are more success stories in the system than you could begin to imagine. Most of those stories are in the classroom, but one of the most conspicuous covers an entire division: Recreation and Community Services.

Better known as Milwaukee Recreation, or simply MKE REC, the division has been enriching the lives of local citizens for more than a century. City-dwellers will be familiar with its ubiquitous program guide, a newsprint marvel that shows up at our doors every semester, crammed with activities that are reasonably priced and broadly appealing.

Like many lifelong city residents, I've been involved in one Milwaukee Recreation program or another for most of my life. When I was six or seven, my parents enrolled me in a nature day camp at US Grant School, not far from our South Side home. We took the yellow bus to a faraway park for a nature hike whose highlight, for me, was being introduced to a wild plant whose leaves smelled like licorice. Years later, I came to recognize the park as Lake and the plant as sweet cicely.

As a full-grown Milwaukeean, I played softball in city leagues well into my fifties, and I logged a few years in the thirty-plus basketball program at the Beulah Brinton Center. In more recent years, my wife and I have developed a gliding acquaintance with the waltz, the rumba, and the foxtrot through ballroom dancing classes at Riverside High School.

Like so many other community assets, Milwaukee Recreation began as a Socialist initiative. In 1910, the city's Socialists rode a wave of reform sentiment into the mayor's office and claimed a Common Council majority as well. Led by Mayor Emil Seidel, the party faithful were firm believers in "scientific government," and they worked hard to make it a reality. Seidel's administration commissioned what would become a small library of studies that addressed municipal problems, from garbage collection to public health.

One team tackled recreation specifically, asking "what the children and young people of Milwaukee were actually doing for recreation" and then examining "the facilities under the control of the Board of School Directors and their adaptability for wider use for recreation purposes outside of school hours." The study's authors concluded that Milwaukee had plenty of for-profit recreational outlets, including ninety-one bowling alleys and twenty-four pool halls, but that the city's young people were spending far too much time in the streets, where their main activity was "doing nothing."

Here was an obvious problem, and the solution was close at hand. Milwaukee already had a large inventory of public school buildings. Why not turn them into social centers when classes were over? The concept of the "lighted schoolhouse" was born, and Milwaukee was its national pioneer. In 1911, the Wisconsin legislature passed enabling legislation that made MPS the first public school system in America to assume responsibility for public recreation. The Extension Department, as it was called, opened two demonstration centers in 1912, one on the North Side and one on the South. They proved so popular that six more were added in the next two years.

Proceeding by trial and error, MPS recreation specialists developed what became a standardized menu of activities for young people in the social centers. Organized play was the entrée, with trained leaders directing a wide array of games and athletic contests. Interest groups were organized around drama, dancing, debate, music (including mandolin clubs), nature study, and journalism. Teenagers could learn dressmaking, shoe repair, cooking, and mechanical drawing. Playgrounds were flooded for ice-skating in winter, and schools with pools offered swimming lessons year-round. Neighborhood residents without indoor plumbing (and that included most of them) took full advantage of the "shower baths" at their nearest social center.

The focus soon broadened to include adults. Milwaukee was still a city of immigrants when the schoolhouse lights went on, and "Americanization classes," introduced in 1913, attracted thousands of newcomers. After a long day of work, aspiring citizens sat at the same desks their children had used only hours before.

Some of the social center protocols seem oddly antique by modern standards. Every center had to have its own yell and song. No male spectators were allowed at girls' athletic contests. Ladies were required to remove their hats at all entertainments, and any boy with short trousers was barred from the ten-cent dance socials "no matter what his age."

Well-organized, closely supervised, and intensely democratic, the social centers developed a huge following. The system required significant outlays for staff, equipment, and supplies,

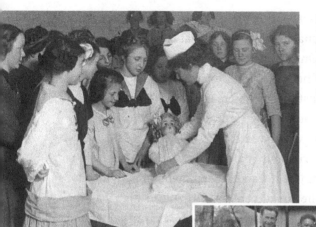

(*Left*) A group of "Little Mothers" learned the fundamentals of baby care at the Seifert School social center in 1912–1913.

(*Right*) Neighborhood boys gathered at a North Side social center, circa 1920s. BOTH PHOTOS: MILWAUKEE RECREATION

but voters approved the necessary tax increases in referendum after referendum. Our ancestors knew that you get what you pay for, and you have to pay for what you get.

The MPS recreation program was an early success, but it shifted into high gear when Dorothy Enderis took the wheel. One of the division's first employees, she became its director in 1920 and stayed until her retirement in 1948. Like her fellow reformers in City Hall, Enderis approached her task with missionary zeal. Recreation, in her view, was far more than fun and games. "During working hours, we make a living," she said. "During leisure hours, we make a life." It was her settled intention to make life richer for every one of her fellow citizens.

Dorothy Enderis was a pure Milwaukee product, equally comfortable in German and English, and she had political skills to spare. Working with officials on all levels of government, she increased the number of social centers from eleven to forty during her long tenure and the number of staffed playgrounds from twenty to seventy-two. Chess tournaments, ethnic festivals, movie nights, theatrical troupes, and community orchestras all flourished on her watch. When Enderis died in 1952, her ashes were spread at Hawthorn Glen, an abandoned quarry that is still Milwaukee Recreation's in-town nature center. The pioneer's name lives on in a UW–Milwaukee classroom building and an MPS playfield.

Dorothy Enderis ran the Milwaukee Recreation program for nearly thirty years with a simple premise: "During leisure hours, we make a life." MILWAUKEE RECREATION

Dorothy Enderis left a permanent imprint on the division, and it continued to evolve under her successors. Golden Age Clubs were introduced in 1949 (my grandmother was a faithful member), programs for children with disabilities were first offered in 1961, and homework help was added to the mix in 1998. Recent programs include old standbys—Sheepshead Club, Coupon Boot Camp, Ballroom Survival—but they also reflect current community interests, from hair braiding to salsa dancing to African drumming.

There is, in fact, something for everyone, whether you want to try cross-country skiing, learn to paint, explore conversational Spanish, get a coaching or CPR certificate, "strum your way to fun" on the guitar, master the basics of Facebook, experiment with Chinese cooking, or participate in any number of athletic activities. If you can't find something in the catalog that piques your interest, you might want to check your pulse to make sure you still have a heartbeat.

Even Dorothy Enderis would be impressed. The program she pioneered has evolved in directions she couldn't have predicted, but Milwaukee Recreation remains a vital component of our common wealth. More than a century after they first flickered on, the schoolhouse lights are still burning bright.

A Healing Street

Regional Medical Care Began on North Fourth

Medicine wasn't always like this. If you visit the Milwaukee Regional Medical Center today, you'll find yourself in a virtual city, with six major institutions employing fifteen thousand people who serve a million patients and clients every year. Although it's technically in Wauwatosa, the Medical Center has its own street system, its own security force, and a skyline that's visible for miles.

On a recent drive through that rather overwhelming complex—known as the County Institutions in earlier days—I marveled at how much it had changed since the 1970s, when I was playing softball on a local diamond called "the pig farm" in the shadow of some decrepit old buildings. I wondered at the scale of the center, and I also began to wonder where our ancestors had gone for medical care. Adjusting for population size, did Milwaukee ever have anything resembling the Regional Medical Center? Was there a comparable cluster of skills, technology, and bedpans anywhere in town?

There were two, as it turns out. The more recent concentration was in the area just west of downtown, where at least seven hospitals admitted patients as late as the 1970s. They included Deaconess (my birthplace), Children's, Lutheran, Mount Sinai, County Emergency, Family, and West Side.

There was an even earlier cluster of health-care institutions, and its location may be surprising. Milwaukee's first "regional medical center" was the two-block stretch of North Fourth Street between Walnut and Reservoir Streets. The area is part of Halyard Park today, a historically Black neighborhood that is in the throes of renewal.

In the late 1800s, the same blocks were covered with the homes of German immigrants, many of them Catholics who had limited access to hospital services. According to Earl Thayer, whose book *Seeking to Serve* is easily Milwaukee's best medical history, Archbishop John Martin Henni decided to remedy the situation. Henni persuaded a group of German-speaking nuns, today's Wheaton Franciscans, to step into the breach. In 1883, the sisters opened St. Joseph's Hospital on the southwest corner of Fourth and Reservoir. Four stories tall with a classic mansard roof, St. Joseph's had beds for fifty patients and coal stoves on every floor. The hospital's customary room rate, which included hearty German cooking, was five dollars a week.

St. Joseph's was so highly regarded that in 1898 a medical school moved in across the street. The Wisconsin College of Physicians and Surgeons, a for-profit venture, built a five-story brick landmark on the southeast corner of Fourth and Reservoir. Faculty members were soon working side by side with the Franciscans, and St. Joseph's became a genuine teaching hospital.

Five years later and two blocks south, another prominent institution took root. The neighborhood south of Walnut Street was filled with eastern European Jews who had fled both persecution and poverty in their homelands. In 1903, Mount Sinai Hospital opened to serve that community and, not incidentally, to provide a professional home for Jewish physicians who were not welcome to practice in Christian hospitals.

Unlike St. Joseph's, which was built from scratch, Mount Sinai took over an older building that still stands on the northeast

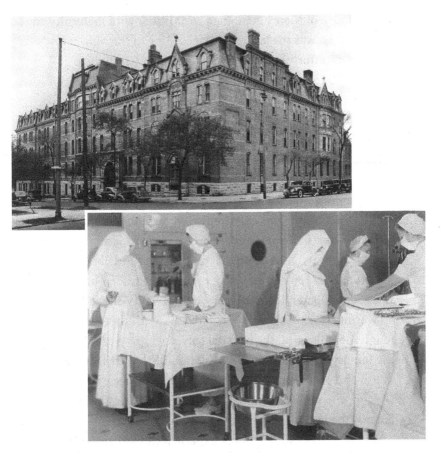

(*Top*) Franciscan nuns opened St. Joseph's Hospital on Fourth and Reservoir in 1883. MILWAUKEE PUBLIC LIBRARY (*Bottom*) Sisters in full habit assisted in St. Joseph's operating room. MILWAUKEE COUNTY HISTORICAL SOCIETY

corner of Fourth and Walnut. It is still used, in fact, by Aurora Health Care as a day center for frail and disabled adults. The landmark has a fascinating backstory of its own. Originally the "German branch" of the YMCA, it became the House of Mercy in 1894, a residence for "fallen women." That category included both unwed mothers and recovering prostitutes—a revealing glimpse at the sexual mores of the time.

The House of Mercy combined social work with maternity services, and it was the last refuge, according to the *Milwaukee Sentinel*, for "unfortunate girls" who "had no other place to go." Although admission was voluntary, to a degree, there were iron bars on the windows. "Evidences of reform," reported the *Sentinel*, "will be required before the inmates will be permitted to return to the world."

There was no shortage of prostitutes to reform. The House of Mercy's superintendent, Julia Kurtz, estimated that Milwaukee supported 121 brothels, including 45 on River Street alone, that housed a total of 400 girls and women, with another 1,600 working on the streets. Mrs. Kurtz resigned in 1899, declaring herself "unequal to the nervous strain that comes with the daily life."

Mount Sinai refitted the former refuge as a fifteen-bed hospital in 1903. Demand was so robust that a twenty-six-bed addition was necessary just six years later, and still there was not enough room. In 1914, the hospital solved its space problem, at least temporarily, by moving to a state-of-the-art facility at Twelfth and Kilbourn. Mount Sinai has been there ever since, although it is now the much-enlarged Aurora Sinai Medical Center—the last hospital in downtown Milwaukee.

Mount Sinai's old neighbors experienced changes of their own. In 1913, after years of financial shortfalls, the for-profit Wisconsin College of Physicians and Surgeons became the nonprofit Marquette University School of Medicine. Aspiring physicians continued to attend classes on Fourth Street until 1932, when Marquette erected a new building near the heart of its campus.

The Jesuit affiliation lasted until 1970, when Marquette's medical school became the nonsectarian Medical College of Wisconsin. The school moved west in 1978 to become a mainstay of the emerging Regional Medical Center. Its original building on Fourth Street has been converted to condos, but, amazingly, a reminder of its first purpose remains; painted letters identifying the Wisconsin College of Physicians and Surgeons are still faintly visible high atop the building's east facade.

Across the street, St. Joseph's Hospital experienced familiar growing pains. In 1930, the Franciscans moved St. Joseph's to a larger facility on Fifty-First and Chambers, where it became a regional anchor in the heart of the Sherman Park neighborhood. The sisters did not abandon their old community. The Fourth Street hospital became St. Joseph's Annex, a clinic that was largely outpatient and largely free.

That clinic was spun off, in turn, as St. Michael Hospital in 1941, still under Franciscan leadership. In 1957, St. Michael relocated to a modern 250-bed facility at 2400 West Villard Avenue. The hospital served patients in its "new" location for almost fifty years, but declining admissions and growing deficits forced the Franciscans to close it in 2006. St. Michael was leveled in 2011, although a clinic still operates on the site.

Meanwhile, back on Fourth Street, the hospital building that started it all became a nursing home when St. Michael departed (I recall Christmas-caroling there in high school) and was ultimately demolished. An upscale housing development now occupies the site, sure evidence of the Halyard Park neighborhood's continuing rebirth.

In brief summary, these are the institutions that came to life on North Fourth Street between Walnut and Reservoir: St. Joseph's Hospital, the Medical College of Wisconsin, Mount Sinai Hospital, and St. Michael Hospital. That's a remarkable concentration for a two-block stretch in any American city, and it has the added distinction of being entirely organic. Milwaukeeans of various backgrounds saw community needs and took steps to meet them. The result was a regional medical center that set a healthy precedent for the exponentially larger Regional Medical Center of today.

The Other Pandemic

Spanish Flu Presaged COVID-19

The parallels are striking. In early 2020, when the novel coronavirus began to make headlines in the US, historians looked back for precedents, and they quickly found one: the Spanish flu pandemic of 1918. In both cases, a submicroscopic menace brought the entire world to its knees, causing catastrophic economic damage, pervasive insecurity, and anguished questions about when it all would end.

The Spanish flu, which had nothing in particular to do with Spain, surfaced in Europe during the waning months of World War I and spread like wildfire to other continents. It probably came to the United States in the respiratory tracts of returning soldiers. What began as a bad cold frequently led to complete debility. Some victims died within hours, and even those who had apparently recovered often came down with a pneumonia that proved fatal. By the time this global scourge had run its course, more than twenty million people were dead, including hundreds of Milwaukeeans.

The city's reputation as a good "leave town" for those in the armed forces may have sparked the local outbreak. Like COVID-19, the 1918 influenza spread most rapidly wherever people were concentrated, and military installations were prime sites. In late September, two sailors from the Great Lakes Naval Training Station in Illinois visited Milwaukee. Before their leaves were over, both had sought treatment for what turned out to be the flu.

More than thirty thousand cases were reported in the city over the next three months. One cough in a crowded streetcar was enough to infect scores of people, and they spread the virus to others in a virulent chain reaction.

Milwaukee, fortunately, had an exemplary public health program already in place. Since the mid-1800s, the city had been struggling with health problems that ranged from cholera flare-ups to contaminated water, but efforts to address them had generally been uncoordinated and inconsistent. It was not until

PREVENT INFLUENZA!

"Prevention is better than cure, but it does not get its name in the paper so often."
Poor Richard Jr.'s Almanack

With the present shortage of doctors and trained nurses, it behooves the citizens of Milwaukee to unite in the fight to prevent the spread of Influenza.

Consider your near and dear ones and elect yourself as a special health officer to see that the dangerous Influenza germs do not menace your home and the homes of your neighbors.

With cool head and common health-sense observe the simple rules of health and fight this danger to a finish.

Adopt the Following Precautionary Measures! Help Wage the War Against the Flu!

Walk to work if possible. Avoid persons who cough or sneeze.
Should you cough or sneeze, cover nose and mouth with a handkerchief.
Wash your hands before eating. Get plenty of fresh air, night and day.
Do not use common towel—it spreads disease.
Keep out of crowded places. Eat good, plain food, plenty of it.
Sleep is necessary to well-being—avoid over-exertion.
Keep away from houses where there are influenza cases.
If sick, no matter how slightly, see a physician.
If you have had influenza, stay in bed until your doctor says you can safely get up.
Worry is Harmful—Keep your mind at ease.

GEORGE C. RUHLAND, M. D.
Commissioner of Health, Milwaukee, Wis.

The Milwaukee Health Department mounted an aggressive educational campaign to keep the 1918 flu in check. The final directive may have been the most difficult to follow: "Keep your mind at ease." *MILWAUKEE SENTINEL,* DEC. 8, 1918

the Socialists swept into office in 1910 that the city's public health efforts acquired focus and direction. Working with reform-minded citizens of all backgrounds, including devout capitalists, Mayor Emil Seidel's team gave public health such a high priority that it transcended politics. City-run hospitals treated the sick, but the heart of the program was education and prevention.

Milwaukee's health commissioner when the flu arrived was Dr. George Ruhland. Trustworthy, diplomatic, and passionately devoted to public health, Ruhland was the city's own Dr. Anthony Fauci, vintage 1918. He went into action immediately. Ruhland and his staff set up a reporting network among the

city's physicians, established a broad-based advisory committee, and created what Ruhland called "an intensive publicity
campaign unparalleled in the history of the city."

There was no cure for the influenza virus; the only "treat-
ments" were bed rest for the patient and isolation from the rest
of the population. Although they never used the phrase "social
distancing," Ruhland and his team preached the gospel of prevention, launching a barrage of posters, pamphlets, streetcar
placards, newspaper ads, and "four-minute" talks. One poster
featured a "Catechism of Caution" that urged citizens to wear
masks, wash their hands, keep away from crowds, avoid people
who sneezed, and, as if it were remotely possible, "Keep your
mind at ease."

The disease spread anyway. On October 11, 1918, Ruhland
was forced to close most of the city's gathering places "until further notice." The list included "theaters, movies, public dances,
churches and indoor amusements and entertainments." Schools
were added a day later, and the closed-door policy on saloons
was clarified. The ban, ruled Ruhland, "will not prevent a person
from entering the saloon, purchasing a drink and leaving the
place." As long as you didn't warm a barstool, in other words,
you could still imbibe. This was, after all, Milwaukee.

Ruhland's order was the medical equivalent of martial law.
For weeks, there were no parties, no parades, no political rallies,
no bowling leagues, no school, no sports, and no religious services. Churches were open only for weddings and funerals, and
attendance then was limited to "near relatives." Factories and
offices were exempt, but gauze masks became standard apparel
in many workplaces. In the meantime, flu cases multiplied so
fast that the Milwaukee Auditorium (today's Miller High Life
Theatre) was pressed into service as an emergency hospital.

Some people grumbled about the restrictions, of course, but
the overwhelming response was complete cooperation. The

"Because Air Infection Is Probably the Most Common Method of Spreading Influenza, the Use of Masks Is Based Upon Rational Principles."

Mask mandates were imposed at the height of the pandemic. *MILWAUKEE SENTINEL*, DEC. 15, 1918

public's faith in its government was apparently rewarded on November 4. After twenty-three days of virtual lockdown, the epidemic had slowed enough to allow the Health Department to lift its ban on public gatherings.

The 1918 influenza was not about to depart that easily. One week after the ban was lifted, the armistice ending World War I was signed. Milwaukee's downtown was thronged with revelers, creating what a later generation would recognize as a super-spreader event. With a boost from Armistice Day crowds, influenza cases spiked again in the weeks that followed, prompting Ruhland to reinstate his ban on December 11.

There were a few modifications. Churches and theaters were allowed to operate at half-capacity, with worshipers and patrons seated in every other row. Archbishop Sebastian Messmer banned midnight Masses on Christmas Eve, prohibited children under fifteen from attending services, and instructed his priests to dispense with their regular sermons. On the other hand, Milwaukee's Catholics were allowed to eat meat on Friday, presumably to keep up their strength.

On December 25, finally, just in time for Christmas, the

infection rate had fallen far enough for Dr. Ruhland to lift the ban permanently. The news was welcome, but it came too late to save the holiday. "Christmas Day in Milwaukee Quiet," read the *Milwaukee Sentinel* headline on the morning after. New Year's Eve dances were held a week later as in previous years, with one new wrinkle: celebrants were required to wear six-layer gauze masks, which made them resemble, wrote the *Sentinel*, "a band of holdup men from the neck up."

The Spanish flu was a national catastrophe. Nearly five hundred thousand people died—more than four times the number of American military fatalities in World War I. But Milwaukee, relatively speaking, was an island of good health. Of the thirty thousand citizens who came down with the flu at its peak, fewer than five hundred died. The city's death rate during the worst weeks of the crisis (September 14 to December 21) was 0.6 per 1,000 people—tragic, certainly, but the lowest of any large city in America. The death rate in the second-healthiest city, Minneapolis, was more than three times higher. All those Germans and Scandinavians in the upper Midwest apparently found it easy to keep their distance.

Milwaukee's record was remarkable, and it demonstrated the wisdom of aggressive public health policies. In her book *The Healthiest City: Milwaukee and the Politics of Health Reform*, historian Judith Walzer Leavitt summarized the city's response: "In a very short time, the health commissioner mobilized an army of volunteers, coordinated the efforts of numerous community organizations, plastered the city with educational literature, isolated the sick in their homes or in city-aided hospitals, and assuaged the doubts of business people and politicians who feared personal loss from the emergency regulations."

There may be an object lesson in that response, one that applies across the decades. Although they were separated by more than a century, the 1918 influenza pandemic and its

Hospitalized for the Spanish flu before Christmas in 1918, the Knepfel sisters were not told that their parents had died of the same disease during their convalescence. Three-year-old Kate kept asking for her mother "'cause she knows when Santa Claus is coming to us." *MILWAUKEE SENTINEL*, DEC. 1, 1918

Unaware That Influenza Has Taken Their Parents, These Sick Tots Confidently Await Visit from Santa

COVID-19 counterpart are twins below the surface. Both were caused by highly contagious viruses that targeted their victims' respiratory systems, and both forced a radical reordering of daily life across the planet. With the possible exception of a visit from aliens, it's hard to imagine a more potent demonstration of our common humanity.

Shared misery, however, did not usher in a new era of brotherhood and sisterhood during the more recent outbreak. In 1918, the American people, conditioned by the need for national unity during World War I, generally accepted the restrictions on their normal activities. In sharp contrast, the COVID-19 pandemic was politicized. Highly partisan divisions emerged, splitting the American people into opposing camps: mask vs. no mask, lockdowns vs. liberty, science vs. opinion.

Despite abundant challenges on multiple fronts, science prevailed, giving us vaccines that greatly diminish the chances of hospitalization or death from the coronavirus—for those who take the shots. But the questions remain: How much suffering might have been avoided, and how many deaths prevented, if a nation beset by COVID-19 had followed the example set by Milwaukee in 1918?

The Missing Middle

American Politics Is Stuck at the Extremes

I didn't realize how bad it was until I went Up North. For several years, I'd sensed a deep change afoot in our country, a seismic shift in how we relate to each other and to our government, but that feeling crystallized during a solo camping trip just weeks before the 2020 election. The Trump signs in northern Wisconsin seemed as thick as the pine trees, a definite shock to someone on the left side of the political spectrum. Although I was visiting a region I've loved since adolescence, I felt like I was in enemy territory. I was frankly embarrassed by the small-mindedness of my reaction, which was something like, "What's wrong with these rednecks? How could they be so duped by that fake-baked carnival barker in the White House?" Then I wondered what they made of me, with the bike rack and the Milwaukee sticker on my Subaru Outback.

After taking more than one deep breath, I concluded that there was a singular tragedy in our current political situation. Without giving our conscious assent, we have all allowed ourselves to be reduced to cultural stereotypes. People on the other side, whichever that side happens to be, have become little more than stick figures. Conservatives bad, liberals good—or the polar opposite.

That oversimplification flies in the face of common sense, not to mention basic charity. Nobody is one-dimensional. I may

MILWAUKEE JOURNAL SENTINEL

be liberal, but I also go to church, cheer the Packers, drink plenty of beer, and own at least five Lyle Lovett albums. I don't doubt that there are people on the right who read Shakespeare, drink only French wine, and would gladly invite an immigrant neighbor over for dinner. During my days Up North, we were all washed by the same golden light in the forest, braced by the same brisk north wind.

So what happened to us? How did we lose our sense of shared humanity? The answer, I think, lies in what might be called the militarization of American politics. It's no longer about policy, really; it's about power—getting it, keeping it, and using it to inflict damage on your enemies, who were merely opponents in a friendlier time. Politics has become a zero-sum game with winners, losers, and nothing in between. Reformers Katherine Gehl and Michael Porter offer a telling assessment of what they call the "political industrial complex." The major parties, they argue, form a "duopoly" fueled by single-interest donors on either side of an ideological divide, and their hardened financial allegiances make both parties unresponsive to the broader public interest. The result is a state of constant partisan warfare that leads inevitably to governmental gridlock.

I generally vote Democratic, but my favored party is obviously part of the problem. The Affordable Care Act did, in fact, pass with barely a whisper of Republican support, and Nancy Pelosi can be as hard-headed as the most obdurate GOP leader. In recent years, however, Republicans have generally held sway. Although Democrats might be just as self-serving if given the chance, the GOP's tactics offer stark evidence of the prevailing problems. Following the 2010 census, Wisconsin Republicans completely redrew the state's legislative map, packing Democrats like sardines into some districts and giving their own candidates a statistical edge in most others. The results are not only skewed electoral results but a rise in extremism. When everyone runs in a politically safe district, no one in either party has any reason to compromise.

Just as troubling are Republican efforts, on both the state and national levels, to make voting more difficult. Despite clear evidence that voter fraud is rare to nonexistent in our country, Republicans in Wisconsin and elsewhere have made voter IDs mandatory, limited the number of polling places, curtailed voting hours, and fueled distrust of mail-in ballots, all in a poorly concealed effort to suppress Democratic turnout. Shouldn't our goal be to make it easier for every citizen to vote, rather than harder? Whenever one party retools the electoral machinery to its own advantage, democracy dies a little.

Even the judiciary is affected. Mitch McConnell, a senator elected only by the people of Kentucky, spent years blocking the judicial appointments of Barack Obama, a president elected by a majority of the American people. When Donald Trump became president, McConnell moved quickly to remake the federal judiciary, including the Supreme Court, in his own conservative image. With the election of Joe Biden as Trump's successor, the shoe shifted overnight to the other foot. There was a time when "judicial" meant "impartial." At our nation's peril, it has increasingly come to signify partisans in black robes.

And so it goes, with one party blithely stacking the deck while the other howls in impotent outrage. The result is either a flagrant abuse of power by one party or a well-oiled stalemate, with each side refusing to give the other an inch, or even the time of day. I find it remarkable that both the Trump and the Biden campaigns portrayed the 2020 election as a battle for America's soul. They pictured the country either descending into a socialist hell or becoming the Western world's first dictatorship.

As the parties move farther apart and America's middle ground shrinks to the vanishing point, we've become, to ourselves and to each other, primitive caricatures, the crudest cartoons. A new tribalism now rules the land: red vs. blue, left vs. right, butter side up vs. butter side down. Are there genuine policy differences behind the stereotypes? There are, and plenty of them, but they've been torched beyond recognition by the scorched-earth politics of the current electoral landscape.

The underlying dynamic, the magma beneath the volcano, is fear. One side fears runaway spending, oppressive taxation, and the death of individual liberty. The other fears runaway climate change, economic inequity, and the death of the common good. Isn't there some place, even one, where we can all tremble together? A single enemy we can agree to fight as a people united? A global pandemic couldn't do it. Will it take an alien invasion? A burning planet?

It's time to find our way out of the current morass. The most urgent task we face, and the hardest, is to depoliticize our politics and bring back the nation's middle. It's self-evident that neither side is going away, and it's equally obvious that neither is going to get everything it wants. Thinking otherwise, for left or right, is a totalitarian fantasy.

Both parties need to start acting as if they understand that
stark reality, and there are ways we can help them. The Institute
for Political Innovation, founded by reformers Gehl and Porter,
advocates top-four nonpartisan primaries and ranked-choice
voting in general elections. Another group called No Labels sug-
gests something smaller but simpler: promoting bipartisanship
by requiring every House speaker to win the post with at least
60 percent of the chamber's votes. And gerrymandering must
end. The legislature has the final say in Wisconsin, but the foxes
shouldn't be allowed to choose their own hens. The job properly
belongs to citizens who can put party aside and draw our legislative maps with a focus on competitive balance and geographic
common sense.

America may have changed presidents in the 2020 election, but the basic problems remain. I, for one, am sick to death
of discord, demonizing, and demagoguery. It's high time to try
something new. If we are to move beyond the manifest ugliness
of current American politics, we all need to give up the feel-
good self-righteousness of our entrenched positions. The only
way forward is to embrace the creative discomfort of compromise. If our republic is to have a sustainable future, we need to
move, together, toward a new American middle.

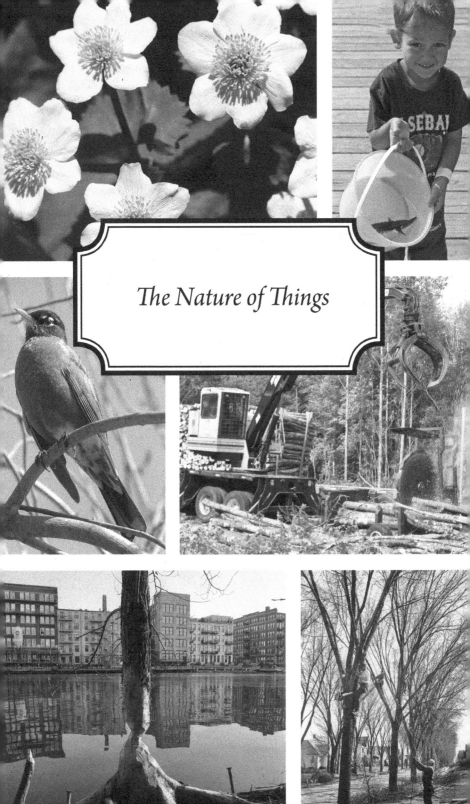

The Nature of Things

Saner Outside

Spring in the Time of Coronavirus

I n an unnatural time, I sought the solace of nature. While millions sheltered indoors, I found a different kind of shelter outdoors. As we kept our distance from each other, I established closer contact with an older order. I was not the only one. When COVID-19 reached America's shores in the early months of 2020, so many people shared my instinct that Wisconsin had to shut down its most popular parks and Milwaukee was forced to close its beaches.

There was still plenty of nature to go around. My favorite spot was Seminary Woods, a lovely remnant of native Wisconsin near my home in Bay View. I walked over almost every day that first spring, sometimes more than once, witnessing the progress of the season more closely than I ever had before. Runners and dog walkers used the same woods, but social distancing was never a problem; I generally saw more birds than people. Safer at Home? Absolutely, but also Saner Outside.

The coronavirus shutdown was like a medically induced coma. The idea was to keep us in suspended animation until the worst of the danger had passed. The natural world, as always, went on without us, keeping a rhythm that predates our arrival by billions of years. While we spent our days in lockdown, nearly every other species in our hemisphere was utterly mobile and, with the return of spring, constantly in motion.

Whatever misfortunes befall its
human occupants, the earth comes
surging back to life each spring.
(A) Trout lily. JOHN GURDA
(B) Trillium. JOHN GURDA
(C) Marsh marigold. JOHN GURDA
(D) Red-breasted nuthatch. DAVE
MENKE, USFWS ON PIXNIO
(E) Baltimore oriole. DANIELLE
KORNITZ
(F) Wood duck. DANIELLE KORNITZ

A

B

C

D

E

F

By the time northern Italy's miseries began to make the news in 2020, spring was definitely on its way to my neighborhood woods, as tentative but unstoppable as a child's first steps. Wave after wave of green started to roll across the forest floor, tumbling together but maintaining a semblance of order. Wild leek, the pungent perennial prized by cooks, came up at the same time as paper-white bloodroot, wrapped in the cloak of its solitary leaf. Both were soon joined by the lance-shaped leaves of trout lily and the peppermint-striped flowers of spring beauty. The mottled fronds of waterleaf came next, followed by mayapples unfurling their glossy umbrellas and the extravagant white of the first trilliums. Just as crocuses bloom before daffodils and daffodils appear before tulips in our home gardens, forest wildflowers have a sequence of their own. All have evolved the good sense to leaf out, blossom, and set seed before the summer canopy puts them in the dark for good.

As plants sprouted and insects hatched, birds entered the procession in their own prescribed order. Slate-colored juncos, last to leave and first to return, joined the hardy year-rounders like chickadees and cardinals. Soon after, there was an explosion of kinglets, golden- and ruby-crowned balls of feathers so small they would barely fill a child's hand. Then the circus came to town: warblers flying, flitting, rolling, and tumbling through the treetops like a rollicking chorus of clowns. They arrived in waves, first the yellow rumps (known affectionately in birding circles as "butter butts"), then the palms, and finally all of them, diminutive daubs of feathered paint with names as colorful as their plumage: chestnut-sided, bay-breasted, yellow-throated, golden-winged, black-throated green. One day, I saw five species in a single tree in Seminary Woods, lighting it up like tiny Christmas ornaments.

Soon the flood of birds became general. Every day brought new arrivals, most only passing through. With my Sibley guide in one hand and binoculars in the other, I identified, in a single morning, a fair sample of Midwestern migrants: hermit thrush, goldfinch, house finch, song sparrow, chipping sparrow, bluebird, brown creeper, white-breasted nuthatch, cowbird, yellow-bellied sapsucker, phoebe, towhee, kingfisher, and winter wren. Some birds escaped my amateur stabs at classification. There's a whole category, particularly numerous in my case, known as LBJs—little brown jobs.

As the players assembled, the action began.

A pair of yellow-bellied sapsuckers climbed up and down an old maple tree like linemen on a utility pole, sipping sap from holes they'd tapped. A few days later, a cardinal and a warbler were sampling the same thin nectar.

A bluebird perched precariously on a thistle stalk in an old soccer field going rapidly back to nature. *If he knew how blue his wings were,* I thought, *that bird would be insufferable.*

One day, I surprised a Cooper's hawk—barred chest, gray wings, banded tail—hunched over the mangled remains of what might have been a chipmunk. He regarded me with fierce attention—a hawk's sole expression—and lifted gracefully into a nearby tree.

In a small wetland near the seminary's main building, a pair of wood ducks, those painted ladies of the waterfowl set, quacked and craned their necks in the direction of the shore. Out onto the marsh grass waddled a fat raccoon. Only when he retreated were the birds quiet again. Another time, it was a sleek black housecat that set off the alarm. I could only hope that its owner had declawed the pampered predator.

On the lakefront below the seminary, male red-breasted mergansers were putting on their courtship display. Stylish birds, with stickpin beaks and natty white collars, they stretched their necks and dipped sharply toward the females of their flock again and again in the avian equivalent of a deep bow.

A red fox trotted along the bank of a small stream across from my sitting spot one afternoon. It paused to nibble some tufts of grass and then headed in my direction, crossing the narrow footbridge right in front of me. It froze for a second and then made a half-hearted run at a kinglet hopping through the grass. When the bird flew off, the fox was no more than ten yards from me. It looked up, noticed me with instant distrust, and then bounded into the underbrush on the softest paws.

All of these creatures are as unique as the characters in any human drama. The more you look, the more you see, and with repeated visits I began to notice their patterns. The brown creeper, a long-tailed bug-eater, starts at the base of a tree in search of food, hops all the way up the trunk, and then flies down to start over at the base of the next tree. Nuthatches, by contrast, apparently immune to vertigo, climb headfirst *down* a tree. Some birds, robins and blackbirds among them, find social distancing impossible, while flycatchers dine alone.

There are also fleeting moments of unexpected beauty: a crow freefalling from its perch and flaring its wings just in time to take flight, four deer seeming almost weightless as they bound across the abandoned soccer field, and high overhead the resonant call of a sandhill crane on its way to some distant northern wetland.

Seminary Woods is a special place, but it's hardly unique. This remnant of Milwaukee's past is a decidedly urban oasis, only four miles from downtown, and I'm confident that similar scenes play out every year in scores of parks, cemeteries, woodlots, and golf courses across the region. A trip to any woods will demonstrate that you can walk alone and never be without company.

As the pandemic ground on, laying waste to lives and livelihoods, billions of people around the world wondered when the siege would lift. It's a question that only we were asking. While our hearts beat faster with fear and anxiety, the rhythm of our planet remained as steady as ever. The earth continues to carry us all—every opening flower, hatching insect, lovestruck animal, and worried human being—around the sun with miraculous precision, and each spring it turns toward our only source of warmth and light. All around us, if we would only look, is a commodious world where we find welcome and our woes find their limit.

Robin Rudebreast

A Dyspeptic Take on Wisconsin's Official Bird

The idiot bird was at it again this morning. For the third spring in a row, a robin has made its nest in a cedar tree not ten feet from my bedroom window. Its singing typically begins at four o'clock in the morning, before the faintest trace of first light, but *singing* is the grossest euphemism for the tuneless iterations rising from this bird's throat. It's more a vagrant, meandering mumble that finds one annoying pitch and stays there without pause or variation for what seems like hours. At this morning's thousandth repetition, when it became clear that sleep would not return, I wanted to shout, "Resolve, already!" but the robin continued its drunken muttering.

These early morning concerts have only confirmed my long-standing dislike for this most noisome of American birds. The scientific name says it all: *Turdus migratorius*—the traveling, well, you know. Not that they travel far. Adaptable beyond our understanding, robins have made themselves at home from Texas to the tundra. They can hatch three broods in a single season, enabling them to spread like measles, and they're still chirping away at twenty below when their smarter cousins have long since relocated to Florida.

Other songbirds get whacked by the propellers of wind turbines or break their necks on picture windows, but not our darling. The robin's hardiness and general ubiquity have made it the

official bird of Wisconsin and
two other states, Connecticut
and Michigan; only the cardinal and the meadowlark have
more stripes on their wings. In
all but the coldest months, it's
hard *not* to see robins. When
birders scan a wood's edge and
notice a flash of color in their
binoculars, hoping for a towhee, perhaps, or maybe an oriole, it's usually just old *Turdus*
again.

The wonder is that these
feathered commoners are
native Americans. European
starlings spread inland from
Central Park, and house sparrows began as lowly weaver

The robin isn't every Wisconsinite's favorite bird. MILWAUKEE JOURNAL SENTINEL

finches in England, but those avian interlopers are hardly less
common than our own omnipresent robins. They were here
when the Potawatomi were the dominant tribe in Milwaukee
and the Ojibwe ruled northern Wisconsin, but they have multiplied mightily since the arrival of the Europeans. They seem to
like our cities especially, for reasons that may mirror our own
motley provenance.

And they come from such a nice family! The *Turdidae* have
some real aristocrats in their tree, beginning with the bluebird—that blithe symbol of rural America—and ascending to
the wood thrush. There is no more melodious melody in all of
birddom than the song of the wood thrush: clear, resounding,
flutelike, and repeated at stately intervals, so unlike the slop that
issues from its Cockney cousin's beak. And the wood thrush

needs a territory of four hundred acres to breed successfully, while the feckless robin's eggs end up splattered on every sidewalk in North America.

The bird has, I'll grant, a few virtues, starting with its eerily acute vision. When a robin pauses in its silly kangaroo hopping on the lawn to cock its head and then spear a worm crawling below the surface, well, grudging admiration is in order. And its egg, admittedly, is of a compelling hue: an ethereal blue found nowhere else in nature. But it's all downhill from there. Even the hatchlings have rheumy eyes that make them look old before they leave the nest, and who could ignore this bird's audial incoherence, its habit of slinging torrents of notes into the air without regard for meter or melody?

It's bad form, I know, to let a mere bird disturb your equilibrium, but I enjoy getting away from the deranged scat singer in my backyard on occasion. Last fall, I was hiking on a windless day in the woods of Upper Michigan, far enough from any road to make cougars, as well as bears, a concern. There was a sudden rustling in the dry underbrush and a flash of color. Startled, I turned to find that it was only *Turdus migratorius.* As the bird winged its way into the deeper woods, I could have sworn I heard it chuckling.

Epidemics in the Treetops

Emerald Ash Borer Picks Up Where Dutch Elm Beetle Left Off

Wisconsin's woods aren't the same these days. When buds unfurl and rivers of sap start to run with the return of warmer weather, a disturbing number of trees fail to rise from their winter torpor. Thousands of ashes, in particular, carry their bare bones into spring, killed by a tiny bug as deadly as it is pretty. The result is a chorus of chain saws that's particularly audible in southern Wisconsin.

The emerald ash borer, a jewel-like beetle native to Asia, began chomping its way toward the state in 2002, when it first turned up in the Detroit area, probably as a stowaway in packing crates from China. By 2008, when the state's first case was confirmed in Newburg, just north of Milwaukee, more than twenty million trees across the upper Midwest had died, their vascular systems choked by the tunneling larvae of this imported pest.

The scourge reached Milwaukee County in 2009, surfacing in Franklin, and by 2012 emerald ash borers were detected on Milwaukee's Northwest Side. "The whole city is at risk," warned David Sivyer, Milwaukee's forestry services manager. A careful survey determined that 17 percent of the city's urban forest was ash—a total of 587,000 trees, the vast majority of them on private property.

The ash borer's progress since 2012 has been horrendously swift. Within a decade, mortality in the Milwaukee area

Elm trees came down by the thousands at the peak of the Dutch elm beetle infestation in the 1960s. MILWAUKEE PUBLIC LIBRARY

A small pest with a huge appetite, the emerald ash borer has brought down millions of ash trees. DAVID CAPPAERT, BUGWOOD.ORG

approached its peak; virtually every mature tree that hadn't been injected with an insecticide was dead or dying.

With a foresight that our Socialist park planners would have applauded, the City of Milwaukee has been treating its 28,218 street ashes—the ones planted between sidewalk and curb—every year since 2009, injecting one third of them annually. With a much larger tree census—356,000 ashes on 15,000 acres of parkland—Milwaukee County limits its treatment efforts to high-use and high-visibility areas, particularly golf courses. Ash trees standing on private land—well over 500,000 of them—are subject to the whims of their owners. Whether in parks or backyards, the number of trees coming down in the Milwaukee area every year numbers in the thousands, and the destruction will continue indefinitely.

We've been here before. Similar epidemics have wreaked havoc on individual species, not once but twice. In 1904, New York City's chestnut trees began to die off in alarming numbers. The culprit was an earlier accidental import from Asia: a wind-borne fungus that affected only the chestnut. "America's perfect tree," novelist Richard Powers calls the species: majestically large and full, prized for its wood, its nuts, and its shade. When the spores of the Asian fungus blew inland, four billion trees were dead by 1940—nearly the entire population of the American chestnut.

Wisconsin was one state removed from the tree's native range; the only chestnuts here were isolated stands planted by nostalgic pioneers. The next invader hit us like a tidal wave. Dutch elm disease—despite its name, yet another Asian import—arrived in a load of logs shipped to an Ohio furniture manufacturer in 1930. Actually a fungus carried by the elm bark beetle, it spread radially from Ohio, traveling at the rate of a few miles a year unless unwitting humans carried it farther afield. Wisconsin's first case of Dutch elm disease was confirmed at 317 Highland Avenue in Beloit on July 6, 1956. Three weeks later, it was in Milwaukee County.

The blight's acronym—DED—is brutally appropriate. Mortality approached 100 percent wherever a beetle breached an elm's bark, and the tree's ubiquity accelerated its demise. The elm's elegant vase-shaped profile made it a perfect street tree. With branches spreading upward from curb to curb and meeting over the center of our roadways to form perfect arches, elms created cathedrals of green in countless American communities. They were virtually the only species the nation's urban foresters planted for decades. In 1956, elms accounted for 70 percent of Milwaukee's street trees.

When Dutch elm disease struck, it spread, block by block, through intertwined root systems as well as marauding beetles. As the scale of the potential damage became clear, Milwaukee shifted into military mode; newspapers chronicled every "battle" in the ongoing "war" against the "invader."

In Milwaukee and elsewhere, the favored weapons were "spraying and sanitation," i.e., DDT and chain saws. Both had their drawbacks. Transporting downed trees may actually have accelerated the spread of the disease, and DDT's pernicious side effects became increasingly hard to ignore. In 1957, Wisconsin game pathologists reported massive die-offs of robins, grackles, sparrows, and other songbirds in the vicinity of spraying activity. A 1959 study found that Shorewood had lost 82 percent of its robins. That was three years before Rachel

Carson's *Silent Spring* helped ignite the environmental movement. The spraying continued anyway. In 1966, a Milwaukee
County official responded to the chemical's critics. "I'm not saying we don't kill birds with DDT," Stanley Rynearson admitted,
but losing them, he opined, was preferable to "a million dollar
tree removal bill."

Even before DDT was banned nationwide in 1972, new tools
had been developed, including growth inhibitors, fungicide
injections, and helicopter spraying. None could halt, much less
reverse, the beetle's progress. The number of Milwaukee County
elm trees that met the chain saw soared from 11 in 1956 to 689 in
1960, 6,789 in 1965, and a historic peak of 19,618 in 1968, when the
disease was reported in "epidemic proportions."

The devastation had multiple impacts. As the urban forest
dwindled, less oxygen was produced, less water was retained,
and less shade was provided. Showcase streets like Prospect
Avenue, Highland Boulevard, and Lake Drive were suddenly as
naked as the rawest subdivision in any newly minted suburb.
Front yards and public squares lost stately centerpieces that had
been decades in the making, and property values dropped as
fast as the trees that supported them.

There was also the emotional trauma of seeing familiar
haunts denatured. The *Milwaukee Journal* of September 5, 1965,
described the catastrophic impact of Dutch elm disease on Wisconsin's countryside: "They rise like grim, dark skeletons along
our highways, souring the rolling beauty of a rural landscape.
They stand out, stark and ugly, in the fresh green of forest and
farm wood lot. Dead and dying elms are a blot on the fresh love-
liness of our state. Their number is increasing and spreading
relentlessly northward." Substitute "ashes" for "elms" in the passage, and the same description would apply today.

The progress of Dutch elm disease slowed as there were
fewer trees to infect, but the fungus is still among us. From a

total of 106,738 American elms on Milwaukee's streets in 1956, the number plunged to 482 in 2020. Replacement efforts began in the first years of the epidemic. One of the favored new species was—you guessed it—ash.

The sad saga of the chestnut, the elm, and the ash is, in the end, a tale as old as Columbus. Ever since Europeans crossed the Atlantic in 1492 and, seventy years later, traversed the Pacific as well, there has been an increasingly free exchange of plants, people, and pathogens across the continents. Potatoes, corn, tobacco, tomatoes, and rubber from the Americas transformed life in the Old World. Horses, wheat, cows, apples, chickens, and, tragically, enslaved people crossed in the opposite direction.

By 1800, writes Charles Mann, a leading authority on the Columbian Exchange, the world had become "a single ecological system." COVID-19 is only the most recent example of what can happen when the barriers are down. In North America's forests, species that had been thriving for millennia were ravaged practically overnight by diseases to which they had evolved no resistance, and the same was true on the other side of the ocean.

Nature, like the average dog, abhors a vacuum. As ash trees fall, the blank spots in our forests and on our streets will eventually fill in—not in my lifetime, but certainly in my children's. Wisconsin will once again leaf out in a uniform surge of green each spring—until the next invader comes.

Return of the Beaver

They're Redeveloping Downtown, One Tree at a Time

The beavers are back. For the first time in nearly two centuries, the buck-toothed rodents have been gnawing away at trees in the very heart of downtown Milwaukee. What better response than to cheer the return of these water-loving natives to their ancestral home?

I first noticed their presence on a boat trip down the Milwaukee River in the summer of 2018. On the west bank, just south of St. Paul Avenue, several small trees had fallen into the water, and a much larger one was leaning precariously over the stream. I went back on foot a few days later, and it was beavers, all right. They had been munching away on the white poplar and green ash that line the riverbank, and wood chips were scattered liberally among the plastic bags and empty bottles that littered the scruffy little grove. I had to look around to remind myself that I was just east of the Pritzlaff Building and directly across the river from some of the trendiest nightspots in the Third Ward.

There was a time when beavers wouldn't have seemed wildly out of place in the center of Milwaukee. They were once among the most ubiquitous mammals in North America, damming streams and gnawing bark from Hudson Bay to the Gulf of Mexico. Prized for their meat as well as their fur, beavers were a staple of both diet and dress for countless generations of American Indians.

Beavers have been busy just across the river from the Third Ward entertainment district. JOHN GURDA

(I had a chance to sample beaver meat at a game feed in Stoughton many years ago. I recall it as rich and dark—much better than muskrat, which tasted like a swamp and was filled with pieces of cartilage that resembled plastic ball bearings.)

Unfortunately for the beaver, Europeans began to develop an absolute mania for the animals in the late 1500s, not for their meat but for their thick, water-repellent underfur. Milliners shaved that fur from the tanned hides and boiled it to produce a heavy felt that they could mold into any shape desired, from elegant top hats to military tricorns. Brushed to a high gloss, beaver hats were the height of fashion for nearly two hundred years.

After depopulating the beaver streams on their own continent, Europeans turned to the apparently inexhaustible lodges of North America. It was beaver that brought the first French traders to Wisconsin in the 1600s. It was beaver that put Green

Bay, Prairie du Chien, and numerous other settlements on the map. And it was beaver, or more precisely European demand for it, that fundamentally altered the Indian way of life.

Millions of hides crossed the Atlantic in the holds of sailing ships after 1600, and the same vessels brought trade goods west on their return voyages: muskets, kettles, traps, beads, blankets, and alcohol. French rum, English brandy, and then American whiskey were all solvents that threatened to dissolve ancient native traditions.

One of the most important of those traditions was conservation. The tribes of the upper Midwest had harvested animals sustainably for thousands of years, but that changed as beaver pelts became the equivalent of currency. Two hides would buy one musket or twenty knives in some years, and the temptation to overtrap proved irresistible. Beavers became scarce around the trading capital of Mackinac Island as early as 1700, and a century later they were nearly as hard to find in eastern Wisconsin.

The market turned to other furs, particularly when the silk top hat came into vogue after 1800. Exports of North American beaver pelts had generated more revenue than all other furs combined, but raccoon took the lead after 1822, and deer, bear, wolf, and otter were all part of the mix.

Solomon Juneau, Milwaukee's last trader and first mayor, left clear evidence of the beaver's fall from dominance. Juneau's papers in the Milwaukee County Historical Society include a letter he received from the American Fur Company in 1840, five years after the county's first public land sale. American Fur announced that it would pay seven cents for one raccoon skin, forty cents for deer, fifty cents for wolf, and a whopping four dollars for a beaver pelt. By that time, however, beavers were not to be had for any price. After thousands of years as a fixture in the Milwaukee area's landscape, they were completely gone.

Until 2013, that is. That's when the staff of the Urban Ecology Center, whose flagship facility borders Riverside Park, noticed that beavers had been exercising their incisors on trees in the Milwaukee River floodplain. Cleaner water, a more continuous forest, and the removal of the North Avenue dam had all created suitable habitat, and a family of furry pioneers had moved in from wilder points upstream. Smart enough to know that they had no hope of damming the Milwaukee River, the beavers set up house in a lodge on the east bank.

Ironically, the UEC was in the process of establishing an arboretum on the same bank, using funds from the Milwaukee Rotary Club and a federal restoration program. Nearly fourteen thousand trees have gone into the ground so far, representing more than seventy species native to Wisconsin. Allowing beavers to live in an arboretum seems dangerously akin to putting pyromaniacs in charge of a fireworks factory. Some stout trees have been dropped and others are on the way down, but the Urban Ecology Center, true to its mission, is determined to let nature take its course. Caitlin Reinartz, the UEC's forester, put it succinctly: "We can't be mad about a species coming back when the whole goal was to create a place animals would want to come back to. The beaver are here, and we're going to find a way to coexist."

It's likely, but by no means certain, that the beavers whose work is on display downtown are "dispersers" from the arboretum colony, adolescents trying to establish their own territories. Unless they can be trapped and fitted with GPS devices, their whereabouts, including where they sleep or even if they're still present, will remain one of downtown's more intriguing mysteries.

There's much more to discover, but for now I like the image of young beavers sluicing down the rapids below North Avenue, paddling south through a gauntlet of steel and concrete walls, and then finding, just below St. Paul Avenue, a natural stream-bank with mature trees. Home again, finally!

Have they become more streetwise, these urban migrants, than their country cousins? Do they swim with more swagger? Active largely at night, have they heard the bartenders holler "Last call!" from the taverns across the river?

I have no idea, but welcome home, old familiars, welcome home.

The Cost of Paper

Witnessing the Death of a Forest

In the waning days of a recent August, a double-bottom flat-bed truck shuttled across the Upper Peninsula of Michigan, carrying loads of eight-foot, eight-inch logs from a forest landing near Ontonagon, on the southern shore of Lake Superior, to a paper mill in Escanaba, on the northern shore of Lake Michigan.

The sight was hardly unusual—logging trucks are nearly as common as RVs on the lake-to-lake route in late summer—but the loads making that 175-mile journey were different in one particular: I knew those trees. They were part of the disassembled forest that had graced the end of the gravel road running past my family's cabin outside Ontonagon. The trees were a stately northern blend of hemlock, white pine, balsam fir, paper birch, and the occasional white cedar—some of them, a ring-count autopsy would later reveal, more than a century old.

I had spent hours in their company since we built the cabin in 2007. When snow sifted through the branches of those trees and covered the ground to a depth of two or three feet, I had followed the comings and goings of the forest's residents, once tracing the tracks of a coyote to where they met a snowshoe hare's trail in a still life of blood and fur. One August, I heard a dry scratching sound at the top of a hemlock and looked up to see a fat porcupine chewing away at the thick bark. Ruffed grouse had exploded from spruce trees a foot or two from my head, and bald eagles were a common sight in the wispy branches of the tallest white pines. I had picked wild leeks in spring, blueberries in late summer, and blackberries in fall, occasionally finding fresh wolf tracks as wide as my hand.

Our first hint that this capacious home was coming down was the sound of chain saws. My wife and I woke one morning to their mosquito-like drone in the mile-away woods, a sound thoroughly alien on a road normally as quiet as a church on Monday. With a growing sense of unease, I walked down to investigate. A crew of four men had already cut a clearing for their machines and were busily gouging roads into the interior.

Concealing my distress as best I could, I asked the nearest logger, a grizzled man in his sixties, what was going on. The logger's family—"100 percent Finn," he declared with pride—had been in the woods for four generations, and this parcel was a two-hundred-acre fraction of the thousands he and his brother owned in the western Upper Peninsula. They were cutting the hemlock first, then the hardwoods, and finally the popple, all bound for the Escanaba mill, where the logs would be pulped, bleached, and turned into paper. A load or two of "saw logs"—straight and stout enough to be used for lumber or veneer—would go to a Wisconsin mill.

In spite of my dismay, I found the spectacle unfolding around me fascinating: a backwoods ballet of ponderous grace. I walked down to the shrinking forest every day that week, not in pointless protest but to witness the demise of a community and to chronicle its passing. The loggers never objected to my presence. The older guys even came over to chat during their infrequent breaks.

The process began with the feller buncher, a mechanical praying mantis whose oversized pincers gripped each tree in a hydraulic embrace and cut it off at the base with a "hot saw."

Sixty-foot maples were sheared to stumps with as little effort as a child picks daisies. Once the feller buncher had dropped the trees, one of the younger loggers—a member of the fourth generation, I learned—scampered across them with a chain saw, cutting off limbs until each tree was pared down to its main trunk. Gathering all the trimmed logs was the job of the grapple skidder, a monstrous vehicle with lugged rubber tires five feet in diameter and wrapped in chains for maximum traction on the soft forest floor. The skidder grasped the logs in its hydraulic jaws and hauled them, perhaps a dozen at a time, to the waiting slasher, an all-in-one machine that resembled a portable sawmill. The slasher's hydraulic boom lifted the trees like so many matchsticks onto a steel bed for the final steps. After a hinged mechanical gate had evened out the bunch at its base, a rotary saw mounted on a moving arm cut the trees to the eight-foot, eight-inch length required by the mill. The slasher's boom then transferred the logs to a waiting eight-axle truck for final delivery, fifty tons to the load.

Viewed from a safe distance, the machines moved like ants swollen to science-fiction proportions, making short work of a thick woods. With such powerful equipment at their command, a crew of three or four could clear five acres in a day—a pace that would have made loggers green with envy in the days of double-bit axes and crosscut saws. Although the process is not indelicate, it is as wasteful as it is fast. The loggers left enough slash on the former forest floor—tree tops, limbs, small trees—to heat my family's cabin for years.

One week after they started, the crew and their formidable machines were gone. I walked down the road one last time to a scene of quiet devastation so complete it took my breath away. A tornado could not have done a more thorough job. Splintered wood of all sizes and dimensions practically carpeted the ground. Discarded soda cans and oil containers provided odd

A

B

C

D

Logging proceeds in a well-defined sequence of steps. *Opposite:* (A) The feller buncher drops the trees, (B) each is "limbed" to a single trunk, (C) the skidder hauls them to the slasher, (D) and the slasher cuts them to size and loads them for transport. *Above:* When the men and their machines leave, the forest floor is strewn with wreckage. ALL PHOTOS: JOHN GURDA

notes of color. The skidder had gouged ruts deep enough to become frog ponds, and limp green plants were strewn across the ground like tattered rags. Rising from the wreckage was the incongruous smell of Christmas.

Witnessing the destruction of such a favorite, familiar place was painful in the extreme. This wasn't an Amazonian rain forest or African savanna disappearing—losses I lament in the abstract—but my home woods, and the pain was made all the sharper by the knowledge that I won't live long enough to see the forest's full recovery.

But my sorrow was complicated by a rising awareness. Standing in the shorn landscape, I had to reflect that here, after all, was humankind at work. We are a species of uncommon rapacity, using the materials at hand to fashion our chosen worlds, even to the point of using them up. Loggers log, just as miners mine and farmers farm, because the rest of us buy what they have to sell; for many, the color of the forest is the color of money.

How, I had to ask myself, was witnessing this crew at work any different from watching someone else kill the fish, chickens, and cows that end up on my dinner plate? How many trees had it taken—local spruce and fir, pine from the Pacific Northwest—to build my family's little cabin down the road? Hadn't our road itself begun as a narrow-gauge rail line carrying virgin logs to the old Ontonagon mill? How many cords of firewood had I cut to stoke our stove? How many wooden playthings—paddles, bats, beach toys—were stored in our wooden shed? And unless you're using an e-reader at the moment, how many trees were fed into the indiscriminate maw of a paper mill to make the material on which you're reading these words?

What I observed during that difficult August week was neither the slaughter of the innocents nor a happy instance of renewable forestry. Something deeper and more ambiguous was happening in the woods, and at its heart was a discomfiting lesson as old as Eve and Adam: In the loss of Eden, we're all original sinners.

Swimming Upstream

Lake Sturgeon Begin Their Long Trip Back

I went fishing in reverse on a recent fall Saturday. Instead of putting a line in the water and pulling up dinner, I pulled a fingerling out of a plastic bucket and gently put it in the waters of Lake Michigan. It was a sturgeon, one of nearly twelve hundred young fish carefully raised at Riveredge Nature Center in Ozaukee County and now deemed ready for the big lake.

The occasion was Sturgeon Fest, an annual celebration of ongoing efforts to restore this ancient native to its original home waters. Hundreds of us gathered at Lakeshore State Park for talks, tours, and finally the release of the newest generation.

As one of Sturgeon Fest's speakers, I was in the first group entrusted with the fingerlings. Viewed up close, I must say, a sturgeon is not a particularly attractive creature. It lacks the sleek iridescence of a trout, the vivid patterns of a bluegill, or even the bars and stripes of a bass. But the young ones, with their upcurved snouts and ridged backs, are cute in a homely sort of way, like basset hounds or bulldogs. They resemble horizontal seahorses: bony, whimsical creatures you might find in a children's book, or perhaps on a cave wall.

The word that kept coming to mind was *prehistoric*. It's easy to imagine sturgeon swimming in a Cretaceous river with dinosaurs milling around on shore—which, in fact, they did. Sturgeon have been on earth for 150 million years, give or take an eon.

Then as now, they were large and long-lived. Modern sturgeon can weigh up to two hundred pounds and live for a century or more. They are the biggest and the oldest creatures in the Great Lakes—the giant redwoods of the inland deep.

The fish don't score particularly high in the libido department. Sturgeon finally reach puberty in their twenties, and they spawn only every few years after that. Their reproductive torpor and great age help to explain why they've changed so little over the millennia; there have simply been fewer generations. The same factors explain their vulnerability: once sturgeon are gone, they're very difficult to bring back.

When the first European immigrants reached the shores of the Great Lakes, sturgeon were super-abundant. They had provided sustenance for innumerable generations of Indian families, but the newcomers didn't quite know what to do with these freshwater giants. The fish ripped holes in nets designed for smaller quarry, raising the ire of commercial fishermen. Sturgeon were so undervalued that in 1866, one Lake Erie steamboat captain began to use overripe specimens for boiler fuel. "The oil from the fish assists the combustion of the wood very much," reported the *Cleveland Herald*. "It is said that twenty sturgeon make as much steam as a cord of wood."

By 1880, tastes had changed. I've eaten sturgeon only once— at a Milwaukee seafood restaurant—and I recall the meat as dark, dense, and rich, somewhere between salmon and tuna on the firmness scale. Residents of the Great Lakes region finally discovered that sturgeon were both tasty and nutritious. The smoked variety was especially popular, and a number of entrepreneurs began to market sturgeon eggs as caviar. As demand for the fish increased, the Great Lakes harvest climbed to four million pounds a year between 1880 and 1900.

Sturgeon were definitely on Milwaukee's menu. The fishermen of Jones Island, many of them immigrants from the Baltic

The next generation: a young Milwaukeean with a young sturgeon.
KATE REDMOND FOR RIVEREDGE NATURE CENTER

seacoast of Poland, hauled up two million pounds of fish in a typical year. Their catch included trout, whitefish, perch, herring, and significant quantities of sturgeon. In 1897, sturgeon brought ten cents a pound in local fish markets—the same price consumers paid for perch, cisco, and sunfish. They were a relatively inexpensive source of protein in those days; pickerel, rock bass, and small crappie cost twelve and a half cents a pound, trout and whitefish fifteen cents.

The sturgeon harvest fell sharply after 1900. Overfishing was certainly to blame, and Milwaukee didn't make it easy for these

slow breeders to recover. Dams blocked access to their traditional spawning beds, and sewage-choked rivers were poor
spawning habitat in any case.

On Green Bay, a different human practice affected bottom-
feeders like whitefish and sturgeon. "The scarcity of these fish,"
reported the *Milwaukee Sentinel* in 1892, "is said to be due to the
large amount of sawdust, which is disposed of by throwing into
the water, this method being practiced by a majority of the mills
in this region, and as the sawdust becomes water-soaked it
settles over their feeding grounds, compelling the fish to go
elsewhere." In the waters off Sturgeon Bay, ironically, sturgeon
became a rarity.

As their Great Lakes population crashed, sturgeon still had
one place they could call home: Lake Winnebago and its tribu-
taries. Shallow and fertile, the lake had always been unusually
good habitat for the fish, and harvests were particularly impressive during the spring spawning run. "It is a common thing,"
wrote the *Milwaukee Sentinel* in 1892, "to see two boys with
a spear on each one's shoulders, and between them a 75 to a
100-pound sturgeon." The 1899 catch at Oshkosh included a
118-pounder, and one greedy spearman, Fred Meyer, killed
twenty-four fish all by himself.

With laudable foresight, Wisconsin began to manage its
sturgeon population in 1903, bringing such indiscriminate
slaughter to an end. As a direct result, the Lake Winnebago system today has the largest population of lake sturgeon on the
entire planet.

It was Winnebago sturgeon that we released at Lakeshore
State Park. The eggs were harvested by the Wisconsin DNR
on the Wolf River, reared to fingerling status at the Riveredge
Nature Center on the Milwaukee River near Newburg, and
finally set free in Lake Michigan. They represented a continuing

The sturgeon reintroduction program is already showing results. WISCONSIN DEPARTMENT OF NATURAL RESOURCES

attempt to restore a naturally reproducing population to the lake for the first time in more than a century.

Releasing a sturgeon is, on the most elemental level, an act of faith. By the time the fingerlings in their buckets return to spawn, the eager children who gathered at Sturgeon Fest to set them free will be adults, and many of the adults present will have shuffled off to make room for the next generation. It's much like planting a tree whose shade we'll never live to enjoy. We have faith that many of the fish we released will survive to maturity, and we have faith that the river they return to will be healthy enough to allow them to begin their own next generation.

But releasing a sturgeon is also an act of justice. It represents an effort, however small, to restore some balance to an ecosystem that has been disrupted beyond calculation by human activity. Faith, justice, and fish: a potent combination on a memorable Saturday afternoon.

A Vote for Autumn

There's Something Bigger than an Election Going On Out There

Our nation goes through the same exhausting exercise every four years. We winnow a field of hopefuls down to two candidates and then watch them pummel each other for what seems like an eternity. The obscene spending levels are matched only by the general level of ugliness. We are subjected to an endless barrage of invective, untruth, and oversimplification that can exhaust even the most patient citizen.

Another season is underway during the thick of every presidential campaign, one of considerably greater breadth than anything happening on the political front. That would be autumn. In the first week of a recent October, I voted early and got out of town. It was a retreat of sorts, the same solo camping trip I've been taking for forty years or more—always in fall, usually on Lake Superior.

This time my destination was the Grand Sable Dunes area in Upper Michigan. For three days I fielded no robocalls, heard no news, and expressed no opinions. No one was running for anything, except the pair of young deer prancing across the trail in front of me. The only attack I witnessed was the ancient assault of water on rock—storm waves this time, five-footers smashing themselves to spray against the sandstone cliffs at the Au Sable lighthouse.

No candidates made an appearance in the Grand Sable Dunes during a recent fall election season. JOHN GURDA

The resident ravens had no positions but the ones that kept them airborne in the updrafts over the dunes. A red squirrel's only policy seemed to be to stay alive, judging from the way it went after the remains of my peanut butter sandwich. The sole evidence of urgent national business was the ore boats far out on the lake, downbound with some of their last loads before freeze-up. I saw just one national symbol: a bald eagle, this one unceremoniously picking at the bones of a roadkill deer in the company of three crows.

I can further report that it was a yellow year in the woods; the weather was too warm and too wet, apparently, for the oranges and reds to shine through in their transient glory. Autumn's flame always burns like a candle—from the top down; some tree-tops were raked clean, while the saplings on the ground below were still green. There was no other color in the landscape, no flowers except the odd stragglers—knapweed, campion, evening primrose—practically daring the frost to cut them down.

I spent an entire day hiking through the lakeside forest and across the dunes. All the creeks were brimful and even higher after a tent-buckling thunderstorm the night before. The thimble-berries were long gone, but the wintergreen plants had pro-duced more than enough bright red seeds for a minty trailside snack. The juncos had returned from Canada, and they were flitting through the underbrush with the kinglets, the chicka-dees, and the warblers. The chickadees will stay, but all the other little ones were rafting up for the long trip south, forming a feath-ered convoy that would soon sweep south across Wisconsin.

In the evening, as I stood above the beach with the comfort of a campfire at my back, I noticed that the stars had wheeled toward winter since the last time I'd really looked. The North-ern Cross had slipped from its midsummer perch at the top of the sky, the Big Dipper hung just above the horizon as if it were about to scoop water from the lake, and the great square of Peg-asus was well up in the southeast.

I came home after three days with a subtly altered perspec-tive. A stay in the woods is always an antidote to angst. Yes, dark-ness is coming, but it doesn't spell the twilight of the republic. All of us—Republicans, Democrats, and independents alike—are merely and marvelously riding the earth's tilt away from the sun into a new season.

I always vote for president, but I also vote for autumn. The turn of the year reminds us that we belong to something larger, something that was here ages before the current election and that will be here long after the latest candidates become foot-notes in some twenty-third-century history. In that knowledge there is comfort, and humility, that will linger when the bom-bast and blather have faded to a distant memory.

A Milwaukeean Abroad

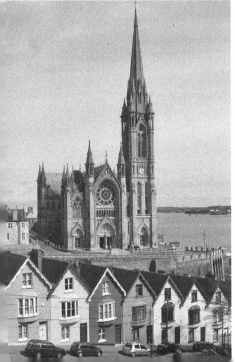

A Polish Pilgrimage

Search for Roots Has Unexpected Results

I flew to Europe expecting to feel more Polish. Poland, after all, is where my grandfather, another John Gurda, was born in 1885, and it was Poland that he and his parents, Franciszek and Apolonia Gurda, left to find a new home in Milwaukee four years later. I had long known that my own story flowed directly from theirs, but what happened across the ocean surprised me. Instead of feeling more Polish, I came home feeling more American.

My wife, Sonja, and I spent more than two weeks in Poland in 2005, covering fifteen hundred miles in the process. Like many third-generation ethnics, I had high hopes of narrowing the gap between my family's past and our present. I believed that if I could just see the graves of my ancestors, or find my grandfather's name in the baptismal records, or even—holy of holies—locate a relative still on the family's land, I'd be a satisfied pilgrim.

We knew from earlier genealogical research that the Gurdas had emigrated from a small farm outside Slawianowo, a tiny town bordering a long, narrow lake in northwestern Poland. Slawianowo, we soon found out, is literally off the beaten path. The village lies at the dead end of a lightly traveled road forty miles west of Bydgoszcz, the nearest major city. This is the "big sky" country of Poland, and you're unlikely to find a more pastoral landscape anywhere.

My grandfather and his family attended this venerable half-timbered church in the tiny village of Slawianowo. JOHN GURDA

As we turned off the main road, the village church rose like a beacon on the prairie to greet us. It's a half-timbered structure of indeterminate but advanced age, and I sensed immediately that this was the place where my ancestors had worshiped. We scoured the stone-walled graveyard surrounding the church for familiar names, but it was innocent of Gurdas. It was innocent, in fact, of any burials earlier than about 1920. Following a common European practice, when a graveyard is full, Poles simply put new graves on top of the oldest ones.

Three elderly women were tending their family plots near the church. In halting and thoroughly non-standard Polish, I explained to them that my grandfather was born in Slawianowo and asked if they knew anyone named Gurda. "*Nie wiem*," came the reply—"I don't know." I would get the same answer again and again in the next hour or two: "*Nie wiem*"—your family doesn't live here anymore.

As we strolled down Slawianowo's single main street,

admiring the neatly tended gardens and the scattering of older homes, it became obvious that the old peasant farmsteads had long since been collectivized out of existence. Fields of wheat, barley, and potatoes stretched from horizon to horizon beyond the village borders—picturesque, certainly, but empty of human habitation. Walking the barnyard of my ancestors was not an option. Even the church records, we learned, were stored elsewhere. All documents more than a century old had been transferred to archives in Koszalin, a city two or three hours away.

What I'd intended as a journey to the past was fast becoming an encounter with the unvarnished present. The bridges were down; the lines had been cut. It was increasingly obvious that, when my ancestors left, Poland had gone on without them.

We would learn to appreciate, in the days ahead, just how much the nation had endured since my family's departure. Poland did not even exist when Gurdas still lived in Slawianowo; the country had been divided among Prussia, Russia, and Austria in 1795. The Poles weathered 123 years of occupation and oppression that did not end until 1918, when the Allies were victorious in World War I.

After twenty years of fractious freedom, Poland became Hitler's first target in 1939. World War II began in Gdansk, and it created unspeakable havoc. Well over six million Poles—nearly 20 percent of the population, both Christians and Jews—were killed, and numerous cities, notably Warsaw, were annihilated.

At war's end, the Soviet "liberators" never left. For nearly fifty years, Poles suffered under a Communist regime that was by turns capricious, corrupt, and cruel. It was in large part the Catholic Church that preserved the soul, as well as the souls, of the Polish people during those years of darkness, and the election of a Polish pope in 1978 helped keep the spirit alive.

The wheat fields stretch to the horizon in northern Poland, erasing all hope of finding a nineteenth-century family farmstead. JOHN GURDA

Long-simmering discontent finally boiled over in the Solidarity movement of the 1980s. Lech Walesa and his fellow Gdansk shipyard workers said "Enough," and the rest of the country rose with them. It was in 1989—exactly a century after Franciszek and Apolonia Gurda left—that Poles tasted at last the freedom they had sought for generations. That century was full of such devastation and dislocation that it's a wonder anyone can find even a vestige of an ancestral memory.

As Poland changed over time, so did the immigrants who left it. For my ancestors and millions like them, ties to the homeland frayed with each passing year until they were all but severed. After a decade or two in Milwaukee, Franciszek and Apolonia became simply Frank and Pauline. Their children learned a different language and absorbed different mythologies. My grandfather had scant knowledge of the Battle of Grunwald or the glories of the Jagiellonian dynasty. Despite the best efforts of

Polish cultural groups, the Fourth of July had more resonance for his generation than Constitution Day. In less than a century, Poles and Polish Americans became two different peoples with the same genetic background.

And then one day a grandson returned, hoping to drink from the old well, only to find that the waters had changed. There was no particular sorrow in that discovery, only a faintly wistful longing for roots that will remain buried without significantly more travel and research.

Sonja and I spent the rest of our stay in the company of familiar-looking strangers. There was plenty to see—the stunning Renaissance city of Krakow, the lush meadows of the Carpathian Mountains, the sprawling beaches of the Baltic seacoast, the bucolic beauty of the Polish countryside—but I saw it all as a tourist, not a long-lost relative visiting an ancient homeland.

We also developed, along the way, a profound admiration for the Polish spirit. Lodged between two assertive neighbors— Germany to the west and Russia to the east—Poland has nevertheless managed to preserve a rich and robust cultural identity. You sense a stubborn, almost defiant pride in nearly every Pole you meet. But that's the spirit of today's nation, not the partitioned Poland my family left behind.

What I felt most strongly after visiting Slawianowo was a new awareness of my own identity, summarized in the phrase I used every time I introduced myself to a Pole: *"Jestem Amerykaninem"*—"I am an American." Your country is fascinating, but it's not mine.

I sensed, after returning to Milwaukee, a more subtle distinction. I realized that I represent, in a way, the culmination of a journey my great-grandparents started more than a century ago. They were rooted in a culture stretching back more than a thousand years, but they chose to become Americans. Peasants in the Old World, they became laborers in the New, and they found prejudice as well as promise on this side of the Atlantic. But they managed to make a life, and here I am, just three generations later, enjoying privileges they probably never imagined, including the luxury of looking back.

Yes, I am an American. My native land has determined everything from the way I hold a fork to my perception of space. But perhaps the richness of America—and the source of its unending wonder—lies in the profusion of stories that have mixed and mingled to create our national narrative. My Americanness, like yours, is tempered by what came before. The Polish connection is an irreducible part of my heritage, shaping my genetic makeup, my attitudes, and above all, my story.

The story continues on both sides of the ocean. As the Slawianowo church bell tolled for evening Mass—the same bell, perhaps, that my grandfather heard when he toddled down the same streets—Sonja and I drove out to fields at the edge of town and gazed back. I picked three stalks of wheat, one for myself and one for each of my brothers. They survived the trip home. The stalk I saved rests in a small vase on my bedroom dresser, a tangible daily reminder that the soil our ancestors tilled so long ago is still bearing abundant fruit.

Luck of the Irish

It Was Better Here than in Ireland

Irish Fest is the big one. Milwaukeeans have been attending ethnic festivals on the downtown lakefront since 1978, absorbing the cultures (and the beer) of a shifting cast of ancestry groups, including Italian, Mexican, German, Polish, African, Asian, Arab, and American Indian. The energy required to sustain those spectacles year after year with only volunteer help has proven too much for some groups, but Irish Fest has endured to become the largest of the lot. Rain or shine, it is reliably the champion, drawing well over a hundred thousand revelers to the largest celebration of Irish music, culture, and cuisine on the planet.

I went back to the source in 2015. Over the course of two weeks in Ireland, my wife and I saw the home regions of Milwaukee's early Irish families, visited the ports they sailed from, and learned more about the conditions that compelled them to leave. The connections between Old World and New were as impressive as the contrasts.

The Irish were Milwaukee's first major immigrant group, establishing a foothold just before legions of German newcomers arrived and made the city uniquely their own. The sons and daughters of Eire reached Milwaukee in the mid-1830s and swelled to 15 percent of the new city's population in 1848, which would prove to be their historic high point. (Residents who

The lofty spire of the Cobh cathedral was the last thing millions of Irish emigrants saw as they departed their homeland, most never to return. JOHN GURDA

claim at least some Irish ancestry now make up about 11 percent of the metro area's residents.)

The greatest number of immigrants came from the west of Ireland, including counties Clare and Galway, where rocks are as abundant as the bubbles in a barrel of Guinness. You can drive for miles in the west today and see nothing but meandering stone walls enclosing sheep pastures whose topsoil is just inches thick. Hundreds more immigrants came from Cork and Tipperary in the south, where the farmland is better but the people were just as Catholic and, in colonial days, just as poor.

Ireland, like the United States, bore the oppressive weight of England in that nation's imperial phase. Americans had the distinct advantage of occupying a continent across an ocean rather than an island across a channel, and the rebels who won

America's independence shared the ancestry of their oppressors. The Irish, by contrast, were exiles in their own land. Although they had been more or less Christianized since the fifth century, they were viewed as an alien culture and a constant threat to the empire's security. Literary lion John Milton, author of *Paradise Lost*, dismissed the Irish in the mid-1600s as "indocile and averse from every civility and amendment."

Periodic Irish rebellions were put down with brutal force, and by the mid-1800s, Ireland was a thoroughly dependent vassal state. Irish forests were cut down to build English ships, Irish sheep were sheared to make English wool, and the majority of the Irish people, particularly in the south and west, were either hardscrabble farmers paying high rents to English landlords or landless peasants who wondered where their next meal might be coming from.

It was the potato, a plant introduced from the Americas, ironically, that kept the poorer Irish classes alive and, in fact, spurred an increase in population. In a cruel turn of fate, it was the potato's failure that transformed a relative trickle of emigrants into a flood. When a pestilential blight turned much of the 1845 harvest black and practically wiped out succeeding crops, poverty became destitution and frustration became desperation.

England grudgingly organized relief efforts that were woefully inadequate. Ireland still has miles of pointless "famine fences" erected by Irish paupers forced to work for their daily gruel. Shiploads of American provisions arrived too late to save many from starvation. For those who were still mobile, emigration was the only alternative, frequently in the holds of the infamous "coffin ships" bound for the United States, Canada, South America, or Australia. In appallingly symmetrical numbers, one million people died in Ireland and one million left the country during the famine years. A scholar combing the countryside for folk songs in 1855 found that Ireland was "no longer tuneful"; the music had either died or departed with the masses.

The famine passed, but persistent economic pressures and Ireland's continuing status as a colony, which would last until 1921, made emigration the only hope for millions of Irish citizens, particularly the young. In the early years, they sailed from whatever port was nearest, but the emigrant trade centered increasingly on Cobh (pronounced Cove), a protected deepwater harbor just south of Cork. Roughly half of the six million people who left Ireland between 1848 and 1950 sailed from Cobh.

The vast majority bought one-way tickets. "America wakes," with plenty of food, drink, and dancing, were customary send-offs for the emigrants, who, once they had ascended the gangplank, were just as dearly departed as the loved ones lying in Irish cemeteries. One of those who boarded was Annie Moore, a fifteen-year-old girl from county Cork, who in 1892 became the very first immigrant to be processed at the brand-new facilities on Ellis Island. She received a ten-dollar gold piece from US authorities and spent the rest of her life in New York City, where she married a German butcher and had at least eleven children with him. Her statue now graces the Cobh waterfront. On the day we visited, the *Queen Victoria*, a posh two-thousand-passenger cruise ship, was in port. Annie, who crossed the Atlantic in steerage, would have been astonished.

An untold number of emigrants who passed through Cobh eventually made their way to Milwaukee. Most settled in the Third Ward, where they found a poverty analogous to what they had known across the ocean. They also experienced new troubles, including the 1860 sinking of the excursion steamer *Lady Elgin* off Winnetka, Illinois, a tragedy that killed nearly three hundred people, most of them Irish residents of the Third Ward.

Poverty and tragedy notwithstanding, the Irish prospered here. Aside from the scenery, the main difference between

Kerry or Clare and Milwaukee was hope, and the immigrants, after a slow start, made the most of their opportunities. Decade by decade they moved up and out, first to neighborhoods like Tory Hill and Merrill Park, then to Wauwatosa and other suburbs, their incomes growing all the while. Today, their descendants can be found everywhere from judicial chambers to the boardrooms of our largest corporations.

And what do their cousins across the sea make of it all? The Irish seem genuinely fond of American visitors, in part because we drop so much cash on our way to the Book of Kells and the Cliffs of Moher. But it's not just the money. Because so many children of Eire have emigrated over the years, virtually everyone has relatives in America, and many of the people we met had visited the United States for work, school, or pleasure. (A Sligo woman was spellbound by our roads. "They're so straight!" she exclaimed.) Milwaukee has a special connection with the hundreds of Irish musicians who have performed at Irish Fest, and it's not unusual to see Irish Fest stickers and posters on the walls of pubs in the western counties.

For Americans, identification with all things Irish may have reached a historic high. There are probably more children named Molly and Brigid, Liam and Seamus in the United States than in Ireland, and St. Patrick's Day is celebrated here with a fervor that would surprise the average Dubliner. For any American with Irish roots, a trip across the ocean can be a powerful exercise in ancestral nostalgia. Who can resist the earthy smell of a turf fire on the hearth, the snugness of even the humblest pub, the lilting cadence of the Irish tongue, and the country's obvious delight in language?

But it is in America that the Irish found their luck, and it is in America that their descendants abide. Would many of our O'Briens and O'Mearas, Murphys and Kellys seriously consider emigrating in reverse? Not for all the rocks in county Clare.

Lost and Found

Hmong Refugees Reinvent Themselves in America

The scene practically defined the word *poignant*. At the Hmong New Year, which is celebrated every December in State Fair Park, one vendor had set up a photo booth with a mural of a sun-splashed, vibrantly green bamboo grove as his backdrop. As snow swirled outside and temperatures plunged toward zero, the children and grandchildren of Hmong refugees posed in traditional costumes before a scene from a tropical homeland most of them had never seen.

I got to visit that homeland on a 2019 trip to Southeast Asia. Traveling in February, my wife and I weathered a temperature swing of 120 degrees, from 25 below in Wisconsin to 95 above in Laos and Vietnam. The Hmong have experienced the same extremes but in reverse, and they didn't get to fly home when the trip was over. Spending four weeks in their native lands gave me a healthy respect for the group's resilience.

Most Hmong residents are not in Wisconsin by choice. Of all the newcomers who have made their homes in this state—and that includes everyone but American Indians—few have traveled such a circuitous path to get here, and fewer still endured so much hardship before they arrived.

The Hmong story, in fact, is an epic of survival. The group emerged thousands of years ago in China, where they were a beleaguered minority frequently at odds with the ruling dynasties. In the mid- to late 1800s, many crossed the border into Laos, Thailand, and Vietnam, where they became a marginalized minority for the second time. The Hmong settled in the region's mountainous northern region, sharing it with other so-called hill tribes. There they practiced slash-and-burn agriculture, exhausting the soil on one steep site after another and moving every ten or fifteen years.

What the Hmong carried with them from place to place was a clan structure that has been a key to their survival. There are eighteen clans in all—Her, Xiong, Yang, Thao, Lee, Lor, and a dozen others—with the result that some four million people worldwide have the same eighteen last names, a looming challenge for genealogists of the future. Strong clans and traditionally powerful elders have kept this distinctly stateless group together through multiple dislocations.

When France colonized Vietnam, Laos, and Cambodia in the late 1800s, some Hmong clans in Laos sided with the European occupiers in hopes of improving their status. In the early 1950s, with French influence waning and Communism on the rise, the United States decided to intervene. As American troops waded into the morass that became the Vietnam War, the pro-French Hmong transferred their allegiance to the United States. By the early 1960s, they were in the thick of the fighting.

Vang Pao, a charismatic but controversial Hmong general in the Royal Lao Army, recruited legions of his countrymen to defend their homeland by fighting in what is now called the Secret War, a clandestine campaign the CIA was conducting outside Vietnam's borders. Hmong farmers couldn't drive cars because there were none to drive, but they learned to fly American fighter planes. The pilots made thousands of sorties against the North Vietnamese, and their clansmen on the ground gathered intelligence, rescued downed American pilots, and engaged in direct combat. Tens of thousands of Hmong died as the result of military action, hunger, disease, and massacres.

When the United States pulled out of the region in 1975, the Hmong in Laos were basically hung out to dry. They faced three choices, none enviable. Thousands crossed the Mekong River into Thailand, sometimes under a hail of bullets, and eventually found homes of a sort in refugee camps sponsored by the United Nations. Their ordeal is preserved in meticulously embroidered "story cloths" that have become collector's items. Other Hmong who had fought with the United States stayed in Laos by choice and took their chances with the new Communist regime, a decision that led to execution for some and extended time in "re-education camps" for others. An uncounted number fled into the jungle and, against impossible odds, continued to fight. In a country roughly comparable to Wisconsin in size and population, their hit-and-run attacks drew quick reprisals.

The Hmong in Wisconsin came largely from the Thai refugee camps, where the enemies were not bullets and bombs but boredom and poor living conditions. The United States, after some hesitation, acknowledged its debt to its former allies. In a migration that began in the mid-1970s and continued into the early 2000s, more than 130,000 Hmong refugees were resettled in America. After losing so much—their possessions, their traditional way of life, and too many of their loved ones—the Hmong suffered one more loss: their place on the continent that had been their home for millennia.

The wonder is where they ended up. California, which has the country's largest Hmong population, was perhaps an obvious destination, given its location on the Pacific. But the states with the second- and third-highest numbers of Hmong refugees were, and are, Minnesota and Wisconsin, where the climate and culture could hardly be more different from what they left behind. The Hmong presence in our region reflects the influence of resettlement agencies run by Catholics and Lutherans, religions carried across the ocean by the standard Midwestern mix of immigrants from Germany, Scandinavia, Ireland, Poland, Italy, and elsewhere in Europe. In a wonderfully symmetrical act of generational payback, the descendants of one wave of transplants helped another put down roots.

In Minnesota, St. Paul has become a Hmong capital of national importance, comparable to Fresno, California. In Wisconsin, the Hmong are easily the largest Asian ethnic group, outnumbering Indian and Chinese residents combined. Their settlement pattern, however, has been one of extreme dispersal, and it is by no means limited to large cities. In 2017, according to US Census estimates, Sheboygan had 4,691 Hmong residents, Wausau 4,399, Appleton 3,874, Madison 3,858, and Green Bay 2,879. Those are significant numbers, and several other communities—Eau Claire, La Crosse, Manitowoc, and Oshkosh—were each home to more than 1,000 Hmong.

The group's impact on Wisconsin's smaller cities has been profound. In Wausau, for instance, the number of Hmong students in the public schools exploded from 160 in 1981 to 1,010 a decade later and 2,214 in 1998. Classrooms were quickly overcrowded, and English became a minority language in several schools. In Wausau and elsewhere, the inevitable process of mutual adjustment has not taken place without tension or even tragedy, but the Hmong presence has broadened the worldview of communities whose diversity had always been measured by the relative ratios of their European groups. In Sheboygan, a Hmong war memorial has been accorded a place of particular pride on the downtown lakefront. Dedicated in 2006, the circular wall of polished stone panels was just the third Hmong monument in America, following earlier projects in Arlington National Cemetery and downtown Fresno.

It will come as no surprise that Milwaukee County has the

Milwaukee's celebration of the Hmong New Year is a showcase for both tradition and adaptation. MILWAUKEE JOURNAL SENTINEL

largest Hmong population in Wisconsin—14,192 people, more than a quarter of the 55,792 Hmong who live in the state. The first arrived in 1976, and they gravitated to both sides of the Twenty-Seventh Street viaduct, settling in Merrill Park on the north side and Clarke Square and Silver City on the south. What followed was a slow mass migration to the north and west. One cluster formed in the Midtown neighborhood, where many found a spiritual home at St. Michael's Catholic Church and homes to buy through ACTS Housing. A second, larger community has emerged on the Northwest Side, in the general vicinity of North Seventy-Sixth Street and Mill Road, where post–World War II ranch homes and duplexes are both abundant and affordable.

Like every other group who arrived with basically nothing—a plight magnified by their refugee status—the Hmong have not had an easy time in their new surroundings. Poverty, under-employment, racism, and intergenerational tensions have all hindered their transition to life in America. They have, at the same time, demonstrated a remarkable ability to adapt. The Hmong clan structure has given them a solidarity that other groups can only envy, and the result is a robust array of mutual aid groups, religious congregations, businesses, and schools. The Hmong American Peace Academy, a K–12 charter school established in 2004, enrolls seventeen hundred students on two Northwest Side campuses. HAPA's goal, says founder and director Chris Her Xiong, is to get kids "to and through college," and the results to date have been impressive. Many HAPA graduates move on to UW–Milwaukee, which now enrolls nearly seven hundred Hmong American students, easily the most of any UW campus. New traditions are being formed, but old ones are still honored. The Hmong have renewed their ties to the land in Wisconsin, and they are a fixture in virtually every farmer's market in the state.

As the Wisconsin Hmong move forward, how are their relatives doing back in Southeast Asia? On our 2019 tour, my wife and I spent time in three villages with significant Hmong populations. The good news is that the fighting is over. Hmong villagers have been repatriated back to Laos on a massive scale, and there are welcome signs of integration in both Laos and Vietnam. The exquisite needlework created by Hmong women is a staple of the tourist trade, and Hmong farmers are as much a presence in the local markets as they are in Wausau or Milwaukee.

The person who stands out in my memory is a minuscule matriarch whose two grandchildren never left her side during our visit. The eighty-year-old welcomed us into her home, a dwelling with dirt floors and two main rooms. The first was both a bedroom and a kitchen, with an open cooking fire that had coated the ceiling with soot. The second room was a shared living space whose most conspicuous feature was a shrine to her family's ancestors made of chicken feathers dipped in blood. In the loft above was an enormous wicker basket filled with rice. Of the woman's nine children, one daughter had died and another had been kidnapped by Chinese Hmong and sold into prostitution.

As we left her modest home, the clouds that had surrounded us all morning parted to reveal a panorama of rice paddies and

A Hmong matriarch with her grandchildren in the hill country of northern Vietnam.
JOHN GURDA

green mountainsides that could have illustrated any calendar. I was left to ponder questions of beauty and hardship, loss and gain. Where, I wondered, was the connection between traditional life in the highlands of Southeast Asia and Westernized life in cities like Milwaukee? What had the Hmong gained in their involuntary flight to the New World, and what had they lost?

What these hardworking wanderers brought with them to America was an identity born in struggle, tested in battle, and passed from one generation to the next as both an ancestral obligation and a continuing act of love. Despite the obstacles, that identity has survived, even thrived, in the United States, and it has also evolved. Traditional dance groups have added hip-hop moves to their routines, and Hmong American women are starting businesses, managing organizations, and running schools—opportunities unattainable on the far side of the Pacific.

In just two or three generations, Wisconsin's Hmong have created lives light-years removed from the jungles of Southeast Asia, and yet they remain identifiably, insistently Hmong. As flexible as bamboo, as tough as teak, they have adapted old ways and adopted new ones. After so many moves and so much suffering, where is home? Home is here.

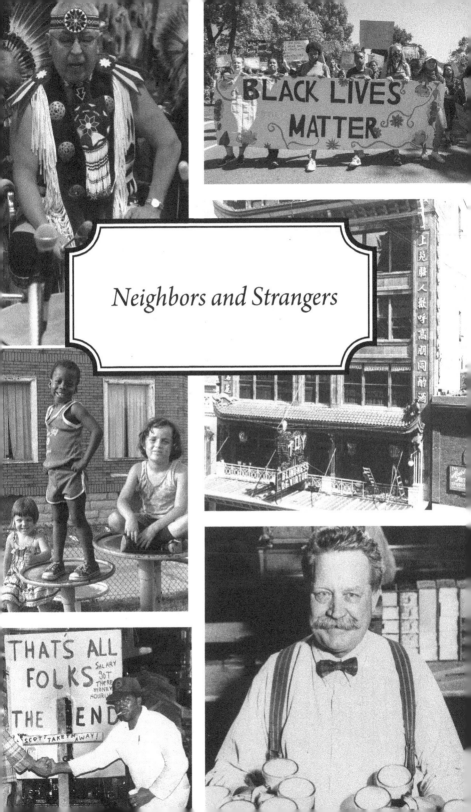

Neighbors and Strangers

Ein Prosit, Milwaukee!

German Traditions Shaped the City's Character

There's a word for it. If you want to express the traditional essence of Milwaukee, look no further than *Gemütlichkeit*. It's not easy to define, much less pronounce, but *Gemütlichkeit* describes the feeling of contentment that wells up after a hearty meal shared with close friends and accompanied by a good glass of lager. It signifies a fondness for the simple pleasures of home and hearth—flowers in the front yard, tomato plants in the back—pursued without undue haste. *Gemütlichkeit* is a key component of Milwaukee's civic character, and it is perhaps the most durable gift of the city's Germans to the rest of the community.

Those Germans got in on the ground floor. The first immigrants arrived in 1839, just four years after the United States began to sell the land it had taken from local Indian nations. The German pioneers were responding to the same attractions that drew Yankee, Irish, Norwegian, and Czech newcomers to the tiny settlement: one of the best natural harbors on the Great Lakes and the prospect, at least, of becoming the upper Midwest's commercial center. Milwaukee was, in fact, evenly matched with nearby Chicago for almost fifteen years—until railroads arrived from the east and made the Windy City a world-class transportation hub.

There was still plenty of opportunity in Milwaukee, and Germans made the most of it. They were a majority of the population

Beer, the classic German beverage, has always been at the center of Milwaukee's self-image as well as its national reputation. MILWAUKEE PUBLIC LIBRARY

as early as 1860. Milwaukee became the most German city in the United States, and its character developed accordingly. By the later 1800s, German musical societies, dramatic groups, and visual artists had earned the city a reputation as *das Deutsch-Athen Amerikas*—the German Athens of America. During the same years, immigrant brewers made their national beverage the foundation of an industry that is still synonymous with the city. Pabst became the country's largest brewer for the first time in 1874, and Schlitz and Blatz were in the top dozen.

And there were the less tangible issues of personality. Travel writer Willard Glazier offered a trenchant summary of the Teutonic influence in 1884: "Germans constitute nearly one-half the entire population of Milwaukee, and have impressed their character upon the people and the city itself in other ways than socially. Steady-going plodders, with their love for music and flowers, they have yet no keen taste for display, and every time choose the substantial rather than the ornamental." In a word, *Gemütlichkeit.*

Although they played a formative role, Germans were hardly the only group to make Milwaukee their home before 1900. As the city became a major industrial center—giving rise to titans like Allis-Chalmers, Harley-Davidson, Allen-Bradley, A. O. Smith, and Johnson Controls—a host of newcomers kept the factories humming. Poles put their unique stamp on the South Side, covering the neighborhood with small homes and large churches, including the magnificent St. Josaphat's Basilica, a National Register landmark built with materials salvaged from the Chicago post office. Italian immigrants, most of them Sicilians, settled in the Third Ward, just south of downtown, where they dominated the city's fruit and vegetable trade. Greeks, Serbs, Slovaks, Croatians, and eastern European Jews developed distinct enclaves, each with its own shops, societies, and places of worship. In 1890, immigrants and their children made up 86 percent of Milwaukee's population—the highest proportion of any city in the country.

The pattern of diversity has only intensified since then. Black Milwaukeeans, whose presence goes back to pioneer days, came north by the thousands to take industrial jobs after World War I. Mexicans arrived on the same wave, many of them

The men and women of the Turner movement, which promoted both physical and mental fitness, helped make Milwaukee the "German Athens of America." MILWAUKEE COUNTY HISTORICAL SOCIETY

recruited by labor agents for leather tanneries on the near South Side. In more recent decades, Southeast Asians—particularly Hmong, Laotian, and Vietnamese refugees and immigrants— have added their unique flavors to the cultural stew. The Black and Latino communities have grown dramatically, and newer groups ranging from Russian Jews to Burmese refugees have kept the pot at a steady boil.

Milwaukee today is a center of truly global diversity but, after all these years, the German presence is still unmistakable. In the 2010 census, 38 percent of the metro area's population claimed at least some German ancestry—the highest proportion of any metropolis in America. Recent city directories contain more than fifty pages of names beginning with the classically German "Sch-" (including such formidable entries as Schimmelpfennig, Schwabenlender, and Schneggenburger), and there are nearly as many Schmidts as there are Smiths. And where else but Milwaukee would someone say his name was Miller and then spell it—to avoid confusion with the German-derived Mueller?

But it's not just surnames and census numbers that testify to the persistence of German culture. City Hall itself, a marvel of stepped gables and ornamental stonework, is a classic example of Teutonic design. Mader's, Kegel's, and other German-themed restaurants offer some of the tastiest sauerbraten and schnitzel this side of Berlin. The aroma inside Usinger's sausage shop is so rich that the proprietors could practically charge for it. The Pabst Mansion offers an up-close look at the opulent life of a German beer baron. And Milwaukee has a well-deserved reputation as a city of festivals in the best European tradition. Summerfest, a lakefront extravaganza that draws up to a million revelers each year, is billed as the world's largest music festival, but it's also an updated and expanded version of the German beer gardens that once dotted Milwaukee's landscape. You might even hear an occasional *Ein prosit!* as someone hoists a cold can of Milwaukee lager. During the rest of the summer, the lakefront grounds host what is probably the most extensive lineup of ethnic festivals in the country—a reflection of the diversity that began with the Germans.

More fundamental than all of these is the tenor of life in the old German Athens. Milwaukee's diversity is obvious, and it has not evolved without struggle or strife, but residents of all backgrounds have created a city like no other in America. Visitors tend to notice the clean streets, the abundant parks, the unforced friendliness of the people, and the manageable scale of the city as a whole. Underlying these qualities is something deeper: a shared desire for domestic tranquility and a high quality of life that goes back to Milwaukee's beginnings.

The word is *Gemütlichkeit*, and it translates easily.

Latino Milwaukee

Los Primeros Left a Rich Legacy

A trip down the aisles of Mercado El Rey is always educational for me. As I peruse the tomatillos, drop a gingerbread marranito into my paper sack, and wonder how in the world you cook something as massive as maguey or as prickly as chayote, I have the extraordinarily useful sensation of being a minority in my hometown. Neither the clerks nor the customers are speaking English, and I know that my differentness is being observed. The El Rey supermarket anchors South Chavez Drive, but I knew the street as South Sixteenth in my earlier years. Visiting the neighborhood today feels like entering a new world, a complete community set down only recently in the midst of traditional Milwaukee.

That impression is wildly inaccurate. Latinos may seem like recent arrivals to older Anglos like myself, but they've actually had a solid presence in the community for more than a century. A few adventurers came as early as the 1880s—organist and music teacher Rafael Baez was probably the first—but it was in the years after World War I that a significant number of Latinos began to call Milwaukee home, and the vast majority came from Mexico.

Most were attracted by the usual magnet: jobs. A short, sharp recession followed the Allied victory in 1918, but the 1920s began to roar soon enough. Facing labor shortages and, in some cases, labor unrest, local industries that had always relied on

European immigrant labor turned to sources closer to home. Foundries, railroads, and above all, tanneries hired laborers from Mexico—nearly all of them younger men—to fill their entry-level positions. Some arrived on their own, and others were recruited as strikebreakers, often unknowingly, with the employers paying their train fares and housing them on company grounds.

During that first wave of settlement, the largest tanner in Milwaukee, and in the United States, was Pfister & Vogel, whose flagship facility sprawled across thirty-eight buildings on fifteen acres at the south end of the Sixth Street viaduct. *Los primeros*—the pioneers—began to arrive in 1920, when one hundred immigrants recruited by labor agents went to work at P&V. They were soon joined by another hundred.

The seeds were planted, but they did not produce a community—not yet. The first arrivals were sequestered inside the P&V complex, perhaps to avoid conflict with European immigrants who were out on strike. "The men sleep on sanitary cots in a room adjoining one of the factory buildings," reported the *Milwaukee Journal* on May 15, 1920, "and eat their meals in the company's dining room." The public school system offered English classes, and there were other diversions. "On their recreational evenings," the paper continued, "the YMCA provides moving pictures, athletics and games."

Los primeros soon filtered out into the polyglot neighborhood bordering the tannery district. Walker's Point was a virtual League of Nations in the 1920s; Serbs, Slovenes, Greeks, Norwegians, Austrians, Poles, Bulgarians, and a variety of other groups made it the most diverse neighborhood in Milwaukee. Spanish-speakers added one more element to the linguistic mix. Relatively steady work and relatively high wages (twenty-seven dollars a week in the tanneries) encouraged the immigrants to put down roots.

Los primeros—the pioneers, nearly all of them male—planted the seeds of Milwaukee's Latino community in the early 1920s. ARNOLDO SEVILLA

As Mexican women began to arrive in significant numbers, families were formed and community institutions launched, among them social clubs, a short-lived newspaper, and a church. In 1926, with crucial support from Milwaukee's lay Catholic leaders, the Mission of Our Lady of Guadalupe opened in a former blacksmith shop on South Fifth Street just north of National Avenue.

The community's growth accelerated after 1924, when a racist federal law virtually ended immigration from southern and eastern Europe. The predictable result was a labor shortage that brought hundreds more Mexicans to Milwaukee. By 1930, the community had swelled to nearly four thousand people, still centered on the near South Side.

What a difference a decade makes. In the 1930s, as the American economy collapsed, some Mexican workers left voluntarily and hundreds more were deported, under the guise of repatriation, to their homeland. They were not allowed to come back until the industrial build-up for World War II, and they kept on coming with the return of peacetime in 1945. Although Mexicans remained the largest single Spanish-speaking group in

Milwaukee after the war, a significant number of Puerto Ricans also made the city their home, some in the vicinity of St. John's Cathedral downtown and others on the South Side. Because they were American citizens by birth, the Caribbean newcomers could come and go without papers.

Milwaukee's Mexican and Puerto Rican families were joined in the following decades by new arrivals from Cuba, Central America, and South America. The result was a loose-knit community that may have seemed monolithic to English-speaking outsiders but was in fact among the most diverse in Milwaukee. Patterns of diet, dialect, dance, and dress varied widely from one group to the next.

In 1970, the US Census counted 15,589 "persons of Spanish language" in the city—2.2 percent of Milwaukee's population. The near South Side housed what was easily the largest

With the arrival of women later in the 1920s, a genuine community began to take shape, with family life at its center. ARNOLDO SEVILLA

Spanish-speaking community in the state, but it was extremely concentrated. In 1970, I was working at Journey House, which was then a youth center on South Sixteenth and West Washington Streets. Even though we were just blocks from the center of the Latino community at Sixth and National, most Journey House participants were white and working-class, typically with roots in rural Wisconsin; the Lopez, Morales, and Pacheco kids were distinctly in the minority. If you wanted to go out for Mexican food, there was just one choice in the neighborhood: the Texas Restaurant on South Fifth Street, a little Tex-Mex place run by the Luna family.

Thirty years later, the neighborhood had been transformed. Sixteenth Street became Cesar Chavez Drive in 1996 and took on a new identity as the city's leading center of Latino commerce. The roster of Latino-owned restaurants in the area—Mexican, Puerto Rican, even Salvadoran—grew to number in the dozens. Spanish was heard much more often than English on South Side streets, and it wasn't hard for an Anglo to imagine he'd been transported to El Paso or Nogales—when it wasn't snowing.

What the demographic shift reflects is a pattern of uninterrupted growth that has lasted for decades. Latinos have continued to come to Milwaukee even in a post-industrial economy, finding work in any number of fields. Although the census nomenclature seems to change every decade—from persons of "Spanish language" to "Spanish origin" to "Hispanic origin" and most recently to "Spanish or Latino"—the count has continued to rise whatever the label. The city's official Latino population skyrocketed from 26,111 in 1980 to 71,646 in 2000 and 116,306 in 2020—more than quadrupling in forty years. Given the reality of undocumented workers in the city, there is not the slightest doubt that those numbers are undercounts. Even as it grows, the Latino population remains diverse; the current community is roughly two-thirds Mexican and a quarter Puerto Rican, with the balance divided among Caribbeans and Central and South Americans.

Expanding outward from their original base in Walker's Point, Latinos now dominate parts of the South Side that were once heavily eastern European. First on Mitchell Street, then on Lincoln Avenue, and now increasingly on Oklahoma Avenue— streets roughly one mile apart—Spanish-language signs have steadily replaced those printed in English, and the South Side's playgrounds are filled with Latino children who have swelled the enrollments of local schools. At St. Josaphat's Basilica, that towering landmark of Polish Milwaukee, the parish grade school's student body is now more than 90 percent Latino.

It's all part of the ferment of life in a large city—dynamic, sometimes disorienting, and occasionally unsettling to some, perhaps, but always enlivening. More than a century after *los primeros* arrived, Latinos are at home in Milwaukee, and their presence has made the city a richer place for all of us.

"Why Can't They Be Like Us?"

An Old Question Is Still Being Asked

It is one of the most persistent weeds in the garden of American democracy. Smother it with rhetoric, douse it with good intentions, and it still comes up, hardy as ever. The weed is nativism, and it sprouts most vigorously whenever one group challenges the fitness of another to live in the country we all share. Underlying the calls to close the door, raise the gangplank, or build a wall is a question as old as America: "Why can't they be like us?"

Even acknowledging the question's existence might seem un-American to some citizens. Hasn't the United States always been a nation of newcomers? Haven't we always opened our door to "your tired, your poor, your huddled masses yearning to breathe free"?

Well, no. In fact, hell, no. A broad vein of xenophobia runs through our national narrative, and the evidence begins in our own backyard. One of the first acts of Milwaukee's white settlers was to evict, under federal auspices, the American Indians who had made their homes in the area for millennia; the newcomers did not consider Native people fit to live on their own land.

The white settlers could be a fractious bunch themselves. Even before it became a city, Milwaukee was a community of immigrants—German and Irish, primarily, but also British, Scandinavian, and Czech—who didn't always get along with their American-born neighbors. In 1843, three years before

An 1893 *Puck* magazine cartoon captured the attempts of earlier Americans to raise the gangplank for anyone arriving later. THE OHIO STATE UNIVERSITY, BILLY IRELAND CARTOON LIBRARY AND MUSEUM

incorporation, the immigrants held a mass meeting to demand equal voting rights with the resident "Yankees," most of whom were Anglo-Saxon Protestants with roots in New England or New York. The *Milwaukee Sentinel*, published by and for the Yankee element, made its editorial position crystal-clear:

> If these foreigners, who are unlike ourselves in birth, language, breeding and customs, secure equal rights with the Americans, our institutions will be seriously endangered. It is an injustice to draw these untutored monarchial Barbarians out of their legitimate sphere and coddle them with fine things they do not understand. Already the population is more than half foreign born. If they once gain the upper hand our liberties are lost.

Over the spirited objections of the city's Schneiders, Murphys, Olsons, and other "monarchial Barbarians"—many of whose descendants help run Milwaukee today—the Yankees succeeded in setting the residency requirement for voting at three months and then six.

The sharp distinction drawn by the *Sentinel* between "foreigners" and "Americans" has never lost its razor's edge, but the line separating one group from the other has shifted with time. By the late 1800s, America's German and Irish residents could wrap themselves in the same flag as the early Yankees to face down a new threat to the established order: immigrants from southern and eastern Europe, including Poles, Italians, Jews, Greeks, and a host of other ethnicities.

Groups who had once been viewed as threats themselves vilified the most recent arrivals as cancers on the body politic. One result was a set of frankly racist theories about body type and head size designed to prove that the "new" immigrants—including my ancestors and perhaps yours—were genetically different from the "old" stock. Anti-immigrant sentiment rose to such a fever pitch that Ellwood Cubberley, one of the nation's leading educators, felt free to libel millions of his fellow citizens without the slightest fear of reprisal: "These southern and eastern Europeans are of a very different type from the north Europeans who preceded them. Illiterate, docile, lacking in self-reliance and initiative, and not possessing the Anglo-Teutonic conceptions of law, order, and government, their coming has served to dilute tremendously our national stock, and to corrupt our civic life."

In 1917, as nativist pressures continued to mount, the United States entered World War I. Now it was the Germans' turn to feel the heat. Anti-"Hun" sentiment reached the level of hysteria, and Milwaukee, as the most German city in America, suffered accordingly. The German language, German customs, and even German foods underwent a metamorphosis. Sauerkraut became "liberty cabbage," hamburger became "Salisbury steak," and even beer was suspect. "We have German enemies across the water," declared John Strange, a former Wisconsin lieutenant governor. "We have German enemies in this country too. And the worst of all our German enemies, the most treacherous, the most menacing, are Pabst, Schlitz, Blatz and Miller." Anti-German propaganda played an important supporting role in America's decision to enact Prohibition in 1919. Beer came back, of course, but German American culture never regained its prewar vigor.

The "new" immigrants suffered a similar catastrophe not long after Armistice Day. Responding to economic insecurity, fears of Bolshevism, and racism masquerading as science, Congress passed quota laws in 1921 and 1924 that ended mass emigration from southern and eastern Europe. "I lift my lamp beside the golden door!," promised the poem on the Statue of Liberty. In the 1920s, the lamp was effectively extinguished, and the "golden door" was slammed shut. By that time, most Asians had already been excluded for years.

Another door soon opened. Faced with a critical shortage of immigrant labor, Northern industries turned to groups already on the American continent, fueling a large-scale movement of Black people from the South and Mexicans from the Southwest. Those movements would reach their first peak in the 1920s, taper off in the depressed 1930s, and rise to new heights during World War II and after. Like the Europeans who preceded them, the newcomers faced both prejudice and privation, but their travails have been prolonged by attitudes about people of color that constitute one of our nation's most troubling traditions.

Despite its manifest shortcomings, America, I firmly believe, is a great country, but there have been times when we doubted our destiny and yielded to the all-too-human tendency to lift ourselves up by looking down on those around us, particularly newcomers. The tensions seem to peak during times of dislocation, including wars, recessions, and rapid social change. The dominant dynamic in today's environment is globalization. As people everywhere share the same technologies and compete in a single market, the world is getting smaller every day without shrinking an inch. The flip side of globalization turns out to be nationalism, a pattern plainly evident both here and in Europe. As people struggle to adapt to a new order, they seek stability in the cocoons of their own traditions within their own borders.

One corollary of nationalism is fear of foreigners, including the seeming foreigners in our midst. That fear has blossomed repeatedly, but it needn't be the dominant narrative. Time after time, and without surrendering our national security, Americans of longer tenure have put hatred aside and allowed newcomers to find their way. We have done so grudgingly, more often than not, and rarely without conflict, but the result is a society enriched by its diversity.

The alternative is not just impoverishing but chilling. What if we really were able to shut our doors and close our windows? In the 1850s, during an especially virulent outbreak of nativism, the aptly named Know Nothing Party rose to prominence as one of the first groups that pledged to "keep America American." Abraham Lincoln, a Republican, expressed grave misgivings in an 1855 letter to a friend. Lincoln's words were powerful in 1855, but they seem oddly clairvoyant today, and more than a little ominous:

> Our progress in degeneracy appears to me to be pretty rapid. As a nation, we began by declaring that "all men are created equal." We now practically read it "all men are created equal, except negroes." When the Know-Nothings get control, it will read "all men are created equal, except negroes, and foreigners and Catholics." When it comes to this I should prefer emigrating to some country where they make no pretense of loving liberty—to Russia, for instance, where despotism can be taken pure, and without the base alloy of hypocrisy.

From Beaver Pelts to Poker Chips

Intertribal Disputes Reflect the Diversity of Wisconsin Indians

The brush is impossibly broad. Carrying childhood stereotypes into adulthood, many of us paint American Indians as a single, undifferentiated mass of people—differing in ancestral dress and dialect, perhaps, but not in essence. The same shorthand is often applied to Latinos, Asians, and, for that matter, European Americans. Even though the Potawatomi are as different from the Menominee as Mexicans are from Puerto Ricans, Chinese are from Hmong, and Italians are from Poles, Americans boil their ethnic and racial differences down to a cartoonish notion of skin color: red, brown, yellow, white, and black.

The human rainbow may be a powerful and poetic symbol, but it's hopelessly simplistic, at every band of the spectrum. Cultural realities are always complex, and that applies equally to Native Americans and citizens of more recent tenure. In 2015, vehement Potawatomi opposition to a proposed Menominee casino in Kenosha made it clear that our state's indigenous people are anything but monolithic, and subsequent tension over other sites has only confirmed that fact.

Casino disputes, in fact, are revealing throwbacks to the Wisconsin of three hundred years ago—long before statehood or even nationhood. Tribal diversity was the region's defining quality then as now, and tribal conflict was a common corollary. Just as neighboring nations in Europe went to war with lethal

frequency, North America had its share of armed combat. Beginning in the 1600s, the fighting was over wealth being introduced to the region from elsewhere, including the guns, traps, kettles, blankets, and other material goods of the European fur trade. Today's disputes typically arise over gambling revenue. Beaver pelts have given way to poker chips, but some of the underlying dynamics are virtually identical.

The history of these dynamics is treacherous ground for a historian, particularly a white historian. Although every tribe has a rich oral tradition, more conventional accounts—the maps, memoirs, letters, and official documents that can provide historians with chronology and context—are often lacking. The written record of Native settlement is largely a white record, with all that implies of one-sided accounts and cultural contamination.

Although the terrain is uncertain, the major landmarks are clear. For untold centuries before European contact, the land we know today as Wisconsin was Menominee and Ho-Chunk territory; both groups have lived here longer than the other state tribes who operate casinos. The border between the Menominee and the Ho-Chunk was vague at best (the very idea of "border" meant little to either group), but Lake Winnebago and the Door Peninsula formed an important Ho-Chunk population corridor, and the opposite side of Green Bay was home to a large number of Menominee. Did members of either tribe spend much time around Milwaukee? Maybe.

The region's relative stability ended with the arrival of newcomers seeking refuge in the mid-1600s. The North American fur trade had developed two competing capitals: Montreal for the French and New York City for the Dutch and then the

(*Opposite*) A Ho-Chunk drummer kept time at Milwaukee's Winter Moon powwow in 2009. MILWAUKEE JOURNAL SENTINEL

English. The European companies routinely used their Native suppliers as proxies in an ongoing war for economic and political dominion. The five (later six) nations of the Iroquois Confederacy, including the Oneida, were particularly aggressive allies of the British. Seeking greater control of both fur territory and trade routes, the Iroquois pushed the French-allied tribes of the Great Lakes region farther west every year.

Two of those tribes, the Potawatomi and the Ojibwe, were pushed all the way into Wisconsin, along with Sauk, Fox, Odawa, and other refugees. Dislodged from southern Michigan after long residence even farther east, the Potawatomi became a dominant force in eastern Wisconsin, while the Ojibwe, always a more northerly people, resettled in northern Wisconsin and Upper Michigan.

Inevitably, tensions arose in this reconfigured cultural landscape. As the Indians jockeyed for position with their European trade partners, casting their lots first with one side and then the other, clashes between tribes were not uncommon. It's worth noting that the "tribes" of Europe at the time were just as prone to conflict, and often with much bloodier results.

A genuine wild card was added to the deck in 1821, when the Oneida, fleeing white pressure in New York State, settled in the Fox Valley on what had been Menominee land, not far from the tribes their Iroquoian ancestors had driven west. The Oneida were joined in the next few years by some of the last of the Mohicans: the Stockbridge-Munsee band, also from New York State.

By the 1830s, when white settlement began in earnest, Wisconsin was home to an unusually broad assortment of Indian tribes. Some had been on the scene for centuries (the Menominee and the Ho-Chunk), others were more recent transplants from farther east (the Potawatomi and the Ojibwe), and another (the Oneida) had been partially responsible for the displacement of their neighbors. The tribes represented three different

Casino revenue has been a major stroke of fortune for Wisconsin's Indian tribes, including the Potawatomi. MILWAUKEE JOURNAL SENTINEL

linguistic stocks and, despite the homogenizing influence of the fur trade, there were still sharp cultural differences among them.

Despite those differences, open conflict between the tribes was sporadic, and it became even less common as the United States mounted more aggressive tactics against the Native people. With the slaughter of Black Hawk's band on the banks of the Mississippi in 1832, warfare virtually ended.

The history of white-Native relations since that time has been a shameful record of manipulation, coercion, and outright theft. As the United States broke promise after promise to Wisconsin's Native communities, imported diseases continued to plague them, wiping out up to 90 percent of some tribal populations. The American Indian families who have made it through the slow-motion genocide of the past two centuries are survivors indeed. Is it any wonder, after such a traumatic history, that many of them object to being reduced to mascots for athletic teams?

Until the advent of gaming, American Indians had no dependable ladder out of the economic cellar. In Wisconsin's largest market, the games began with the desire of Milwaukee's

Indian Community School for a stable source of income. Its leaders proposed high-stakes bingo, but that option was available only to recognized tribes, not to a school that served children from several nations. School officials therefore shopped their proposal around to the full range of Wisconsin's tribes. It was the Forest County Potawatomi who finally said "Yes," and their Menomonee Valley casino opened in 1991.

It has been successful, to put it mildly, taking in nearly $400 million a year and lifting one of Wisconsin's smaller tribes out of poverty. Expansion since 1991 has been nearly constant. The newest addition to the Potawatomi complex is a five-hundred-room hotel, which enables gamblers to sleep as close to their favorite slot machines as possible.

I haven't left much of my own cash in the Menomonee Valley. On the rare occasions when I visit the casino for a show or a meal, I zip through my allotted twenty dollars at the machines in about as many minutes. But I don't begrudge the Potawatomi or any other tribe their golden goose. White America has taken so much away from Native America over the centuries that there's a certain amount of poetic justice in winning some back.

Given the hefty sums involved, you can hardly blame any tribe for wanting to build or expand where there is dependable traffic, whether it's Kenosha, Wittenberg, or Beloit. Nor can you fault other tribes for resisting competition. There's nothing like money for drawing lines between old neighbors.

If you listen carefully to the opposing sides in any casino dispute, you might hear faint echoes of the fur trade era, when European settlers gave Wisconsin's resident tribes new reasons for antagonism and competition. Contemporary conflicts are more likely to be fought with ads than arrows, but the battles are familiar. So often, when the chips are down, history is only repeating itself.

Chinese without a Chinatown

Small Community, Colossal Homeland

From New York to San Francisco, Chinatowns are fixtures of America's largest cities. These beehives of humanity are often so dense with commerce, so drenched in color—lacquered red, burnished gold—that they constitute worlds of their own, sometimes feeling as separate from the cities around them as if they were surrounded by walls. That, of course, is the attraction. Non-Chinese visitors experience these self-contained communities as welcome breaks from their daily routines.

Milwaukee has never reached the population threshold necessary to support a real Chinatown; you have to travel ninety miles south for a concentrated dose of Chinese culture. But a community has developed here anyway. Although Milwaukee was historically known as a magnet for Europeans, it has been attracting a steady trickle of Chinese immigrants for well over a century.

The first arrived in the 1870s, all of them from the Canton area, all of them men, and most of them with prior experience on the West Coast. The California gold rush of 1849 sparked the first mass exodus from China. Immigrants came for the gold—or at least the jobs it created—and stayed for the railroads, helping to forge the nation's first transcontinental link in 1869. White backlash against Chinese workers in the West, codified in the Chinese Exclusion Act of 1882, forced them to seek work

Toy's Restaurant, shown in 1922, was an anchor for Milwaukee's small but close-knit Chinese community. MILWAUKEE PUBLIC LIBRARY

elsewhere, and Milwaukee became one of their many destinations in the American interior.

Generations of Chinese men traveled great distances to support their families across the Pacific. As the United States passed more restrictive immigration laws, the adventurers who had made it this far found it nearly impossible to bring relatives across, even their own wives. Maurine Huang, whose 1988 doctoral dissertation is a standard source, described the resulting Chinese community in Milwaukee as "a bachelor society."

The title of Huang's work says it all: "Chinese without a Chinatown." Milwaukee's community never topped twenty or thirty people in the 1800s, and it was not until the 1930s that the population reached the three-hundred mark—far too few to form a distinct geographic enclave. But the immigrants were distinctive in other ways, particularly their occupations. The vast majority—more than 80 percent—worked in either Chinese restaurants or Chinese laundries. The businesses may seem stereotypical today, but they provided a steady flow of cash and enabled the newcomers to operate in all-Chinese environments. Charley Toy opened an extremely popular restaurant (and theater) on North Second Street in 1912. By 1920, Toy's was one of at least eight Chinese restaurants in the city, and there were sixteen Chinese laundries taking in shirts and skirts, including establishments run by Wah Kee, Lee Wah, Sam Wing, and Lee Sing. The greatest number were located on the west side of downtown.

The community's linchpin, writes Maurine Huang, was the tong, a secret society that protected its members' interests, maintained group discipline, and even served as an informal zoning board, setting the minimum distance between Chinese businesses. The tong's leader for decades was Jack Wong, a wealthy importer who had come to Milwaukee in 1902. Wong's word was law among the immigrants, and his shop on Fourth and State served as their informal community center.

Although Milwaukeeans developed a taste for chow mein and a habit of patronizing Chinese laundries, racist attitudes toward the Chinese themselves were commonplace. The *Milwaukee Journal* invoked a typical stereotype in 1894, describing Chinese residents as "absolutely the most un-American of all the people whom steamships bring to our shores." The description appeared in a story about three Chinese immigrants who were applying for citizenship—something denied them by federal law.

Other racist stories about "the celestials," as they were called (a reference to China as the "celestial empire" whose people considered their emperor divine), focused on criminal activity. In 1889, two laundrymen were tried for "debauchery of young girls." Lurid press accounts of "the lust of the vagabond celestials" spurred mobs of vigilantes to vandalize Chinese laundries all over town. Although both defendants spent more than two years in jail, neither was ultimately convicted.

RAID OPIUM DENS; TWO UNDER ARREST

United States Officers Arrest Ho Wah and Sam Wah, Charged With Selling "Dope."

PIPES ARE DISCOVERED

Paraphernalia Is Taken From Rooms Frequented by Chinamen Who Smoked.

Occasional drug raids generated unwelcome publicity. MILWAUKEE SENTINEL, OCT. 12, 1910

Drugs generated the headlines in other cases. In 1910, federal marshals raided opium dens in the back rooms of two more Chinese laundries. According to the *Journal*, they discovered smoking paraphernalia, processed opium, and "four or five unconscious Chinamen reclining on high shelves . . . like stacks of cord wood," completely lost in "the delicious stupor." The offending establishments were quickly closed.

Far removed from the headlines, the vast majority of Milwaukee's Chinese residents, both the single men and the smaller number of families, endured prejudice, loneliness, and long hours, working patiently and sending their money across the Pacific to relatives they hadn't seen, in many cases, for decades.

It was not until the years following World War II that the United States finally began to reopen its doors, first to Chinese intelligentsia fleeing the Maoist takeover of 1949 and ultimately to anyone with the means to make the trip.

It is those more recent arrivals who form the bulk of Milwaukee's current Chinese population. According to federal census estimates, there were 4,314 residents of Chinese ancestry in Milwaukee County in 2019, trailing both Hmong and East Indian Milwaukeeans among the Asian groups. Many of the city's Chinese transplants are single adventurers as in days past, but there is an abundance of families as well. Although Chinese restaurants are more plentiful than ever, the community also includes physicians, engineers, scientists, and a dean's list of other professionals.

New growth has sparked both new pride and new solidarity in a group that includes a remarkable breadth of regional cultures. In 2006, the Milwaukee Chinese Community Center was established to offer language classes, sponsor performance groups, and organize other cultural activities for its members and the general public. Those activities take place against the backdrop of China's remarkable rise as an economic giant and a global superpower. They also remind us that, even as boatloads of Chinese-made products reach US shores every day, the country has been sending something else to America for many more years: its people. There may not be a Milwaukee Chinatown, but there is a Chinese Milwaukee. Its members look back to a past, just as all of us look to a future, that is bound inseparably to the culture of a colossus halfway around the world.

Most Segregated Metro Area?

It's Not That Simple

Is there anything more difficult to write about than race? Is there any subject that carries such an emotional charge, such potential to confuse, enrage, and divide? Race is, after all, with the possible exception of gender, often the first thing we notice about each other, and every encounter triggers a tangle of inherited attitudes, ancient tensions, and unresolved questions.

Let me step directly into the minefield of race by saying that I'm tired of hearing about Milwaukee's status as the most segregated community in America. Segregation is often the first thing mentioned in national news stories and the first problem identified by local activists. It's as if we all had a big scarlet letter "S" emblazoned on our chests, wearing it as a badge of shame for all the world to see. Anyone who hasn't been to another Northern city—almost any other Northern city—might think that Milwaukee is the capital of American apartheid, an oppressive throwback to the Jim Crow South.

That's a false impression, but let me be clear: I'm not giving my hometown a pass. I don't write from wounded pride or naïveté about the racism in our midst. Milwaukee's problems are glaringly obvious, but they are problems we share with the rest of the urban North, aggravated by some unique historical and geographic circumstances. I object to the "most segregated" tag because it reflects an incomplete, often knee-jerk understanding

Milwaukee's children grow up in worlds that are either Black or white but rarely both.
JOHN GURDA

of race in Milwaukee, and because it's both demoralizing and unproductive.

Let's look at the numbers, first of all. One widely used measure of segregation is the index of dissimilarity, which calculates how many Black residents would have to move to achieve an even distribution across a given metropolitan area. In 2017, the most recent census sample year available, Milwaukee would have required the most moves, after finishing second to Detroit in 2010. Another measure, the isolation index, calculates the proportion of a metro area's Black residents who live in census tracts that are at least 80 percent Black. Milwaukee ranked twentieth most isolated in 2017, an improvement from fifth in 2010.

The numbers may be inconclusive, but Milwaukee is always in the same cluster of highly segregated Northern cities that includes Chicago, Detroit, Cleveland, Buffalo, and Philadelphia. The numbers confirm what common sense and personal experience suggest. After visiting all of them, I'm convinced that, viewed from ground level, the North Side of Milwaukee has striking similarities with the South Side of Chicago, the East Side of Cleveland, and the heart of Detroit. The struggling Black ghetto is an American landscape type.

Milwaukee is hardly unique, and yet there are specific conditions that have shaped segregation here. The first reflects the

city's internal geography. For most of our existence, the North
and South Sides have been monolithic districts, ethnic and
racial strongholds where outsiders knew within a minute or two
that they were on another group's turf. For generations the
North Side was German, the South Side was Polish, and they
functioned as two different worlds, with different inscriptions
above the church doors, different sweets on the bakery shelves,
and different languages heard in the saloons. More than a century later, after one of the least-studied transformations in Milwaukee's history, the same North Side is overwhelmingly Black
and the same South Side comparably Latino. The demographics
are different, but the underlying pattern is much the same.

I recently read an essay by a local writer who claimed that
she could tell a Milwaukeean's cultural background by his or
her address. She made that observation as an indictment, one
more proof of the city's hypersegregation. The simple fact is
that she could have done the same thing with equal confidence
125 years ago.

The strength of Milwaukee's European ethnic communities
was another influence on race relations in the city. Any group
with a highly developed sense of "us" will have an equally
strong conception of "them." To the white ethnics of the post–
World War II period, Black residents represented otherness of
a previously unknown order. When they expanded into the
North Side after the war, Black people entered a heavily German enclave whose members yielded ground slowly and resent-
fully. Milwaukee was spared the savage violence that left
thirty-eight people dead in a 1919 Chicago race riot, but the
welcome mat was conspicuously absent. White resistance,
expressed in restrictive housing covenants, racist lending practices, and an array of less obvious measures, created a color line
that changed slowly and painfully.

A third historical/geographic factor was Milwaukee's place

in the region. During the first phase of the Great Migration, from 1910 to 1930, hundreds of thousands of Black sharecroppers traded the fields of the rural South for the factories of the urban North, fleeing the tyranny of Jim Crow laws and seeking "the warmth of other suns," a Richard Wright line that became the title of Isabel Wilkerson's superb study of the mass movement. Like a gigantic sponge, Chicago absorbed the lion's share of migrants coming to the upper Midwest. Milwaukee, lying squarely in the larger city's shadow, attracted relatively few newcomers.

The numbers are telling. In 1920, Black residents made up more than 4 percent of Chicago's population and only 0.5 percent of Milwaukee's, an eightfold difference. In 1950, even after the full-employment years of World War II, the contrast was nearly as stark: Black households made up 14 percent of the Windy City's population and just 3.4 percent of the Cream City's. Ranked by its proportion of Black residents, Milwaukee was nearly always dead last among the nation's fifteen largest cities until 1970.

Why is that important? Because Milwaukee's Black community reached critical mass a full generation later than its peers elsewhere in the North. That's one less generation to put down roots, develop supportive institutions, and grow a middle class. The fact that Milwaukee's Black residents were, on average, more than four years younger than their Chicago counterparts was another likely limiting factor.

A formidable river valley, a cohesive European ethnic population, and the proximity of Chicago all influenced the historical development of Milwaukee's Black community. Those three factors combined to check the community's growth, but they could not check it indefinitely. In 1970, the city's Black population finally crossed the double-digit threshold, rising to 15 percent of the total. Despite stubborn resistance on multiple fronts, the new arrivals made notable headway. Slowly at first, Black residents joined Milwaukee's blue-collar aristocracy, earning union wages in a union town at companies like Allis-Chalmers and A. O. Smith. By 1970, in fact, 54 percent of the metro area's Black men had production jobs, compared to 23 percent of their white counterparts. Homeownership, second cars, and higher education were all within reach.

No sooner had Black workers started to climb the ladder into the middle class, however, than it was rudely yanked out from under them. Milwaukee lost a quarter of its manufacturing jobs between 1979 and 1983, and the losses kept mounting. Deindustrialization claimed giants like Allis-Chalmers and slashed payrolls at virtually every other plant. Black workers made up a disproportionate share of the blue-collar work force, and they bore a disproportionate share of the job cuts. In 1986, Milwaukee's Black unemployment rate approached 26 percent, nearly three times the metro average. Between 1980 and 1990—a decade of recovery for the rest of the economy—the proportion of Black Milwaukeeans living in poverty soared from 28.4 percent to 41.9 percent.

It doesn't take a doctorate in sociology to connect the dots. The great mass of Milwaukee's African Americans began young, arrived late, and had only a decade or two to establish themselves before the roof caved in. They have, in effect, been fighting with one hand tied behind their backs ever since they got here.

One result is a high level of segregation. Racist practices of the past had an obvious geographic impact, and racism is still alive and well in the present, but the legal barriers to Black mobility are down. What has kept the North Side ghetto intact is an economy first flattened and then frozen in place by forces global in scale.

Where is the evidence? Consider Holton Street, the border between Riverwest on the east and Harambee on the west. Holton is as stark a racial dividing line as exists in Milwaukee today: 20 percent Black on the east side and 74 percent on the west. The gap exists despite the fact that Riverwest is celebrated as one of the most open, most tolerant neighborhoods in the city, a community that embraces its diversity and would welcome more.

Why, then, such a vivid color line? Two numbers suggest an answer. In 2015, Riverwest's median housing value was 60 percent higher than Harambee's, and Harambee's median household income was 40 percent lower than Riverwest's. That mismatch reveals a fundamental lack of buying power. Geographic mobility depends on economic capacity; without it, hypersegregation becomes a default state. For households who can't afford even very affordable Riverwest, Brookfield and Mequon might as well be the moon.

Even if today's hurdles are primarily economic—class trumping race—they still rest on a racial foundation. It was race, after all, that produced those class divisions in the first place, going back to the dark days of slavery, and the split in Milwaukee has been aggravated by the specific local conditions described here.

And so we find ourselves living in a community, like many

The loss of major employers like Allis-Chalmers had a catastrophic impact on Milwaukee's Black community, creating economic hardship that impeded upward geographic mobility. MILWAUKEE JOURNAL SENTINEL

others in America, where most people of different races navigate the world in cultural bubbles, their views of each other too often dependent on media reports and tired stereotypes. I know white suburbanites who have written off the entire North Side as hostile territory, a place where they're sure they'll be robbed, raped, or beaten if they so much as try to drive through. I also once met a Black woman with a novel explanation for the loss of factory jobs that has inflicted such harm on her community. White manufacturers, she insisted, were so alarmed by the growth of Milwaukee's Black population that they closed their factories to put a stop to it. Paranoia and blind suspicion flourish on both sides of the color line.

Milwaukee, it seems to me, faces two problems today, related but different. The first is economic. It's been more than thirty years since Allis-Chalmers went bankrupt. Despite good intentions and some promising initiatives, nothing of serious consequence has changed in the North Side's economy since then. What the inner city needs is jobs, jobs, and more jobs—and the educational and social support necessary to sustain them. Until a larger proportion of Black Milwaukeeans have the means to improve their neighborhoods or move into other ones, any discussion of ending segregation will be purely academic.

The second, quite separate, task we face is interpersonal. All across America and more especially in cities like Milwaukee, it takes real effort to cross the color line. I fear that simplistic labels like "most segregated" only aggravate the problem, making us look down at our shoes rather than up to solutions. Our common goal should be to overcome our mutual ignorance. If we remain open to every opportunity to learn each other's stories, if we resist the temptation to point fingers, if we speak with honesty and leave room for nuance, Milwaukeeans, one by one, can build a foundation for progress on both sides of the racial divide.

Birth Pangs of a New Understanding

A White Historian Reflects on Black Lives Matter

Minneapolis? Really? I still find it hard to believe that a global movement to end police brutality and systemic racism began in Milwaukee's neighbor to the northwest. How could the current groundswell have started there? Wasn't Minneapolis known as the progressive, prosperous Star of the Snow Belt? Wasn't it the hipper of the Twin Cities, a community famous for strong neighborhoods, lovely lakes, and a booming white-collar economy? And wasn't Minneapolis so Scandinavian that "ethnics" there have been defined as people with brown hair?

Whether they're accurate or not, those stereotypes have long masked a darker reality. There is a historical hierarchy in the upper Midwest. Just as Milwaukee lagged Chicago for decades in the growth of its Black community, Minneapolis has been steadily catching up to Milwaukee. Even as high-income workers, most of them white, were filling downtown Minneapolis with office towers, condominiums, and luxury apartments in recent decades, the city's Black population, notably devoid of office towers and luxury housing, was quietly surging from less than 8 percent of the total in 1980 to 13 percent in 1990 and 20 percent in 2018. (The comparable figures for Milwaukee are 23, 30, and 39 percent.)

Whether they were coming from Chicago, Somalia, or, in George Floyd's case, Houston, Black Minneapolitans too often

George Floyd's 2020 murder in the custody of Minneapolis police sparked passionate protests in Milwaukee. MILWAUKEE JOURNAL SENTINEL

found themselves out in the cold. In an incredibly myopic 2015 article, *The Atlantic* magazine lauded the "Minneapolis miracle," a dynamic blend of "affordability, opportunity, and wealth." It was abundantly clear that the supposed miracle had bypassed the city's Black neighborhoods. By 2018, the poverty rate among Black residents had climbed to 42 percent—even worse than Milwaukee's dismal 35 percent. The seeds of unrest were present, and they were swelling.

George Floyd's murder on Memorial Day of 2020 burst those seeds wide open. That horrific smirk on Officer Derek Chauvin's face as he calmly, almost casually, killed a man already pinned to the ground was the inhuman opposite of "Minnesota nice." Protests began within hours, sparking worldwide demonstrations and recalling, for many of us baby boomers, the epidemic of racially charged riots in the late 1960s.

The violent unrest in Minneapolis was a wake-up call, an undeniable expression of inchoate rage at a system and a city that had never really worked for people of color. Minneapolis and Milwaukee were among the countless Northern communities that had put roadblock after roadblock in the paths of their Black residents. The obstacles of choice included redlining, racist housing covenants, restrictive union policies, overly aggressive policing, and a generalized assumption of white superiority. The unsurprising result, over many decades, was a staggering number of people with little or no investment in maintaining the status quo. George Floyd's murder handed them a torch.

Although pressures had been building in Minneapolis for years, the scale of the eruption rocked the city to its core. I was reminded of an observation made by Mayor Henry Maier of Milwaukee in 1966, when conditions in the inner city had grown too desperate to ignore. "Milwaukee for years," wrote Maier, "regarded herself somewhat complacently as more fortunate than her sister cities." For Minneapolis now, as well as for Milwaukee, those delusional days are over.

If Minneapolis was rocked, the world was shocked. It mattered that George Floyd was murdered in a Midwestern city with a liberal tradition and a white-bread reputation. Derek Chauvin's final act in uniform was both symbol and substance of white oppression, and the $500 million in property damage that resulted from the ensuing protests was jaw-dropping in this ostensibly most civil of American cities. The troubles there laid bare a malady that afflicts the nation as a whole.

The historical moment mattered as well. For almost everyone but essential workers, one byproduct of the coronavirus pandemic was time. George Floyd's murder occurred when millions of people had ample free time and a heightened awareness of what was going on in the world. The result was a wave of

outrage so powerful that, for a time, at least, it swamped defend-
ers of the status quo. Thousands of Black Lives Matter signs
popped up in Milwaukee's largely white neighborhoods and in
the suburbs as well. Earnest expressions of righteous anger were
heard from some unlikely quarters, including historical societies, real estate developers, temporary help agencies, and the
Milwaukee Symphony. Local protest leaders were amazed by
the outpouring of support from white Milwaukee. "We were
trying to irritate everybody," said organizer Frank Nitty in
June of 2020, "and now everybody's like cheering for us, getting
pictures, and that's crazy."

Why such a tidal wave of support for Black Lives Matter,
both here and elsewhere? Because it was time and then some.
Because George Floyd's murder was irrefutable evidence that
hatred has a home in our basic institutions. And because many
white Americans realized, some of us for the first time, that we
have been quietly complicit. Sure, we may have worked hard for
what we have and, yes, we've cleared hurdles of our own, but the
color of our skin has given white people like me a head start on
everyone else in America. Columnist Maureen Dowd once
offered a deliciously snarky assessment of George W. Bush,
describing him as a man who was "born on third base but
thought he hit a triple." To our mingled surprise and embarrassment, many white Americans have now awakened to the fact
that our skin color confers similar privilege.

My own father, hardly a paragon of racial understanding,
reached that conclusion late in life. One day in the 1990s, he had
a momentary lapse of attention and rear-ended a police car at a
North Side traffic signal. Dad was ticketed but treated with
respect. Driving home, shaken and chastened, he had an epiph-
any. Telling the story later, he asked in wonder, "What if I'd
been Black?"

The Black Lives Matter movement prompted a new reckoning with racism in American society. MILWAUKEE JOURNAL SENTINEL

Where will the current civil rights groundswell roll from here? The hardest work, it seems to me, will be internal. Conditions won't improve unless and until white Americans not only recognize our privilege but muster the courage to apply it to changing the status quo. That doesn't mean ignoring cultural differences or glossing over the all-too-real problems of the inner city. It does mean growing a new awareness of how we treat and, just as important, how we perceive the person of a different race at the next desk, in the next lane, down the next block. For me, as a white Milwaukeean, it means owning my own ignorance, asking uncomfortable questions, and groping my way toward greater understanding. The task we all share is to see "the me in thee" and act accordingly.

After so many movements have come and gone, after so many protests have roiled the waters of our society, will this be the one that takes hold, or will it fade away like sidewalk chalk after a hard rain? The established order has enormous resistance to change. That is, after all, why it's called the establishment. But George Floyd's murder carried us to a pregnant moment in our nation's history. Perhaps the ferment we're experiencing is labor pains. Millions of us are struggling with the stark contrast between the American Dream and America's reality. As our labor continues, I look forward to the birth of a more genuine democracy, one whose people understand and embrace the truth articulated by Martin Luther King Jr. more than sixty years ago: "No one will be free until we are all free."

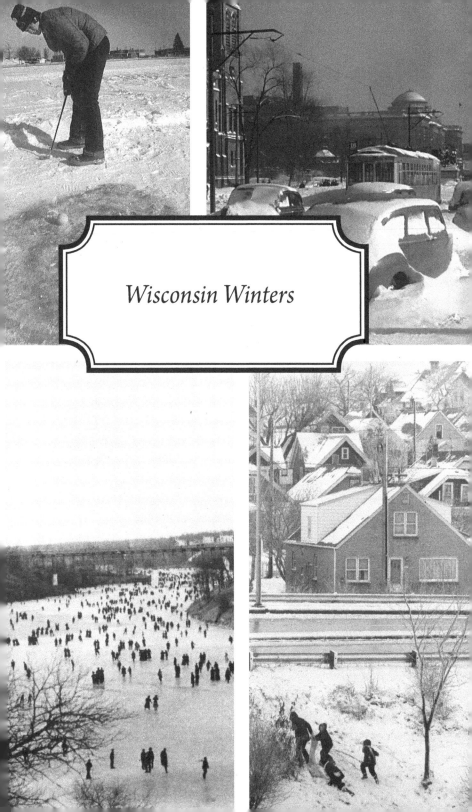

Wisconsin Winters

In Praise of True Winter

Finding Cold Comfort in the Ice and Snow

Today's coldest winters, we baby boomers tell our children, are like the ones we used to know. Back in the good old days—the 1950s, even the 1960s—the snow seemed to begin in November and last into March. Day after day, the temperature dropped below zero and the snowbanks rose to the heavens. It took a pioneer spirit to weather those winters, we insist; there was something heroic about simply making it to spring.

We conveniently forget the brown Christmases and the January thaws. We overlook the fact that the snowbanks seemed twice as high when we were half as tall. And we find it hard to believe that we probably spent more time watching Mickey Mouse and Roy Rogers than we did building snow forts in the backyard. Like so many childhood experiences, the memories dwarf the lived reality.

Even as the climate warms, Wisconsin still has winters that our own children can embellish when they look back from middle age—seasons with luxuriant drifts of snow and prolonged periods of arctic cold. I, for one (and maybe the only one), enjoy those statistical throwbacks. No, I don't welcome the shoveling, the shivering, or the days of endless gray, but whenever a cold winter winds down, I'm glad we had a real one.

My affection for winter may be in part genetic. As a descendant of northern people—Poles and Norwegians—I probably have snowflakes imprinted in my DNA. I crave winter as an absence, an anti-environment, a state of suspension, even gestation, that serves as a respite from the frenetic pace of a typical Milwaukee summer. Just as some seeds require a period of cold and dark to germinate in spring, I seem to need the long time-out of January and February.

I also appreciate winter on philosophical grounds. The northern year reflects the human condition in both its brightness and its bleakness; the cold is a yearly reminder of our innate frailty. You are alone here, says winter; you and your warm-blooded kind are just wayfaring strangers in a broken world. Seek shelter. Find enough.

And, oh yes, the cross-country skiing can be spectacular. What really makes true winters work for me is the steady supply of good snow. I'll ski thirty or forty times if given the opportunity, and I'm not talking about major expeditions. I might make an occasional pilgrimage to Upper Michigan or the Kettle Moraine, but most of my skiing is done in Milwaukee County parks—Whitnall, Brown Deer, and, above all, Grant.

The blizzard of 1947 virtually paralyzed Milwaukee. Motorists at Tenth and Wisconsin abandoned their cars wherever they had stalled in the drifts. MILWAUKEE COUNTY HISTORICAL SOCIETY

The Grant Park golf course and its adjoining woods lie only ten minutes from my home in Bay View. The ski trails there aren't even identified, much less groomed. An informal community of skiers—no more than a dozen, to judge from the pole tracks—creates loops that change after every snowstorm. I've never seen any of my coconspirators, largely because I ski at night. The only reason I'm able to go out so often is that I'm on the course after dark, following a full day of work.

It's brighter than you might think. Clear, moonless nights can be a challenge, but on cloudy evenings the orangish reflection of the city's lights provides all the illumination I need. Full moons are by far my favorites. On moonlit nights, when the broad blanket of snow takes the light whole and beams it back again, the world is so bright that I can read the lettering on my skis.

The advantage of going so often, sometimes every night, is that I get to experience ordinary snow in its remarkable variety. A road is a road is a road, but a ski trail can be an aerobic slog or a shot down an ice-slick chute, depending on the day or even the hour. A lake-effect storm one January buried the well-worn tracks of the previous day under several inches of pure fluff. Breaking trail that night felt like swimming through feathers. Two weeks later, after a hard rain and a harder freeze, I found myself poling gingerly across expanses of glare ice on the same trail. Whatever the conditions, I come home, more often than not, with my jacket soaked, endorphins coursing through my veins, and a smile on my face.

There are times, during a night ski at Grant, when I find it easy to dream back to the winter world of our ancestors. They, too, took pleasure in the cold months, despite the absence of Gore-Tex and Thinsulate. When snow began to fall in the late 1800s, newspapers hailed it with undisguised affection as simply "the beautiful." In the winter of 1885–1886—still the snowiest on record at 109.8 inches—an early storm prompted the *Milwaukee Sentinel* to celebrate the "long avenues of snow-mantled trees, their boughs hidden, weighted down and interlaced by the ermine covering."

Snow-covered sidewalks—the wooden variety—could be an irritant, but no one cared about snow piling up in the streets. It only marked the end of wagon travel and the start of winter sleighing—something many looked forward to all year. The *Milwaukee Journal* described a scene after an 1892 storm that could have been a print from Currier and Ives: "The jingle of a multitude of musical sleigh bells, the clatter of the hoofs of many horses, and flying flecks of snow and ice proclaimed a midwinter carnival yesterday, the principal scene of which was laid on Grand avenue."

Certain realities were absent from this romantic picture, of course. The bones of the poor were always sharper in winter. Downed telegraph lines regularly cut off communication with the outside world, and passenger trains were sometimes buried in drifts for days. In 1886, a trainful of anxious passengers bound for Milwaukee was snowbound in Ozaukee County and getting hungrier by the minute. Their trial ended when a rescue party struggled out from the little town of Belgium with coffee and sandwiches.

In the circumscribed world of our ancestors, Cancun and Captiva were not options. Milwaukeeans of the 1800s realized that winter would stay for as long as it had to, and they knew instinctively that the season was something to be enjoyed, not just endured. Why not revel in the regular delights and the just-as-regular hardships of the snowy months? In March 1893, the *Milwaukee Sentinel* looked back on months of harsh weather with an odd sense of accomplishment: "Altogether, it has been a winter to be proud of, if one is disposed to be proud of cold winters." That ironic benediction still applies to our infrequent true winters, when we thaw by degrees toward another spring.

Skating into the Past

A Memorable Trip to Thiensville

Good ice has always been a rarity, and it's gotten rarer as the climate changes. Only extended periods of frigid weather with little or no snow will turn our lakes and rivers into the sheets of glass favored by ice skaters, ice fishermen, and ice boaters. More often they'll encounter impassable drifts, uneven crust, or, especially these days, slush.

I hadn't skated in years but, prompted by the rumor of good ice, I drove over to the Humboldt Park lagoon one cold Saturday in 2018. Soon after I had laced up my vintage Bauers and pushed off from shore, it became apparent that my skills had not improved with age. It wasn't the ice's fault. Except for the occasional deposit of frozen goose poop, the surface was smooth, the ice was thick, and the going was easy—for good skaters, anyway.

Not many people were taking advantage of the lagoon's frigid bounty. A spirited game of pickup hockey was underway at one end of the pond, but I had plenty of room to maneuver. I tottered around until my ankles burned and called it a day.

I would have had much more company a century ago. Before we succumbed to the spell of Facebook postings, YouTube videos, sports telecasts, Zoom conversations, Twitter feeds, Netflix movies, electronic games, and a million other Things on Screens, Americans spent much more time outdoors, even in

With good ice, the Milwaukee River attracted legions of skaters.

the depths of winter. When the ice was good, skaters ventured out to glide and spin all over the region.

Their favorite destination was the Milwaukee River. For more than 150 years, from 1843 until the removal of its most recent incarnation in 1997, a dam near North Avenue turned the stream above it into a long, narrow lake stretching as far north as Capitol Drive. It was busiest during the summer months, of course, but hordes of skaters descended on the river as soon as it froze. Someone watching from shore could have seen races, romances, pratfalls, hockey games, and crack-the-whip lines at any point along the stream.

A few skaters were overachievers. One of the minor treasures of the Central Library's Rare Books Room is a slim volume titled *A Little Journey on Skates*. Its author, Joseph Bell Jr., was a draftsman for Ferry & Clas, the architectural firm responsible for the Pabst Mansion, St. John's Cathedral, and the Central Library itself. On New Year's Day in 1895, Bell and nine companions, most of them Ferry & Clas employees, skated on the river from North Avenue all the way to Thiensville—a distance of eighteen miles.

River ice is notoriously more dangerous than the still-water variety, but that didn't deter the adventurers. They carried no life rings and no ropes—only sticks to help in case someone broke through the ice. Bell noted that even those weren't necessary: "As the river is deep enough in but a few places to drown a man standing upright, . . . our precautions on this head were rendered naught." The skaters used the river for drinking water and carried miscellaneous supplies in their knapsacks, including ingredients for Tom and Jerrys.

Wearing knickerbockers, thick sweaters, and strap-on skates, the group left Milwaukee at ten in the morning. "Many skaters were upon the ice for the first few miles north," wrote Bell, "but we had only to climb over the first weir of frozen water falls where the dull roar of the under cataract sounded solemn and uncanny, to leave behind all these ephemeral merrymakers and the last view of the city." That solemn cataract was most likely the modest waterfall below the beer garden in today's Estabrook Park.

The real fun started once they had the river to themselves. "But the skating!" Bell enthused, "such skating as it was! such ice and such a winter's day as one might wait an entire season for to see—not a stirring of the air, save that we made ourselves as we rushed along the smooth black surface."

The skaters were on uncharted ice above the falls, with plenty of hazards ahead. Their leader plunged into waist-deep water at the first flour mill, and Bell himself belly-flopped through "a two-inch layer of slush water spread over a surface of sunken ice." But there were pleasant surprises as well: "In shallow parts of the mid stream we could see the fishes through ice clear as window glass."

The Milwaukeeans reached Thiensville in three hours and forty minutes, traveling at an average speed of five miles an hour. The pot of gold at the end of their rainbow was a prearranged "royal good dinner" of turkey and goose at Memmler's Inn, a German establishment on the river. The skaters, Bell reported, were famished: "I am afraid the smiling folk, who gazed at us through the sliding panel from the kitchen, must have wondered if we had ever had a square meal in our lives. . . . In half an hour the table looked as if a typhoon had struck it amidships."

After a full meal and a few drinks, most of the travelers were ready to take the train back to the city. Not Joseph Bell and two of his hardier companions. Even though night was falling, they decided to skate home by moonlight, and that, according to Bell, was the best part of the journey: "On we sped at ever increasing pace, until we had reached the limit for safety, and only tempering our speed when crackling surface ice and an opaque appearance of the river ahead, warned us of the vicinity of rapids underneath and ticklish skating above."

Despite their best efforts to read the river, the skaters experienced "several somersaults," and one of them plunged into a water hole two feet deep. The trio reached the North Avenue bridge at the stroke of eight, with their clothing "frozen hard and clanking like steel armour." Bell still faced a long streetcar ride home to the West Side, but he had no regrets: "Truly it was entrancing, that return trip, and romantically beautiful—by far the most conspicuous recollection that remains to me of the entire outing."

I'm one of many paddlers who have canoed the river between Thiensville and Milwaukee, but the odds of anyone replicating Joseph Bell's marathon journey on skates are remote indeed. The world is warmer today than it was in 1895, limiting the potential for good ice, and we've become more risk averse as a people. But Bell's chronicle is a welcome reminder of winter's unique potential for fun. You certainly don't have to skate to Thiensville and back, but the draftsman and his buddies had the right idea. Unplug, they might tell their modern-day descendants. Turn off those tyrannical screens. Get outside and enjoy winter like true four-season Wisconsinites.

The End of Winter?

Our Ancestors Also Felt the Heat—Sometimes

Wisconsin has had some strange winters lately, and that's putting it, well, mildly. There have been, in my opinion, too many Christmases in shirtsleeves, too many January bike rides, and far too little snow for dependable cross-country skiing. As our planet's climate continues to change, we are groping by degrees toward a new normal, and the direction we're headed is, to say the least, troubling.

The reality of climate change—the average global temperature has climbed roughly two degrees Fahrenheit since 1880—may lead us to believe that warm winters are a recent phenomenon, that our ancestors experienced nothing but deep snow and bitter cold when the calendar flipped to December. The reality is that long-term averages can conceal some significant aberrations. Since the National Weather Service began keeping records in 1871, Milwaukee's highest average temperature for December, January, and February was 32.6 degrees in 1931–1932—just above freezing—followed closely by 31.7 degrees in both 1877–1878 and 2001–2002.

I suppose some of us, if we tried hard enough, could call up a memory or two from the 2001–2002 season. What about those earlier warm spells? How did our ancestors cope with the balmy winters of 1877–1878 and 1931–1932?

A close look at the *Milwaukee Sentinel* and *Milwaukee Journal* for those seasons turned up a few surprises. Ice harvested from local lakes and rivers was a conspicuous casualty in 1877–1878. As the *Sentinel*'s Oconomowoc correspondent complained, "The warm weather of the present winter has been decidedly unfavorable for the ice crop in this vicinity, and our dealers have felt anxious lest their supply the following season would be insufficient to meet the demand. . . . Pray for cold weather, ye ice dealers."

As the climate warms, winter golf may not be such a novelty in the Milwaukee of the future. MILWAUKEE COUNTY HISTORICAL SOCIETY

Other businesses were affected as well. Bridge-builders were able to "push their work rapidly forward," reported the *Sentinel*, but by mid-January the proprietors of ice-skating rinks were "beginning to despair of a profitable season." Rich & Silber, a downtown clothing store, put its "ladies cloaks" on sale, "owing to the summer-like winter weather which we have been enjoying."

Warm weather also disrupted the rhythm of the meatpacking industry, a mainstay of the local economy. Packers always processed their livestock in winter, when the risk of spoilage was least. Unseasonable temperatures forced them to feed their hogs longer and butcher them later, pushing the entire season back significantly.

Reporters marveled that farmers were still plowing their fields and that pansies were still blooming in front yards even after Christmas. "I picked full blown dandelions in my yard on the 22d of January," recalled pioneer historian James Buck, "and my fruit trees all budded in February. Nothing like it was ever seen before." Some residents, however, grew so tired of muddy roads that they longed to trade their wagon wheels for sleigh runners. "We were favored with a light fall of snow on Jan. 3," wrote a *Sentinel* correspondent. "Enough more to make sleighing would be very welcome."

More than fifty years later, in the record-setting winter of 1931–1932, the sound of sleigh bells was faint indeed. Automobiles had taken over the roads, and even ice was no longer a concern—at least the variety used for refrigeration. "Natural ice has been no great factor in the market for five years," a supplier told the *Milwaukee Journal*, explaining that machines were doing most of the work.

Recreational ice was another matter. Milwaukee had developed a passion for speed skating, and there was widespread disappointment when the city championship meet at Gordon Park was called off. Officials had no choice; there was only half an inch of ice on the Milwaukee River. The opening of the municipal hockey league season was also postponed, and it wasn't until early February that ice fishing was permitted on Waukesha County's lakes.

"The seasons are upside down," declared the *Journal* on January 13: "No frost in the ground, summer time showers, trees budding, grass pushing up and bees humming in their hives— wait a minute, this is not a spring scene, but a picture of southeastern Wisconsin in winter, in January—now!"

"We're dancing now," a local meteorologist warned, "but we'll have to pay the fiddler some day." Well, the fiddler never showed up in the winter of 1931–1932. Although the temperature briefly dipped below zero at the end of January, by February 11 it had soared to 58—warmer than Los Angeles—producing a fog

so thick that mail planes were grounded and freightyard switch-
men could barely see the cars coming at them.

The prolonged warmth allowed city crews to plant locust
trees on the hillsides above Lincoln Memorial Drive in January;
the descendants of those trees are still holding the bluff in place.
By February, park workers were already fertilizing the grass
along the new drive—with locally made Milorganite, of course.

Those workers were among the dwindling ranks of the
gainfully employed. Milwaukee, with the rest of the nation, was
dropping toward the absolute pit of the Depression in the winter
of 1931–1932, and the warm weather provided some welcome relief
to a cash-strapped city. Coal prices fell sharply (to $11.05 per ton
for the buckwheat size and $14.80 for "egg coal"), and the city's
snow-plowing expenses were negligible; a few applications of
sand were sufficient to get local motorists through the winter.

The Depression continued, but the winter of 1931–1932 ended
as the warmest on record in Milwaukee. It was widely viewed
as an aberration and, sure enough, the average December-
through-February temperature dropped from its historic peak
of 32.6 degrees to 27.3 the very next year.

We are leaving behind the world of aberrations. The historic
spikes of our ancestors are fast becoming business as usual. I
find it stunning that climate change is still a matter of debate.
The naysayers have made cold, hard facts "controversial," which
raises the question of how human beings know anything. We
don't doubt that the sun is 93 million miles away from earth, but
no one I know has ever held the tape measure. We have no trouble believing that dinosaurs lived 150 million years ago, but who
can even count back that far? We take it on faith that the continents drift around on tectonic plates like ice floes in a slush
pond, but the ground feels pretty stable to me.

Even though none of us can independently verify any of
these things, most of us accept them as facts, not assertions. We

recognize them as the settled conclusions of qualified experts who have studied the evidence carefully and ruled out every competing hypothesis. That's what science does; it extends our reach and allows us to connect dots that we couldn't possibly link on our own. If we accepted only the evidence of our senses, we'd still think the earth was flat and that the sun and stars revolved around us.

When it comes to climate change, however, many of us still inhabit a flat earth. Scientific facts have somehow become opinions, and carefully researched conclusions are written off as theories or even hoaxes. Climate scientists went to the same schools, earned the same degrees, and follow the same protocols as experts we wouldn't begin to question on other matters, but millions of us find it easy to say, "I don't think so."

Why don't we believe the prognosticators of climate change? Because believing would be, to use Al Gore's favorite word, inconvenient. Because accepting climate change would require a change in our behavior. Once we admitted our collective guilt, we would have to accept, however reluctantly, our collective responsibility for fixing what we and our ancestors have broken.

The key word here is *collective*. Anyone who places the freedom of the individual above all else will instinctively resist subordinating personal privilege to the common good, particularly if it means living more simply. And anyone who puts "America First" will find the idea of meaningful cooperation across international borders repugnant. And so climate change becomes something we seek to manage rather than halt. The bus keeps careening toward the edge of the cliff.

We may be nearing the end of white Christmases and dependable snow for skiing. Although I reserve the right to grumble, I'll continue to live in the state of Wisconsin anyway. But I wonder how long we can continue to live in a state of denial.

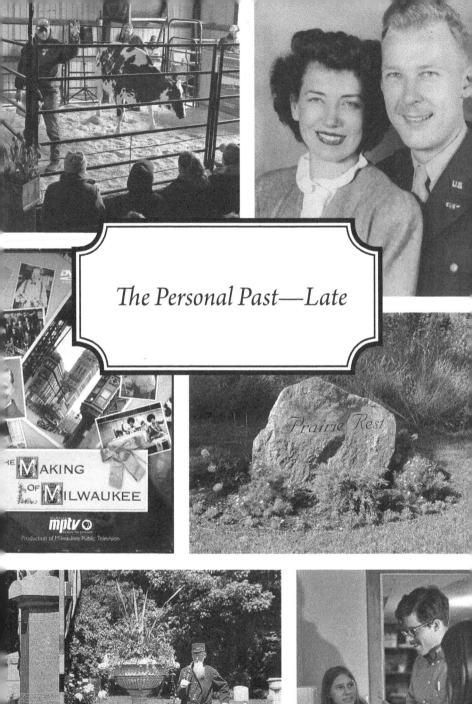

The Personal Past—Late

The Personal Part—Late

Memory Lane

Sometimes It's a State Highway

The past gets more personal as we get older. Events deemed certifiably historic today—Cold War air raid drills, the Watergate hearings, the 9/11 terrorist attacks—are part of the lived experience of thousands of Wisconsinites. Faces that peer out from faded photographs or low-res screen images inhabit our memories as living, breathing human beings. Landscapes altered beyond recognition persist in our imaginations like postcards from a vanished era.

I was reminded of these truths on a recent trip down Highway 45. It's a highway, curiously, that I've always associated with my father, gone these twenty-five years now. I don't mean the entire road, which runs for thirteen hundred miles from Mobile, Alabama, to Ontonagon, Michigan. I'm talking about the thirty-mile stretch between my boyhood home in Hales Corners and the Illinois border. That section is one of the more scenic state highways in our part of Wisconsin, inscribing a straight line across the rolling farm country of western Racine and Kenosha Counties as it connects the demographic dots of Muskego, North Cape, Union Grove, and Bristol.

Highway 45's association with my dad seems strongest during the holidays. I recall in particular one Thanksgiving dinner in the late 1950s that was less than a complete success. With four kids, a mortgage, and the instinctive frugality of their generation, my parents seldom saw the inside of a restaurant. On that Thanksgiving, however, my mother apparently decided that she'd had enough of cooking and left it to my father to pick a dining spot. His choice was a truck stop on Highway 45, just across the Racine County line. The six of us sat at a bare table surrounded by semi drivers whose big rigs were parked on the gravel outside. The turkey was basically lunch meat, but I recall the dressing as excellent. My mother fumed for the entire meal.

Summertime excursions were more harmonious. My father was a one-man sales engineering firm with a steady customer in Bristol: the Charmglow gas grill plant. A few times each summer, he'd take me or one of my brothers along on calls. Our favorite stop was an ice-cream stand on Highway 45 where it briefly joins Highway 20. One July, as we crested an especially scenic rise south of that little drive-in, Dad paused to indulge in what was, for him, a rare moment of reflection. "I don't think I could ever live anywhere else," Art Gurda declared simply. "Wisconsin is so beautiful." Looking out over the verdant fields rolling unbroken to the horizon, I had to agree, and I still do.

The last time the two of us traveled Highway 45 together was probably in the late 1960s, during another holiday season. I flew home from Boston College for Christmas break that year. My half-fare student ticket got me as far as O'Hare Airport, where Dad picked me up late in the evening. Although there was a perfectly good expressway just a few miles east, he took Highway 45 all the way home, hitting every suburb, small town, and stoplight along the route. I'm sure it had a lot to do with avoiding Illinois's tolls, but my father's affection for the road was obvious.

It's an affection I inherited. As a young adult, I'd travel out Highway 45 at odd times when I needed respite from the city. Sometimes I'd bring my bicycle along to explore the honeycomb of town roads east of Wind Lake. Once a friend joined me and we decided, on a whim, to help an elderly farmer finish his haying. What followed was two hours of scratched forearms in the field, non-stop sneezing in the hay-mow, and a glass of country water in the farmhouse kitchen for our reward.

At other times I'd bring my camera and spend a couple of hours photo-graphing the North Cape cemetery, whose residents include a pioneer with the whimsical name of Adam Apple. My wife had been making her case for a third child before one of those

The North Cape graveyard is a perfect place for quiet contemplation on Highway 45. JOHN GURDA

visits, and North Cape was where I decided that, yes, indeed, another baby would be a fine idea.

Years have passed since those youthful excursions. On a recent trip to Kenosha, perhaps channeling my father, I decided to take Highway 45 home rather than Interstate 94. Things, I discovered, had changed. There were still fields of corn, soy-beans, and barley, but sprouting between them were more suburban-style homes than I could count. Hobby farms, their pastures studded with horses, had replaced many of the hard-working dairy operations. Charmglow was no more, at least not in Bristol. The ice-cream stand at Highway 20 was long gone, and the right-angle intersection at its front door had given way to a roundabout. Adam Apple still lay undisturbed in the North Cape graveyard, but the ruins of the tile plant in the nearby village had vanished. My family's Thanksgiving truck stop, which, according to its weather-beaten sign, had last done business as Los Mariachis, was boarded up and for sale. As I neared Racine County's northern border, twin peaks of trash loomed on either side—minor mountains of landfill that had barely been molehills on my last time through.

I had changed as well. I realized with a start that I was older than my father had been during those fondly remembered childhood excursions, and that my own third child, the son I first dreamed of in North Cape, had left home more than a decade ago.

It had all passed, as usual, too fast, but did I mourn the loss of old Highway 45? Did I yearn to return to days past and landscapes lovingly recalled? Not really. The ribbon of road I knew so long ago—ice-cream stand, truck stop, haymow—was just one in a long series of incarnations that continues in the present. Imagine how Indians of the 1800s must have felt when they saw their sprawling prairies plowed up and their towering forests cut down—not that they were given much chance to take in the view. Think of the white settlers behind those first plows, who began with oxen or horses and whose descendants graduated to steam engines and then gasoline tractors. Imagine how a single generation saw kerosene lamps and woodstoves replaced by incandescent lights and electric milking machines. Life once moved at a slow trot down the dusty predecessor of Highway 45. Today's travelers glide by in steel machines at speeds our ancestors couldn't easily comprehend.

The personal past is always a universal past as well. Each of us occupies a narrow niche, a single layer in time that rests on an infinity of older layers. Our layer will someday lie buried under new life as surely as one bed of rock rests atop another, as securely as Adam Apple lies beneath the sod in North Cape. The road runs straight as an arrow from present to future, and its only signpost is change. I will follow my father as my children will follow me into a past that grows denser and deeper with the turn of each season.

Deep in the Heart of Dairyland

Holstein Sale Tells a Wisconsin Story

"Lot 1 is Goldwyn Deidra. Every sale's gotta have a Lot 1, and she's a beauty: seven generations excellent, and fresh in January. Goldwyn's got champions in her bloodline, folks. Who'll give me three thousand dollars?"

Goldwyn Deidra was oblivious, of course. The fifteen-hundred-pound dairy cow, six years old and still a steady producer, was the first of more than 180 purebred Holsteins to parade through a makeshift sales ring in a machine shed south of Sparta. The shed was on Tyrone and Barb Johnson's farm, 240 acres of cropland with a fringe of forest in the rolling hills of southwestern Wisconsin. After a lifetime in dairying, Tyrone, at the age of sixty, was leaving the business.

For an entire week, the cows had been treated like beauty queens primping for a pageant. They'd been clipped, washed, combed, and then photographed, each with her front legs on a small riser to show off her lines. These bovine pinups filled a sales catalog that was widely circulated in the region. Cows that lacked full tail switches were even provided with bushy clip-ons for the camera.

On the day of the sale, a raw Friday in early April 2015, roughly 350 people converged on the Johnson farm. The north cornfield was filled with what must have been the largest gathering of pickup trucks in Monroe County, many of them pulling livestock trailers. These pilgrims, some traveling from two hundred miles away, had obviously come to buy, and why not? Tyrone and Barb's Holsteins were widely considered some of the best dairy animals in Wisconsin.

And what was I doing there, a city kid whose closest contact with a cow is usually the milk on his morning cereal? Tyrone Johnson is my cousin.

> "Next up is Shottle Daphney. She's got a straight back and a crackin' good udder. She's a factory, folks—112 pounds of milk a day. Another one of them good Shiloh daughters. She does more work in three hours than most of my buddies do in three days. Who wants to start?"

My maternal grandfather, John Johnson (from Wisconsin, no less), emigrated as a boy from Norway to Coon Valley, a picturesque hamlet fifteen miles southeast of La Crosse. His father, Torger, was a carpenter, but John became a farmer, writing the first chapter in a family story that mirrors the story of Wisconsin dairying over the past century.

John owned a small general farm, covering just eighty acres on the ridge north of Coon Valley. He maintained a small dairy herd, chickens, pigs, and the tobacco patch that was once obligatory in that region. My grandfather's career ended in 1939, when he suffered a fatal skull fracture after slipping on a patch of barnyard ice.

By the time John died, his third son, Laurence, was already established on his wife Julia's home place a few miles south of Coon Valley. That gorgeous farm, straddling a spring-fed brook between two rocky bluffs, was a fixture of my childhood, and I continued to visit as an adult. Laurence owned a herd of about twenty-five Guernseys whose milk he collected in old-fashioned

Looking for bidders at Tyrone and Barb Johnson's Holstein sale. JOHN GURDA

metal cans and cooled in a spring house. My uncle shipped his Grade B output to the Coon Valley creamery, where it was turned into butter and cheese.

Laurence's son, Monroe, made the transition to the world of Holstein cattle, bulk coolers, and Grade A milk, which went to market in fluid form. In 1954, Monroe and his wife, Beverly, bought a 160-acre farm near Melvina, twenty-five winding miles northeast of Coon Valley, and built a herd of about fifty cows—twice as many as his father owned. Most were "grade" cattle, without pedigrees or papers, but Monroe and Beverly's second son, Tyrone, took an early and active interest in genetics, an interest that really blossomed during his college years—at UW–Madison, of course.

Year by year, the herd's bloodlines improved, and so did its output. By the time Tyrone took over the operation and moved to a farm of his own just up Highway 27, every cow was registered, and the herd grew to about seventy-five in the stalls.

In three generations, the average Johnson herd increased

from twenty-five to fifty to seventy-five, the average farm size doubled and then tripled, machines took over many of the more arduous manual tasks, milk cans gave way to bulk coolers, and management shifted from seat-of-the-pants decision-making to thoroughly scientific methods. That is precisely the evolution of the state's dairy industry. As went the Johnsons, so went Wisconsin.

> "And here's Advent Destiny. She's all business and all pedi-gree. Ninety-six points and earned every one of 'em. Mark her pregnant to Atwood. Goldwyn's her sire. She's carrying a heifer calf, so here's a two-for-one. What'll you give, what'll you give?"

The Johnson family mirrors Wisconsin in one other partic-ular. When they decided to sell their herd, Tyrone and Barb joined an exodus from the dairy business that has been under-way for decades. In 1960, our state was the home of nearly a hundred thousand dairy farms and 2.2 million dairy cows. By 2015, the year of the sale, the number of farms had taken a nose-dive to fewer than ten thousand, and the cattle census had dropped to 1.3 million. Even with those diminished numbers, the state's milk output actually increased more than 50 percent during the same period—the result of better feed, better breed-ing, and more scientific management.

The exodus has accelerated sharply since 2015. Dairy farmers are leaving despite the production gains, and who can blame them? Fiercely independent as individuals, they are vulnerable as a group to market forces that penalize smaller operators and reward those who can spread their costs across larger herds with higher volumes. "Get big or get out" has become standard advice in dairy country.

Achieving economies of scale is prohibitively expensive for most farmers, but that's not the only reason for the continuing exodus. When we city-dwellers visit the countryside, many of us gaze through rose-colored glasses at the neat fields, the orderly outbuildings, and the cows grazing contentedly in their green pastures. What we fail to see is the work. The most skillful breeders have yet to develop a dairy cow that stops producing on weekends.

Tyrone Johnson, my cousin, represented the fourth generation of dairy farmers in our family. JOHN GURDA

Tyrone Johnson routinely put in eighty to a hundred hours every week, and he went fifteen years without a real vacation, even with a full-time hired hand. No one contributes to a farmer's pension plan or writes a check for health insurance premiums, and the price of milk is as volatile as gasoline. "I'm at the place," said Tyrone on the day of the sale, "where I need to slow down a little bit." With the herd in great shape and their son pursuing another career, he and Barb decided on what the industry calls a "complete dispersal."

By the time the auctioneer slammed down his gavel for the last time on that blustery April day—more than three hours after Goldwyn Deidra entered the ring as Lot 1—the most tangible fruits of a lifetime of unremitting labor had passed into other hands, and in their place was a pot of nearly six hundred thousand dollars. With that conversion of cows to cash, the fourth generation of dairy farming in my family came to a bittersweet end.

"Lot 121 is Atwood Paisley. Here's a really nice heifer calf,
folks. Sired by Atwood out of the great Shiloh Desire.
Who'll start us off at two thousand? There's a blue ribbon in
this calf's future for sure."

When I asked Tyrone, a few weeks later, if he had any misgivings about the sale, he said, "Not really. It's fun watching the
good cows develop. You miss the good cows, but not the work."
Although a melancholy presence hovers in the air of every empty
barn, Tyrone and Barb Johnson's decision to leave the dairy business was not a complete farewell to farming. In fact, there were
sixty-five Angus steers in their cow yard a week after the sale,
and the couple continues to raise cash crops—corn, soybeans,
and hay—on their 240 acres. But beef cattle require infinitely
less attention than dairy cows. "Twenty minutes a day," said
Tyrone, "and you're done." Even as his pace slows, a fifth generation of Johnsons is in the wings. Tyrone and Barb's daughter,
Ashley, married into another dairy family, the Hemmersbachs,
who milk cows on nearby St. Mary's Ridge—organically, no less.

A story started by John Johnson in the early twentieth century
continues in the twenty-first. Even though I make my living in the
city, the story is also mine, both as a Johnson and as a citizen of
this state. As I drove back to Milwaukee with hay on my jeans and
manure on my shoes, I knew I had witnessed something purely
and elementally Wisconsin. Bittersweet it may have been, but my
cousin's sale took me to a place where the Johnsons have always
been—at home in the heart of Dairyland.

Owning the Past

Thoughts on Turning Seventy

It was the easiest thing I've ever done. Turn seventy, that is. All I had to do was keep drawing breath, taking nourishment, reading the paper, and suddenly there I was, a newly minted septuagenarian, well past the point of dying young or retiring early. A line from Paul Simon's "Old Friends" sums it up: "How terribly strange to be seventy." Simon recorded the song at the age of twenty-six. He's now past eighty and presumably feeling even stranger.

Old age may be odd, but it's not all bad, at least as I'm experiencing it. I always told my kids that every age has its pluses and minuses, and that's no less true of seventy than it was of forty or four. The physical side would have to be in the minus column. For most guys, the breeding plumage is pretty well shot, gone to gray or gone entirely. Joints creak, the plumbing leaks, and your feet develop strange bumps and gnarls after keeping you upright for so many years. You also face the fact that you're unlikely to get better at anything you attempt. That curveball you could never throw? It will remain forever unthrown. Those tricky guitar chords you never mastered? They will be unmastered to the end of your days. And all these changes occur if you're in good health; never mind the million more serious things that can, and frequently do, go wrong. The simple fact is that we all have front-row seats at the spectacle of our own deterioration.

Grandchildren are the most adamant joy of advancing age. ANDERS GURDA

To a person, my friends and I are paying the wages of age. We wear our medical adventures—a knee surgery here, a hernia repair there—like notches on our belts, and our conversations turn to physical complaints with a frequency that would have appalled us twenty years ago. I've logged enough time in medical settings to come up with a new definition of aging: it's the process whereby your primary doctor hands you off to one specialist after another until the only thing left to do is an autopsy.

Our physical decline has its mental and emotional corollaries. Capacity, stamina, and resilience all take a hit as we age. We ... simply ... need ... more ... time—more time to do things, more time between doing them, and more time to recover. In a neat proportional adjustment, our desire to do large things seems to diminish with our capacity. I have no interest in full retirement, but the prospect of writing another five-hundred-page book seems about as remote as doing fifty pushups or running a five-minute mile.

Time itself changes with advancing age. As your past outweighs your future by an ever-widening margin, you realize how little time there has always been, and how quickly it passes. The passage from pubescence to senescence is much shorter than you'd ever realized. Sometimes I feel like a saloon patron at closing time: "What do you mean it's time to leave? I've still got half a beer and all my change on the bar."

Some of my peers find it easy to deny or at least ignore their fast-approaching last call. Age is just a number, they say. Seventy is the new fifty. That strikes me as a psychological comb-over: we've reached authentic old age. If seventy is the new fifty, dead must be the new eighty.

But there's a plus side to aging as well. We septuagenarians have reached an undeniable sweet spot. If we've been lucky, provident, or both, the house is paid off, the kids are educated, and we have plenty of time, enough money, and the ability and inclination to use both. Within limits that become obvious, we can do whatever we want: travel abroad, read mysteries, take classes, bike, bird-watch, go to concerts, or even take in a Brewers day game. The window may be narrow—we know what comes next—but it's a really nice window.

A guaranteed paycheck helps. After endless miles of open water, we've rowed safely to the shores of Social Security and Medicare. It's going to take me a long time just to get back what I paid into the system, but that monthly direct deposit still feels good. Not that Social Security pays enough to live on. I'm still working, but I've entered my squirrel years, when I, with all my peers in the pensionless class, have to start eating whatever acorns I've stored away on my own.

In addition to greater financial security, there are certain permissions that come with age, among them a growing disregard for appearance. I take an oddly perverse pride in having made it past seventy without once working in food service or wearing a tuxedo. Those are resolutions I'm likely to keep, and I have most certainly bought my last suit. I agree with Charlie McNeer, the former CEO of We Energies, who said when he retired that he wanted his entire wardrobe to come from Farm & Fleet.

But what I like best about my age may be a newly discovered sense of owning the past. Whatever you've done, your life—your entire life—is your single greatest accomplishment. At seventy, you feel the weight and heft of it, the homeward bend of the long arc as you enter the final stretch. You own every nick, scratch, and heartache, every wrong turn and right decision. What poet Theodore Roethke called "the pure serene of memory in one man" becomes more and more tangible each year.

Owning the past applies to us collectively as well as personally. Every generation inhabits a particular slice of time whose shape becomes clearer as we age. Just as our parents remembered ice men and steam trains and FDR, we baby boomers—an odd term for today's senior citizens—are old enough to recall rag men and trackless trolleys and JFK. Some details from my childhood have become genuinely historic: the first TV in the neighborhood (a small black-and-white in Bernie Lindner's house), alphabetical phone-number prefixes, traveling to Madison on two-lane Highway 30, and watching Elvis Presley's first gyrations on *The Ed Sullivan Show*. It goes without saying—but I'll say it anyway—that today's toddlers will have their own fully comparable sets of antiquarian memories.

As the past becomes clearer, the Big Questions loom bigger, particularly the ones about our ultimate future. At seventy, however, you realize that the answers are unlikely to be any clearer than they are right now. Perhaps, like autumn leaves, the life of the spirit grows brighter as the light of the body dims. I know there's a spark at the root of things that feels immortal. What that means for us personally is beyond my comprehension. Although it's damnably hard to remember at times when my brain craves certainty, my own mantra is pretty simple: Do good work. Love your family. Walk in mystery.

Aging, like birthing, is a largely involuntary and completely irreversible process. It's a condition you can't help catching. There's no vaccine, no dietary supplement, no elixir that can halt the onrushing years. To the extent that you can distance yourself from your ongoing decay, it's important not to take the process too personally. Decline is built into the organism. It would be wholly unnatural for it not to occur, and it occurs, at varying rates of speed, for all of us. The young become old and the old leave the scene, as inevitably and organically as the sun sets and the moon rises.

Successful aging, then, is a matter of adjusting our mental expectations to our physical limitations without undue resistance. And remembering that there's always more out there. "Old men ought to be explorers," wrote T. S. Eliot, and I intend to follow his advice as best I can. Stay in the game, Eliot says; resignation, self-satisfaction, and idleness are the wrong responses. There are still things of moment over the horizon. In the meantime, I offer a prayer for those who have joined me on the far side of seventy:

I thank you, Lord, for my good left knee,
and all the times I've found my keys,
for grandkids to spoil in late December
and every name I still remember.

Give me more days when I can sleep past seven
and one or two nights when I'm up till eleven.
Keep me from fear, shield me from doubt,
and help me go with grace when the lights go out.

The Generation Before

My Parents' Struggles Put COVID-19 in Perspective

As pandemic projects go, I came up with a pretty good one. When the coronavirus shrank our social circles to the vanishing point, mine actually grew by two people. As millions of us became high-tech hermits, connected to the outside world by waves and wires, I used technology to renew my ties with a pair who had always been dear to me: my parents. Never mind that they've been dead for years, my father since 1996 and my mother since 2004. I still had the pleasure of their company for hours at a time.

As you've probably guessed, I was listening to recordings— tapes I made with them in the 1990s. In the early stages of the COVID-19 shutdown, I rescued a pile of cassettes from years of oblivion in a dusty shoebox. After having the interviews digitized and transcribed, I spent days checking the accuracy of the transcripts against the original tapes. Hearing my parents' long-silenced voices—his careful diction, her girlish laughter—was a sweet experience, grading at times into bittersweet. Even though I'm past seventy myself, it was like being at their knees again, getting reacquainted with them, not in their complex roles as parents and spouses, but simply as tellers of their own stories.

These stories sound like dispatches from a different world, which in fact they are. From two different worlds, actually. Although they were born only one year apart, he in 1911 and

Clarice Johnson and Art Gurda on their wedding day, September 13, 1944. GURDA FAMILY

she in 1912, my parents had widely divergent backgrounds. Arthur Gurda was a pure product of Milwaukee's Polish South Side, while Clarice Johnson was raised on a Norwegian farm outside Coon Valley, Wisconsin, near the heart of the Driftless Area. (I have the state's only POLNOR license plates in tribute to both of them.)

I started those long-ago interviews by asking my parents to describe their earliest memories—an easy way to prime the conversational pump. My father recalled his excitement as a four-year-old sitting next to the driver on the horse-drawn wagon carrying the Gurda family's worldly goods from their tiny cottage on Third and Maple to their new hardware store on Thirty-Second and Lincoln.

My mother at the same age was confined to a darkened upstairs room with measles for a short time. One day, her father drove into the farmyard with the family's first car, an Overland, and she was so excited that she climbed out onto the porch roof to get a glimpse. When her older sister, Alice, saw what was happening, she ran upstairs and pulled Mom back into the house with such force that she dislocated her right arm. In the long recovery period that followed, Clare Johnson became a leftie for life.

Although they were born in this country, both of my parents

maintained strong connections with the Old World. For Art Gurda, the link was his widowed paternal grandmother, Apolonia, who lived with the family until her death in 1928. Polish was her everyday language, but my great-grandmother spoke fluent German as well—a necessity in the German-occupied section of Poland from which she emigrated. Apolonia taught my father, the firstborn child in his family, to speak Polish, sing Polish songs, and appreciate foods like *czarnina*, or duck blood soup. She also hid him in her voluminous skirts when his father tried to discipline him.

My mother's favorite grandparent was Torger Johnson, an itinerant carpenter who brought his family to Coon Valley in about 1885. After weathering the rigors of uprooting and resettling, Torger and his wife, Johanne, lost four children to diphtheria in a matter of days. Only my grandfather, John Johnson, and his baby sister were spared. My mother remembered Torger as a gentle man "with a sadness about him." Like Apolonia, he spoke very little English, but "he had a readily available lap," my mother recalled. "It was his love for his own children, transposed to his grandchildren."

Religion was perhaps the main point of difference between my parents. Clare Johnson was baptized and confirmed in the Norwegian language, and Upper Coon Valley Lutheran Church (as distinct from Middle and Lower) was her family's primary social outlet. Art Gurda, by contrast, was raised devoutly Catholic, but with a twist. Until the Polish families in his South Side neighborhood built St. Barbara's Church in 1924, he went to church and school at Holy Ghost, the German Catholic congregation that was literally across the street from the hardware store. Religion, in this single instance, trumped ethnicity.

My parents were both on the cusp of adulthood when the bottom fell out. The stock market crash of 1929 ushered in the hardest economic times the nation has ever known, and they soon found themselves swimming upstream. Art Gurda had no desire to spend the rest of his life behind a hardware store counter, and there was no future for a girl on the farm overlooking Coon Valley. Even though none of their parents had made it past sixth grade, college emerged as the best option for both of them—if they could pay for it themselves.

My father worked his way through the University of Wisconsin–Madison with a series of "meal jobs" at the Memorial Union and local restaurants. He was paid in meal tickets—a $5 book for every ten hours he worked. That amounted to only fifty cents an hour, but my dad put in so much overtime that he was able to sell his extra books to other students for $4.50. (Tuition at the time was less than $65 a semester.) Meal money, plus the dollar he earned for every ROTC drill in the Red Gym (and $15 for a two-week ROTC summer camp) enabled my father to graduate in 1936. With his chemical engineering diploma in hand, Art Gurda went to work for the Caterpillar Company in Peoria at sixty-seven cents an hour. He used his first paychecks to buy a tailor-made tuxedo and a pair of French Shriner dress shoes—just like the ones he'd seen the swells wearing when he served them at Memorial Union formals.

My mother's story was similar. Clare Johnson worked her way through the State Teachers College, now UW–La Crosse, as a live-in nanny and maid for affluent families in the campus district—a common pattern for the region's Norwegian farm girls. After graduating in 1934, she went back to Coon Valley and started teaching in a one-room school for eighty-five dollars a month. The first money she earned went to something more down-to-earth than dress shoes: a milking machine for the family farm.

The Depression was far from over when my parents launched their careers. What finally ended the hard times was the military build-up for World War II, a conflict that upended whatever futures Art Gurda and Clare Johnson had imagined for themselves. My father went on active duty early in the fighting and became an officer in the Army's chemical warfare corps, working with poison gas, smokescreens, flamethrowers, and the young men he trained to use them. Before shipping out to the carnage of Iwo Jima, he was sent to the Command and Staff School in Fort Leavenworth, Kansas. There he met my mother, who had quit teaching to do her part as a Red Cross worker at Leavenworth. Their romance started on the tennis court and led to the altar on September 13, 1944. Eleven months later, the war ended.

That's also where my tapes ended. It is a matter of deep regret that I didn't continue the interviews through the war years and beyond, but I'm glad for what I have, and not only as a family record. Although my parents' stories are uniquely their own, they are also the stories of an entire generation. I think especially of the 1930–1945 period, an ordeal dominated by the Depression and World War II. For fifteen long years, my parents and their peers were buffeted by forces beyond their control. They suffered privation in the first instance and pressure in the second, but the period's keynote was constant anxiety.

For a son looking back anxiously from the middle of a pandemic, the old stories provided a welcome perspective. For all the pain that COVID-19 has caused, my parents' generation endured far more turmoil for a much longer period of time. When their multiple crises finally passed, they bound their wounds, counted their strengths, and got on with it, building a world that became the foundation of our own. As the pandemic becomes, in time, a fading memory, may our generation find the fortitude to do precisely the same.

Rest in Peace, Naturally

Green Burial Is One Way to Go

Every age has tasks appropriate to its station. In our twenties, we lay the groundwork for a sustaining career. In our middle years, we reach our height of productivity and nurture those coming up behind us. At seventy, well, maybe it's time to start thinking about an exit strategy. That's why my wife and I acquired two lots in the green burial section of Forest Home Cemetery in 2017. It was one less thing for us, and more importantly for our kids, to worry about.

The decision was surprisingly easy. As an Illinois native with no particular desire to make the Land of Lincoln her final home, Sonja was open-minded. "It won't matter," she sagely pointed out. "I'll be dead." In my case, it became clear that the only real choice was Forest Home. Established in 1850, it is without question the most historic cemetery in the city, filled with artful monuments bearing the names of Kilbourn and Walker, Pabst and Blatz, Falk and Zeidler, and scores of other local luminaries I've studied and written about over the years. I'll also be the only resident who's authored a book about the cemetery: *Silent City*, a slim volume published for Forest Home's 150th anniversary in 2000.

But my connections go far beyond the professional. What will be my last neighborhood was also a major landmark of my first. I lived just seven blocks from Forest Home until I was

The Prairie Rest section of Forest Home Cemetery offers a natural way to go.
JOHN GURDA

eight, and my grandparents' Lincoln Avenue hardware store—
an anchor of my childhood—was even closer. As a boy, I passed
the graveyard with a morbid dread that has weathered with age
to something resembling acceptance.

Despite its patrician reputation, Forest Home is a thoroughly egalitarian burial ground. For every towering stone
maiden or massive mausoleum, there are thousands of simple
markers placed by Milwaukeeans of more modest means. Prairie Rest, the green burial section, is especially unpretentious;
it lies south of Cleveland Avenue, overlooking a railroad corridor and practically across the tracks from the Maynard Steel
foundry. The section fits snugly into the surrounding neighborhood, a historic Polish enclave that has since become a Latino
stronghold. Just beyond the gates is the industrial, immigrant-
centered Milwaukee that has long been one of my central themes
as a writer.

Forest Home makes sense, but why choose green burial
over the alternatives? Because I could never warm to the idea of

cremation, and embalming leaves me cold. The thought of going up in smoke seems somehow profligate; I've gotten attached to these bones, after all. (I do, however, like the funeral industry's term for human ashes: *cremains*, a coinage that always reminds me of *craisins* for dried cranberries.) As an aficionado of old cemeteries, I also like the idea of leaving something tangible behind—a physical remnant, however temporary, of my presence here.

Embalming, on the other hand, is basically human taxidermy. The idea of being drained of blood, pumped full of formaldehyde, and gussied up in a suit with my lips sewn shut and my face coated with wax has never seemed like a particularly attractive option for my body's last hours above ground. Once below, our remains dissolve into a doubly sealed puddle, ruining a perfectly good suit or an expensive dress.

In green burial, by contrast, the body is cleansed, wrapped in a cotton shroud (no buttons, no buckles), and placed in a pine coffin. Biodegradable chemicals are available for those who want to be embalmed for viewing, but the window closes in a day or two. The body is finally lowered into the ground, where it can nourish, in T. S. Eliot's phrase, "the life of significant soil." In Prairie Rest's case, the soil supports a carefully curated selection of sun-loving grasses and wildflowers.

Green burial isn't especially cheap. A single lot cost $3,490 in 2021, compared with a range of $2,000 to $5,000 for one of Forest Home's conventional spaces. (If you want to lie near a beer baron or a governor, expect to pay more for the privilege.) But green burial also eliminates the cost of concrete vaults, shiny metal caskets, and individual monuments. The names of Prairie Rest's residents are inscribed on boulders at the edge of the graveyard, and GPS devices are available at the office for anyone seeking an exact burial location. Sonja and I picked corner lots to make it easy.

Civil War veteran Francis
Collins entertained
numerous visitors to his
gravesite before he finally
went below at 104.
FOREST HOME CEMETERY

I've visited my future grave a couple of times since we signed
the papers. It was a bit eerie, I admit, to stand on the spot where
I'll one day lie down for my eternal dirt nap, but I also found the
experience oddly comforting—like knowing I had a room waiting for me at the end of a long trip.

One of our neighbors-to-be across the road, Francis Collins,
carried the same feeling to an unusual extreme. Collins was a
Civil War veteran who used his oversized lot like a summer
home. After erecting a monument twice his height, he decorated the lot with flower-filled urns, hosta plantings, a large
American flag, and two iron benches for visitors. Collins com-
muted from the National Soldiers Home (now the Veterans
Administration Center) by streetcar every day from spring to
fall, dressed in his blue Union uniform. A confirmed bachelor
and retired salesman, he loved to puff away on his homemade
pipe and tell war stories to anyone who would listen. "Don't fail
to come out and visit me again," Collins told a reporter in 1907.
"I may be down there, but if I am, I want you to come and sit on
my benches and admire this spot just the same as if I was here."
The veteran had above-ground use of his little estate until 1930,
when he finally went below at the age of 104.

Although I have no intention of haunting my own grave like Francis Collins, I'll visit our lots at Forest Home on occasion, if only to stay in touch with some final realities. It's been said that everybody wants to go to heaven but no one wants to die. It'll happen anyway—life's one guarantee is that it will end—so why not exit on your own terms?

I know that my body will some day be joined with the elements of earth and water at Prairie Rest, visited at first and in due course forgotten. What lies beyond? I have no earthly idea. I do, however, like the idea of lying there with my wife and our neighbors as we literally push up daisies—or at least coneflowers—and wait to wake in eternity.

A Life in History

Fifty Years of 1099s

"When are you going to retire?" is a question I heard more often as my seventieth birthday approached. Old friends and close associates were leaving the work force in droves, and there was an unspoken assumption that I would soon follow. "Not yet," I always replied, and I might have added, "Perhaps not ever."

The logic of retirement has always escaped me. Slow down, sure, but when you've done something long enough to get reasonably good at it, when you're still close to what you consider the height of your powers, when people seem to enjoy the fruits of your labors, why quit? Above all, why quit history? Nothing has history's power to explain or history's capacity for story. Why would anyone willingly give that up?

And so I find myself looking back on a half-century (and counting) in the field of local history, all of it spent as a freelancer. I'm surprised to have made a living at it for all these years, and even more surprised to have found the field in the first place. My path has been, you might say, circuitous. I actually came late to a love of the subject. I began on the writing side of my profession, graduating from Boston College in 1969 with a degree in English. This was the 1960s, remember—a decade that America has never entirely forgiven. I came home to Milwaukee with a woolly notion that I'd be a poet.

Telling Milwaukee's story, 2017. LEE MATZ/
MILWAUKEE INDEPENDENT

Well, all those jobs seemed to be taken. I painted houses for six months as one-third of Tom Sawyer Painting Company, which lasted until the weather turned cold and our ladders no longer served as advertisements. With no other options, I accepted a friend's offer to volunteer at a South Side youth center he was running. I was soon working at Journey House full time, and I stayed for three years, teaching photography, organizing small groups, begging supplies, and doing whatever else needed to be done. My roots are actually in social work.

Journey House was a shoestring operation; a forty-five-thousand-dollar budget paid for five staff, rent, utilities, and supplies. It was obvious that we needed to be on a sounder footing. Working with our volunteer from VISTA (Volunteers in Service to America), I co-wrote what today's fundraisers would call a case statement: What were the neighborhood's needs, how had they developed, and what were we doing to meet them? That meant neighborhood research. For reasons still unclear to me, I drew the historical side of the assignment. That's when the legendary light bulb went on above my shaggy head. That's when the clouds began to part and visibility improved dramatically.

My family's roots are on the Polish South Side. I hadn't taken a history course since high school, but here I was, studying the history of my old neighborhood. I met people who had shopped at my grandparents' hardware store on Lincoln Avenue. I found

my father's name on the letterhead
of a Polish student organization at
UW–Madison in the 1930s. I began
to develop a powerful sense of history as story. All these connections
began to surface: between my
story and the stories of my family,
my neighborhood, my city, my
country, and the larger world.

What I discovered, in short, was
historical context—something
that had been sorely lacking in the
1960s. That period was not just ahis-
torical but anti-historical. My generation was determined to create a
new world, so why give a moment's
thought to the old one? The baby
went out with the bathwater.

The darkroom was my province
at Journey House, a South Side
youth center that provided my
first real job after college. JAN
KLECZEWSKI

The product of our research was a little booklet fearlessly
titled *The Near South Side: A Delicate Balance*. To our surprise,
it was published in 1972 by a local social action group, and that
led me to a job with United Way, doing neighborhood research
elsewhere on the South Side. During a period of unemployment
following that project, I wrote, for free, another, somewhat less
primitive pamphlet on the South Side's history, which led to
another research job in Waukesha County.

It began to dawn on me—slowly—that this might be a
career, but it became more and more obvious that I really didn't
know what I was doing. I needed more tools, and that's what
brought me to the University of Wisconsin–Milwaukee. I
quickly found a home in the Geography Department. Neighborhoods were my primary focus then, but I became interested
in the broader intersection between time and place, and that is

historical geography. My master's thesis was on Jones Island, a former fishing village at the mouth of the Milwaukee River. What I do is history, but it has always been informed by a geographic perspective.

As soon as I received my master's degree, I went back to work. I got married in 1977, and Sonja and I soon had one kid in diapers and a second on the way. I wrote a couple of neighborhood histories for a project sponsored by UWM: one on Bay View, where we moved soon after the book was published, and another on the West End, which covered Merrill Park, Concordia, and Pigsville. When the project's funding ended after two years, so did my job.

In a major stroke of luck, the head of our advisory committee was a Northwestern Mutual executive, Ralph Harkness, who asked if I'd write a history of his company. Northwestern has a long tradition of chronicling its evolution every twenty-five years, and another writer had backed out. Now consider this offer from the viewpoint of a 1960s kid. Northwestern virtually embodied The Establishment. It was founded by Yankees in 1857 and had grown to be the largest financial institution in Wisconsin: buttoned-down, traditional, and undeniably conservative. Working for NML would mean working for The Man. Add to that the fact that I knew nothing about life insurance; I literally could not have told you the difference between term and whole life.

Did I agonize? Did I hesitate? Not for a second. I had two little kids and no other prospects.

To my surprise and my great relief, the project turned out to be fascinating. Northwestern was like another neighborhood, with its own culture, its own characters, and its own story. I made a lot of friends there, and twenty-five years later they hired me to do another book-length history. Repeat business is important for freelancers, even if your assignments are a quarter-century apart.

(A) A primitive pamphlet titled *The Near South Side: A Delicate Balance* (1971) was my first publication. (B) *The Quiet Company: A Modern History of Northwestern Mutual Life* (1983) introduced me to commissioned work. (C) *The Making of Milwaukee* was published in 1999 (D) and became the basis of an Emmy Award–winning documentary in 2006.

That's been the rhythm of my career ever since. One part has been commissioned work, sometimes for companies like Northwestern or Miller Brewing or We Energies, at other times for nonprofits like the Jewish Museum or Forest Home Cemetery or St. Josaphat's Basilica. The other part is community work: usually projects I choose and carry out with essential support from local philanthropists.

By the mid-1990s, I'd gathered so many pieces of local history that I felt compelled to put the whole puzzle together. The result, after four years of work, was *The Making of Milwaukee*, the first full-length history of the community to appear since 1948. Published by the Milwaukee County Historical Society, the book has sold more than twenty-eight thousand copies in four editions to date—a solid showing for a local title.

I knew, even before the ink was dry, that Milwaukee's story was too important to be confined to a book. I began to work with Milwaukee Public Television, and the result of that collaboration was a five-hour TV series that premiered in 2006, also called *The Making of Milwaukee*. The series made Channel 10 the most-watched public TV station in America for three nights running, and it went on to win a Midwest Emmy. The documentary is still in Channel 10's broadcast rotation.

What I had obviously tapped into was an enormous appetite for local history, and I kept at it. My next large project was *Milwaukee: City of Neighborhoods*, which is based on a series of ubiquitous neighborhood posters published by the city back in the 1980s. Cleverly concealed on the back of each one of those posters was a historical essay I had written about the neighborhood. If people hung them for display, my words went away forever. Working with Historic Milwaukee, Inc. as the publisher, my chosen task was to update those twenty-seven essays, add ten more, and put them between the covers of a book that has become a sort of grassroots bible. It's about that size as well, weighing in at six and a half pounds.

So that's my story. That's what I've been doing for the past fifty years. What, you might ask, is the point? I wouldn't presume to offer my path as a textbook case of how to pursue a career. It's closer to the opposite, but I've developed some rock-solid beliefs during my years in the field of local history. The first and perhaps most obvious is that history is where the present comes from. There *is* no other possible source. I define history very simply as why things are the way they are. The landscapes around us, the laws we live by, the customs we observe, the assumptions we harbor all rise from deep roots that, however buried they might seem, retain their vitality in the present.

But history has other gifts to offer, and one of the most important is perspective. Although we know better, we grow up thinking that things were always the way they are now, that the world as we know it is somehow preordained, fixed. History explodes that notion. It puts the world in motion. That may be the greatest gift of history, especially local history. It teaches us that nothing had to happen, that nothing is inevitable, and it teaches us that everything is on its way to becoming something else. History, at root, is the study of change.

Just think for a moment of the people around you: your family, your friends, your neighbors. Visualize their hairstyles, their clothing, their glasses and shoes. I can guarantee you with absolute certainty that, fifty years from now, everything they're wearing could be sold in a vintage clothing shop. Every car on the streets outside, if it's still running, will be a classic fifty years from now—something to be seen in parades. Every current song you stream on your mobile device will be an oldie, if it's played at all. And your descendants will some day gaze at your photograph—maybe in the cloud, maybe as a hologram—and think how curiously antique you look. I guarantee it.

We are all sharing a single historical moment, one that places us between a million moments that went before and millions more to come. That means we're all in this together. We are the only link, the living bridge, between past and future, and what we do with, or to, this world, this society, and our communities will shape the lives of generations to come.

That sense of shared fate, that sense of shared responsibility, is something I think is very much endangered in America today.

We elevate the "I" at the expense of the "we." We spend much of our time wandering in what might be termed the digital wilderness, glued to our phones, virtually together but really alone. That isolation feeds a polarization that threatens the very core of our democracy.

There are numerous ways to recover a healthier balance, and the one I've pursued is local history. History, on some fundamental level, is story. I believe in the power of story to shape our understanding of who we are as individuals. I believe in the power of shared story to shape a sense of who we are as communities. The communal story is what I tell—a modest endeavor, to be sure, but one I undertake in the service of something larger. Whether we've lived in a place for generations or arrived just yesterday, our communities provide the context for our story. We shape them as they shape us.

My hope is that by helping people put *their* stories in the context of *our* story, I can help to close some of that troubling distance between the individual and the community. My ultimate goal is to encourage a sense of ownership and finally a sense of belonging for everyone who calls Milwaukee home. It's like Aldo Leopold's land ethic. We need to see place not as something that belongs to us but as something to which we belong. And it all starts with story.

It's been a rare and unexpected privilege to be able to tell Milwaukee's story for the last half-century. I look forward to many more stories in the years still to come.

Index

Page locators in *italics* indicate illustrations.

About the Author

PHOTO BY MAX THOMSEN

John Gurda is a Milwaukee-born writer and historian who has been studying his hometown since 1972. He is the author of twenty-three books, including *The Making of Milwaukee*, the first full-length history of the community published since 1948, and *Milwaukee: City of Neighborhoods*, a geographic companion that has quickly become the standard work on grassroots Milwaukee. In addition to his work as an author, Gurda is a lecturer, tour guide, and local history columnist for the Milwaukee *Journal Sentinel*. The common thread in all of his work is an understanding of history as "why things are the way they are."